Maximum Feasible Participation

Post 45 Loren Glass and Kate Marshall, Editors
Post•45 Group, Editorial Committee

Maximum Feasible Participation

American Literature and the War on Poverty

Stephen Schryer

Stanford University Press
Stanford, California

Stanford University Press
Stanford, California

Printed in the United States of America on acid-free, archival-quality paper

Library of Congress Cataloging-in-Publication Data

Names: Schryer, Stephen, author.
Title: Maximum feasible participation : American literature and the War on Poverty / Stephen Schryer.
Description: Stanford, California : Stanford University Press, 2018. |
Series: Post*45 | Includes bibliographical references and index.
Identifiers: LCCN 2017037235 (print) | LCCN 2017041865 (ebook) | ISBN 9781503606081 (ebook) | ISBN 9781503603677 (cloth: alk. paper)
Subjects: LCSH: American literature—20th century—History and criticism. | American literature—Minority authors—History and criticism. | Literature and state—United States—History—20th century. | Literature and society—United States—History—20th century. | Poverty—Government policy—United States—History—20th century.
Classification: LCC PS225 (ebook) | LCC PS225 .S37 2018 (print) | DDC 810.9/3556—dc23
LC record available at https://lccn.loc.gov/2017037235

Typeset by Bruce Lundquist in 10/15 Minion

Contents

Acknowledgments   vii

Introduction: Maximum Feasible Participation   1

1   Jack Kerouac's Delinquent Art   27

2   Black Arts and the Great Society   51

3   Legal Services and the Cockroach Revolution   79

4   Writing Urban Crisis after Moynihan   99

5   Civil Rights and the Southern Folk Aesthetic   125

6   Who Belongs in the University?   151

Conclusion: Working-Class Community Action   175

Notes   187

Bibliography   219

Index   235

Acknowledgments

Thanks are due, first and foremost, to Emily-Jane Cohen, Loren Glass, Kate Marshall, and the two readers at Stanford University Press. They believed in this project, and their critical feedback transformed it into a much better book.

I also owe a massive debt to Mary Esteve. I started this book in 2008 as a postdoctoral project under her supervision at Concordia University, and she continued to read drafts after I took up a tenure-track position at the University of New Brunswick. As always, I'm indebted to Michael Szalay, who did his best to eradicate my worst critical habits when I was his student at the University of California, Irvine.

The following scholars read individual chapters and/or provided especially helpful comments at conferences: Sean McCann, Andrew Hoberek, Jennifer Andrews, Eric Strand, Marci L. Carrasquillo, Michael Hames-García, Nicola Nixon, Sarah Wilson, Amy Hungerford, Anthony Reed, Abigail Cheever, Deak Nabers, J. D. Connor, Annie McClanahan, Lisa Siraganian, and John Alba Cutler. Excerpts from this project benefited from vigorous discussions at two Post•45 conferences.

Thanks also to my supportive colleagues at the University of New Brunswick and to the graduate student research assistants who helped with this project: Kayla Geitzler, Curran Folkers, Charlie Fiset, and Brittany Lauton. This project was funded by an Insight Grant from the Social Sciences and Humanities Research Council of Canada and by a University Research Fund Grant from the University of New Brunswick.

Early versions of sections of this book appeared in *Arizona Quarterly*, *Modern Fiction Studies*, and *Twentieth-Century Literature*. I thank those journals for permission to include the material here.

This book would not exist without my supportive family: Frans and Catherine Schryer, who introduced me to literature and sociology; Emily Schryer, who set off on her own scholarly adventure; Joanne Minor, who does the kind of social work that I only write about; and Rowan Schryer, who put up with my distracted moments at the dinner table. This book is dedicated to them with love. It's also dedicated to the memory of Scott Eric Kaufman, whose critical voice is sorely missed.

Maximum Feasible Participation

Introduction

Maximum Feasible Participation

One of the most unlikely institutions to benefit from President Johnson's War on Poverty was the Black Arts Repertory Theatre and School (BARTS) in Harlem, founded by Amiri Baraka (LeRoi Jones), Larry Neal, and others. Its immediate patron was Harlem Youth Opportunities Unlimited (HARYOU), a Community Action Agency established under the Kennedy administration to deal with the problems of inner-city youth.[1] In the summer of 1965, the Johnson administration channeled over two million dollars into the program, hoping to cool down tempers after the riots of 1965.[2] Due to the bureaucratic chaos created by the need to spend so much money in a short period of time, it was relatively easy for Baraka and his compatriots to acquire funding for their venture; in his autobiography, Baraka estimates that "we must have got away with a couple hundred grand and even more in services when it was all over."[3] Throughout the summer, BARTS staged black nationalist street dramas that ritualistically enacted the deaths of liberal whites and integrationist blacks, accompanied by avant-garde jazz by Sun Ra, Albert Ayler, and Archie Shepp. It was not what the architects of the War on Poverty had in mind, and Sargent Shriver terminated the theater's funding, denouncing its plays as "scurrilous" and "obscene."[4] For the War on Poverty's congressional critics, the incident highlighted the flaws of the Community Action Program, a key part of the 1964 Economic Opportunity Act.[5] The program established thousands of Community Action Agencies, federally funded organizations located in slum neighborhoods and rural areas that provided services for low-income citizens. The agencies were supposed to encourage racial integration. HARYOU's mandate, in particular, was to prepare black inner-city youth for the integrated workforce supposedly opened up by the 1964 Civil Rights Act.[6] The agency had impeccable liberal credentials; it was founded by Kenneth Clark, coauthor of the famous doll studies on the psychological effects of racial discrimination cited in *Brown v. Board of*

Education (1954). The money for the program, however, ended up in the hands of separatists who followed the philosophies of Ron Karenga and Malcolm X.

The BARTS controversy was not an isolated case. Rather, as Karen Ferguson documents, most of the signature institutions of the Black Power era, including "ghetto-based economic development initiatives, university black studies programs, multicultural and 'affective' school curricula, and race-specific arts and cultural organizations,"[7] were funded by the Community Action Program and the Ford Foundation, the major philanthropic organization focused on improving conditions in the inner city. Huey Newton and Bobby Seale, for example, wrote the Black Panther Party's political platform in an office paid for by the Office of Economic Opportunity (OEO).[8] This pattern of liberal patronage also extended to other minority organizations that espoused cultural nationalist politics—in particular, institutions run by Chicanos/Chicanas and Puerto Ricans.[9] This conjunction of liberal funding and radical politics was controversial at the time, and it has since been criticized by voices from across the political spectrum. Conservatives point to BARTS and other Black Power beneficiaries of the War on Poverty as emblematic of liberalism's loss of pragmatic sense and moral compass during the Great Society. Black Arts scholars, meanwhile, argue that white liberals co-opted Black Power, leading to its safe institutionalization in Black Studies programs and other multicultural initiatives.[10] Commenting on BARTS in particular, Geneviève Fabre complains that "by accepting government grants," Baraka ran the risk "of appearing to blacks to be ideologically bought off, even if only to reach a state of financial autonomy."[11] Gravitating toward the latter thesis, Karen Ferguson argues that philanthropic organizations like the Ford Foundation sought to incorporate Black Power into a refashioned racial liberalism—what she calls "developmental separatism." The Ford Foundation "promoted a balkanizing ethic for the urban poor that emphasized the need for the continuing isolation of minority communities so that they could experience a cultural revitalization" leading to their "eventual assimilation into the mainstream American political economy."[12]

This debate about whether black nationalism infiltrated or was co-opted by the liberal establishment disguises a deeper affinity between BARTS and HARYOU. Both institutions were part of a broader set of experiments that tried to redefine what it meant to be a writer and, more generally, what it meant to be a professional in the years after World War II. When Baraka established BARTS, he hoped it would fulfill a political imperative facing all African American artists in the 1960s. "An artist is supposed to be right in the center of the community," Baraka explained. "The artist has to be fully integrated into the will of his people, has to *be* the people himself, and not be any different."[13] Baraka envisaged BARTS as a people's arts center, enmeshed in the community that it served. Not just a theater, it was a school, day care, spiritual center, and meeting place. The dramas that he staged there similarly enacted the artist and artwork's integration into the community; plays like *Slave Ship* (1968), in which the theater becomes the hold of a slave ship, were participatory rituals, encompassing performers and audience. In spite of Baraka's black nationalist ideology, this participatory aesthetic fit perfectly with the War on Poverty. When Lyndon Johnson addressed the nation after signing the Economic Opportunity Act, he insisted that the War on Poverty would empower the poor to help themselves. Its purpose was "not to make the poor secure in their poverty but to reach down and to help them lift themselves out of poverty."[14] To this end, the Economic Opportunity Act established funding for Community Action Agencies like HARYOU and stipulated that these agencies be "developed, conducted, and administered with the maximum feasible participation of residents of the areas and members of the groups served."[15] The resulting programs attracted young professionals on the vanguard of reformist movements that were reshaping social work, law, medicine, and other public service professions in the 1960s.[16] These professionals, like Baraka, questioned practices and privileges that separated them from their clients. They pushed for a new kind of participatory professionalism that would engage people normally disempowered by the welfare state. Once in charge of Community Action Agencies, many of these idealists interpreted the mandate of "maximum feasible participation" in a fashion unforeseen by Johnson and other architects of the Economic Opportunity Act. Like Baraka, they tried to politicize the poor, organizing them to identify and fight the forces that oppressed their neighborhoods.

Maximum Feasible Participation traces the rise and fall of this Great Society–era participatory imperative in post–World War II American literature and society. The chapters that follow explore postwar writers' efforts to rethink the relationship between artist, artwork, and audience, in ways that reflected and sometimes helped inspire broader changes in the nature of professionalism itself. For Baraka, this new relationship was central to what he called process aesthetics, a theory that he adapted from the white counterculture of the 1950s. This theory, developed by Black Mountain and New York poets like Charles Olson,

Robert Creeley, John Ashbery, and Frank O'Hara, and implicit in the work of Beat writers like Allen Ginsberg, Jack Kerouac, and William S. Burroughs, was a reaction against the New Critical formalism that dominated US English departments after World War II. New Critics like John Crowe Ransom, Cleanth Brooks, William K. Wimsatt, and Monroe Beardsley insisted that literary texts are organic unities, independent from the authors who create them, the historical circumstances that shape them, and the audiences who read them. The 1950s avant-garde, in contrast, emphasized literature's origins in and continuity with lived experience. They developed an improvisatory aesthetic that emphasized orality and performance. Charles Olson, for instance, conceived of poetry as an energy transfer from poet to reader: "A poem is energy transferred from where the poet got it . . . by way of the poem itself, all the way over to, the reader."[17] This conception of literature meant that process writers also emphasized audience response. In Lisa Siraganian's terms, while object artists insist on the "independence of art's *meaning* from a spectator's interpretations,"[18] process artists believe that art cannot be separated from its embodied spectators. In the late 1950s and early 1960s, Baraka claimed this process aesthetic as his own, emphasizing the priority of artistic process over the finished product. The artist, he claimed, "is cursed with his artifact, which exists without and despite him. And even though the process, in good art, is everywhere perceptible, the risk of perfection corrupts the lazy public into accepting the material *in place of* what it is only the remains of."[19] As Baraka evolved from a Beat writer into a black cultural nationalist, he emphasized process art's capacity to create new kinds of political community by incorporating audiences. Participatory dramas like *Slave Ship*, he believed, would fashion a racially specific, politically efficacious version of Olson's energy transfer between artist and audience.

The Community Action Program grew out of parallel assumptions, leading to the creation of what might be called "process professionalism." Many of the welfare idealists who planned and implemented the program conceived of themselves as anti-institutional figures capable of channeling creative energies that threatened the rigidity of established bureaucratic structures. Paul Ylvisaker, the director of the Ford Foundation's Gray Areas program, laid out this vision of the welfare professional in a series of speeches he delivered in 1964. Community organizers should not create new institutions; all welfare agencies fall prey to a "morbid life cycle" that turns them into rigid bureaucracies oblivious to their clients' needs. He imagined Community Action Agencies as provisional organizations that can challenge local welfare establishments, rousing them from their bureaucratic slumbers. The ideal welfare professional is an institutional energizer; his or her goal is "to detect and anticipate; to correlate and differentiate; to probe and carry through; to collect energy and allocate it; to reflect and reformulate; to mobilize and individualize; to gather power and liberate it."[20] Client participation is crucial to this energizing strategy; once clients are empowered, they can function as checks against bureaucratic self-perpetuation, disrupting and restructuring local organizations—including the Community Action Agencies themselves—whenever they depart from their original purpose. HARYOU, one of the earliest test projects that Ylvisaker helped fund, put this imperative to work in a dramatic fashion. Soon after its formation, HARYOU invited a group of Harlem teenagers, known as the HARYOU associates, to become involved in the program's day-to-day planning. The result was a perpetual state of organizational chaos, as youth took over the HARYOU offices and interfered with routine administrative work. As one HARYOU associate explained, unconsciously echoing Baraka's description of the revolutionary artist, "HARYOU must be taught by the young person in Harlem. . . . HARYOU, in essence, must be the young person in Harlem."[21]

This participatory professionalism, which aligned writers with a new generation of politically engaged welfare workers, transformed American literary culture in the 1960s. Originating in the work of the white counterculture, it became central to the various hyphenated minority literatures that proliferated after the Black Power era. More broadly, it functioned as the postwar period's most influential model for politically engaged art. Participatory professionalism gave rise to what might be called a "process era" in American literature that persisted long after many of the War on Poverty's legislative achievements were dismantled by subsequent Republican and Democratic administrations. I adapt this phrase from Mark McGurl's *The Program Era* (2009), which in turn borrows it from Hugh Kenner's *The Pound Era* (1971). McGurl's work locates the American literary field's institutional center in the university—specifically, in the creative writing programs that flourished after World War II: "The rise of the creative writing program stands as the most important event in postwar American literary history, and . . . paying attention to the increasingly intimate relation between literary production and the practices of higher education is the key to understanding the originality of postwar American literature."[22] McGurl's focus on these programs leads him to develop an autopoietic model of literary production. Serious (non-genre) literature is written by college-educated writers for college-educated readers. Much of that literature comes out of creative writing workshops and is consumed in English classrooms. In other words, postwar literature circulates within what sociologists call the professional-managerial or new class—a class defined by its acquisition of postsecondary educational capital.[23] This internal circulation is the condition of possibility for postwar literature, including minority literature that seems to give voice to communities largely excluded from the academy. According to McGurl, the "high cultural pluralism" of writers like Maxine Hong Kingston, Chang-Rae Lee, Ishmael Reed, Toni Morrison, and Sandra Cisneros is a product of the "partially overlapping institutionalizations of elitist high modernism and cultural pluralism in university English departments of the postwar period." Minority writers perform their racial and ethnic difference for a university audience who are "taught to savor their own open-mindedness."[24]

Maximum Feasible Participation complicates this autotelic model of literary production by tracing a looping strand of institutional influence that branches out from the academy and passes through the activist welfare agencies of the War on Poverty and their beleaguered post-1970s successors. This institutional loop left an especially visible mark on the careers of minority writers in the 1960s. Writers such as Amiri Baraka, Gwendolyn Brooks, Oscar Zeta Acosta, Alice Walker, and Toni Cade Bambara all participated in War on Poverty programs. Together with the Ford Foundation, the War on Poverty provided patronage for enough fledgling writers that it should be considered a rebooted version of the Works Progress Administration, one that specifically targeted minority artists.[25] For these writers, participatory professionalism provided a solution to what Madhu Dubey calls a "crisis in the category of racial community,"[26] generated by the Great Migration and the growing divide between minority professionals and the underclass. The Community Action Program offered a model for how professional expertise could circulate outside the academy and directly impact lower-class constituencies, often through alternative pedagogical institutions like Baraka's BARTS and Spirit House or Gwendolyn Brooks's poetry workshop for Chicago's Blackstone Rangers. This model became postwar writers' most influential account of how a university-centered literary field might interact with its outside, and it recurs throughout the work of writers with no direct experience with the War on Poverty, such as Tom Wolfe, Joyce Carol Oates, Philip Roth, and Carolyn Chute. At the same time, the process aesthetic developed by the white counterculture and 1960s cultural nationalists provided writers with examples of how they might loosen or break free from the formalism characteristic of the late modernism institutionalized in the American academy after World War II. Process art thus contributed to several important strands of what later became known as postmodernism, whose critics and adherents often defined it in terms of its incorporation of audience response and challenge to traditional forms of literary expertise.[27]

As the writers discussed in the chapters that follow show, participatory professionalism was a divided enterprise, with ambivalent effects. The paradigm's heyday was extremely short; the 1967 Quie Amendment, attached to the congressional funding bill for the OEO, put an end to maximum feasible participation by stipulating that two-thirds of the seats on Community Action Agencies must be reserved for elected officials and private-sector representatives. At its best, participatory professionalism challenged the nature of expertise itself and promised a radical democratization of the new class. At its worst, it perpetuated the very welfare paternalism it sought to dispel and lent itself to appropriation by conservatives bent on dismantling key institutions of the post–New Deal welfare state. Participatory professionalism did an immense amount of good; it established institutions that provided desperately needed help to the poor: free clinics, preschool programs, legal aid offices, and art and recreational centers. All too often, however, the strategies that participatory professionals used to bring their expertise to the inner city were manifestations of what, in an earlier book, I call "new class fantasy": the professional-managerial class's belief that it could reshape postwar society by disseminating practices and styles of thinking peculiar to that class.[28] In particular, most War on Poverty programs, including the Community Action Program, hinged on a theory of poverty that defined it in cultural terms, as a way of life passed on from generation to generation. War on Poverty programs hoped to intervene in that culture, reconditioning the poor to make them more middle class. This project of cultural engineering neglected the profound structural changes needed to eradicate poverty in a society that was shifting from an industrial to a postindustrial base—the kind of changes increasingly demanded by the civil rights movement in the early to mid-1960s.[29] Moreover, it helped establish an essentialist view of the poor that influenced the conservatives who increasingly shaped welfare policy as the War on Poverty of the 1960s gave way to the War on Welfare of the 1980s and 1990s. Paradoxically, participatory professionalism did as much to reinforce as to dismantle divisions between professionals and the poor, and it alternately undergirded and challenged existing forms of middle-class privilege.

Sutured Professionals

At its core, the participatory professionalism cultivated by postwar writers and welfare workers was an attempt to close the gap between the academy and its outside at the very moment that this gap was becoming a defining feature of American society. In the years after World War II, the professional-managerial class expanded at an unprecedented rate in response to the postwar economy's demand for university-educated knowledge workers. This expansion coincided with an even more dramatic shift: the migration of increasing numbers of African Americans, Mexicans, and Puerto Ricans to America's cities. Unlike the whites who attended America's postsecondary institutions in unprecedented numbers, most of these urban migrants were not poised to benefit from the transition to a postindustrial economy. Faced with racial discrimination and urban deindustrialization, they could not take advantage of the mechanisms of upward mobility used by previous generations of white ethnics; most joined the vast, surplus army of unskilled workers growing in America's cities. In the 1960s, many members of the new class, especially those in public professions like law, social work, and health care, tried to suture this class divide. In Steven Brint's terms, their participatory ethos was the last major expression of the "social trustee professionalism" that guided many professionals in the first half of the twentieth century. This ideology "promised competent performance of skilled work involving the application of broad and complex knowledge, the acquisition of which required formal academic study. Morally, it promised to be guided by an appreciation of the important social ends it served."[30] However, whereas traditional social trustee professionals envisaged the poor as a client population subject to paternalistic management, participatory professionals called this relationship into question. They imagined middle-class professionals and the poor working side by side to improve conditions in the inner city. This idea found a ready home within the Democratic Party, which increasingly imagined itself as the party that would fashion a coalition of urban professionals and minorities. The Community Action Program, which brought idealistic young professionals into poor communities, while also helping select members of those communities join the professional class, was one of the initiatives that the Johnson administration used to bring this coalition into being.[31]

For postwar writers and welfare professionals, this belief in audience and client participation paradoxically grew out of their perception of the poor's cultural difference. This perception at once motivated and frustrated participatory professionalism, inciting professionals to cross the gap between themselves and the poor while ensuring that it could never be fully closed. From the 1950s to the mid-1960s, most American commentators agreed that the nature of American poverty differed markedly before and after World War II.[32] Michael Harrington outlined this thesis in *The Other America* (1962), the book that rediscovered poverty for a generation of middle-class readers. Before the war, poverty "was general. It was the condition of life of an entire society, or at least of that huge majority who were without special skills or the luck of birth." As a result, poverty was the central political problem of the New Deal; the poor were America's most important voting constituency. Postwar affluence solved mass poverty for most Americans, but it left behind "the first minority poor in history,"[33] consisting of people who could not benefit from general improvements in the economy because of racial discrimination, lack of education, and other factors.[34] The new minority poor, Harrington argued, are "invisible," isolated from the great mass of Americans who live in the burgeoning suburbs. They are also politically silent; the poor "are without lobbies of their own; they put forward no legislative program. As a group, they are atomized. They have no face; they have no voice." Last, the minority poor are without aspiration—the saving characteristic of the New Deal's impoverished majority. The other America "is populated by the failures, by those driven from the land and bewildered by the city, by old people suddenly confronted with the torments of loneliness and poverty, and by minorities facing a wall of prejudice." This loss of aspiration colors every aspect of the minority poor's lives, making them entirely different from other Americans. "There is in short," Harrington concluded, "a language of the poor, a psychology of the poor, a world view of the poor. To be impoverished is to be an internal alien, to grow up in a culture that is radically different from the one that dominates society."[35]

This conception of the poor's cultural difference took on a number of competing forms in postwar social science. The best-known version is Oscar Lewis's culture of poverty thesis, developed in his 1950s and 1960s ethnographies of Mexican and Puerto Rican slum life. For Lewis, the poor's isolation from the institutional mechanisms of upward mobility makes them "present-time oriented." They seek immediate gratification and are compulsively promiscuous and violent. Because of their deficient impulse control, their families are female centered, with single mothers rearing children from multiple fathers. These traits originate as an adaptation to a slum environment; passed on from generation to generation, however, they become a cause rather than an effect of poverty. "By the time slum children are six or seven," Lewis argued, "they have usually absorbed the basic values and attitudes of their subculture and are not psychologically geared to take full advantage of changing conditions or increased opportunities which may occur in their lifetime."[36] Harrington drew on Lewis's work in *The Other America*, as did Daniel Moynihan in his leaked government report, *The Negro Family* (1965), which identified female-centered families as a leading cause of poverty among African Americans. Richard Cloward and Lloyd Ohlin offered a different formulation of the poor's cultural distinctiveness in their differential opportunity theory of juvenile delinquency, outlined in their study *Delinquency and Opportunity* (1960). In contrast to Lewis, they argued that the poor share the same aspirations as middle-class Americans; like all Americans, they want social status and the rewards that accompany it. Cut off from legitimate ways of achieving that status, however, they pursue deviant shortcuts, such as gang banging, theft, and drug abuse.[37] Both of these theories influenced the Community Action Program during its planning phase. President Kennedy read *The Other America* in preparation for developing a poverty program,[38] and he included Lloyd Ohlin in the President's Committee on Juvenile Delinquency and Youth Crime that established HARYOU and other antipoverty pilot programs.[39] Both theories led to similar conclusions about the need for a special kind of welfare activism that encouraged participation by the poor. For Lewis, the best way to disrupt the culture of poverty is to politicize the poor. "Any movement," he argued, "be it religious, pacifist, or revolutionary, which organizes and gives hope to the poor and effectively promotes solidarity and a sense of identification with larger groups, destroys the psychological and social core of the culture of poverty."[40] For Cloward and Ohlin, community action helps delinquent youth integrate into the national culture, giving them alternatives to the aberrant shortcuts normalized within the gang. For War on Poverty planners in general, the poor needed to be culturally reconditioned, and this change could be accomplished only through welfare activism that brought social workers and other professionals closer to the people they wanted to help.[41]

This perception of a cultural gap that experts must cross was also central to postwar process art. For the white counterculture, this gap was the condition of possibility for their work. In Michael Szalay's terms, these writers cultivated a "hip aesthetic"; they showed "how members of the professional-managerial class might . . . view themselves as simultaneously inside and cast out from the center of political power, as possessed of both white and black skin."[42] Beat writers like Kerouac, Ginsberg, and Burroughs identified product art with the academy and white middle class. They went on the road, seeking out the class and racial outsiders who embodied the alternative, process aesthetic they hoped to realize in their work. In an oft-cited passage from *On the Road* (1957), Sal Paradise walks through Denver's black neighborhood, "wishing I were a Negro, feeling that the best the white world had offered was not enough for me, not enough life, joys, kicks, darkness, music, not enough night. . . . I wished I were a Denver Mexican, or even a poor overworked Jap, anything but what I was so drearily, a 'white man' disillusioned."[43] Charles Olson, similarly reflecting on the Maya Indians of Mexico, claimed that they lived the bodily poetics he wanted to achieve with his poetry. They maintained "one thing no modern knows the secret of, however he is still by nature possessed of it: they wear their flesh with that difference which the understanding that it is common leads to."[44]

Baraka, in his writings on the white counterculture, disavowed their racist romanticism; in Werner Sollors's terms, Baraka diagnosed the counterculture's admiration for African Americans as a form of "Jim Crowism," an "inversion of white segregationist Jim Crow society in the Bohemian subculture."[45] However, he also took up and radicalized their racial ontology, making it central to the participatory art and community activism that he cultivated in the mid- to late 1960s. He embraced the idea that lower-class African Americans were the bearers of an antirationalistic black soul that challenged the rationalism of white America and the black bourgeoisie. In order to evoke this black soul in his work, he needed to destroy his own bourgeois psyche by immersing himself in the culture of the ghetto. Unlike writers such as Kerouac and Olson, who channeled the experience of poverty for middle-class readers, Baraka viewed those who lived in the ghetto as his natural audience, necessitating his move from Greenwich Village to Harlem. This radicalization of white countercultural aesthetics led him to embrace the cultural engineering espoused by many War on Poverty planners. In works like *The System of Dante's Hell* (1965), discussed in Chapter 2, Baraka imagined that lower-class African Americans were prone to the alleged pathologies identified by writers like Lewis and Moynihan. In bringing his art to the black lower class, Baraka did not want to reinforce those pathologies. Rather, he wanted to rectify them; he became one of the chief promoters of Ron Karenga's Kawaida—an Afrocentric philosophy that supposedly encapsulated the traditional ethical values and metaphysical beliefs of preconquest African societies. According to Jerry Watts, this philosophy, like the Nation of Islam's political program, "attempted to homogenize and rationalize the black urban working classes."[46] As Madhu Dubey and other critics have pointed out, it did so by appropriating many key ideas from liberal poverty discourse—in particular, its emphasis on eradicating black, female-headed households in favor of a more conventional, patriarchal family structure.[47]

Participatory professionalism's response to poverty was ambivalent. The process aesthetic that Baraka used to mediate his relationship with his inner-city audience was drawn from a white counterculture that explicitly conceived of the poor as a resource to be exploited by the middle-class writer. The process professionalism that HARYOU's Kenneth Clark and other community action pioneers put into play in their programs similarly insisted on the expert's ultimate authority over his or her clients. This authority was evoked by the phrase "maximum *feasible* participation" of the poor. Although professionals must question the protocols governing their interaction with the poor, they initiate that interaction and know best how to manage their clients. Baraka, in his application for BARTS funding, captured the resulting ambiguity about professional-client relationships in Community Action Agencies: "Acting, Writing, Directing, Set Designing, Production Management workshops will open aimed at gathering young Negroes interested in entering the professional theater world. The Black Arts will in turn make use of these 'students' in its own repertory company."[48] By putting the word "students" in quotation marks, Baraka highlighted his desire to challenge conventional distinctions between teacher and inner-city pupil. At the same time, he pitched BARTS as outwardly conforming to the institutional shape and purpose of conventional theater schools. BARTS would transform lower-class black youth into upwardly mobile artists capable of negotiating the New York cultural institutions that Baraka himself so ably mastered in the first half of the 1960s.

As a result of this ambiguity, one of the key complaints that the War on Poverty's critics made about Community Action Agencies was that they merely consolidated the authority of already-established professional elites. Kenneth Marshall, one of HARYOU's planners, complained, "The major immediate beneficiaries of these programs have been non-poor persons who have been afforded the opportunity of executive, technical and professional positions in the program."[49] Daniel Moynihan, unchastened by the controversy surrounding *The Negro Family* and installed as a domestic adviser for Richard Nixon, published a retrospective on the Community Action Program called *Maximum Feasible Misunderstanding* (1969), in which he insisted that the War on Poverty was a war fought by professionals with little impact on actual poverty rates. The War on Poverty was a consequence of what he called the "professionalization of reform." Instituted at a time when "the American poor, black and white, were surpassingly inert,"[50] the War on Poverty was the creation of social scientists whose profession was to identify society's ills. Moynihan's diagnosis of the class interests of the liberals who fashioned the War on Poverty prefigured neoconservatives' claim that American politics was dominated by what they called the new class: a liberal segment of the professional-managerial class with a vested interest in the welfare state.[51] The argument neglected the idealism of many welfare professionals involved in the Community Action Program and other 1960s manifestations of participatory professionalism. These professionals sometimes put their careers in jeopardy in the service of mobilizing the poor; Southern antipoverty workers occasionally risked their lives. However, most of the social scientists, social workers, lawyers, and writers who embraced the Community Action Program's dictum of maximum feasible participation struggled with the question of whether they were serving their own professional interests or those of the poor. This problem especially plagued minority writers and social scientists like Amiri Baraka and Kenneth Clark. These intellectuals experienced the split between professionalism and lower-class identification as an internal division, one that they tried to suture through their activism and writing. In Clark's terms, the minority professional who tries to improve the ghetto is an "involved observer." Unlike the participant observer of cultural anthropology, the involved observer participates "not only in rituals and customs but in the social competition with the hierarchy in dealing with the problems of the people he is seeking to understand."[52] The minority professional, in other words, is always enmeshed in the ghetto's struggle for status and power; however, she is never fully integrated into the community. Rather, through her acquired expertise, she provides a complex, insider/outsider's perspective on the community's problems.

Cultures of Poverty

Discussing the relative neglect of poverty in literary studies, Gavin Jones argues that this neglect derives, in part, from the culture of poverty thesis espoused by postwar social theorists like Lewis and Moynihan. In the 1960s, this theory provoked a backlash from minority intellectuals, resulting in books like Joyce Ladner's anthology, *The Death of White Sociology* (1973).[53] For African American literary critics since the 1960s, Moynihan has been emblematic of everything wrong with American perceptions of black cultural pathology, and Lewis plays a similar role in Latino/Latina literary studies.[54] Postwar theories of cultural deprivation, Jones argues, placed material deprivation "culturally off limits" and led literary critics to develop affirmative, identitarian projects that emphasized race, gender, and sexuality.[55] These projects downplayed poverty since, as Walter Benn Michaels remarks, it is "hard to see how appreciating the poor—as opposed to, say, eliminating them—can count as a contribution toward progressive politics."[56] However, the belief that the poor inhabit a separate culture never disappeared from American politics and culture. Indeed, as Kenneth Warren argues, this belief became interwoven with many of the identitarian projects that supposedly supplanted theories of cultural deprivation; writing about Henry Louis Gates Jr. and Houston Baker, Warren claims that their commitment to lower-class black cultural difference leads them to echo white sociologists like Daniel Moynihan.[57] Belief in the poor's cultural specificity continues to lend itself to political projects aimed at expanding and dismantling the welfare state and to professional practices aimed at eliminating, appreciating, and neglecting the poor.

The culture of poverty thesis resulted from postwar social theorists' muddled conception of class, which led them to conflate economic inequality with cultural difference. This conflation was most obvious in Oscar Lewis's work, which attempted to synthesize cultural anthropology and Marxist class theory. In the 1930s, Lewis completed his PhD under the supervision of Ruth Benedict, the founder of the Culture and Personality school of anthropology. In *Patterns of Culture* (1934), Benedict argued that culture is personality writ large: "A culture, like an individual, is a more or less consistent pattern of thought and action."[58] When analyzing indigenous cultures, she reduced them to archetypes: the Apollonian culture of the Pueblo Indians versus the Dionysian cultures of the Great Plains. When Lewis began his family studies in Mexico, he rejected Benedict's model as excessively reductive: "It was my dissatisfaction with the high level of abstraction inherent in the concept of culture patterns which led me to turn away from anthropological community studies to the intensive study of families." Benedict's theory, in particular, failed to account for cultural

differences between classes; it was ill suited to analyzing complex, modern societies with a rapidly changing capitalist economic base. Attempting to bring
Marxist insights to bear on cultural anthropology, however, Lewis developed
an even more reductive version of Benedict's theory. Accepting Benedict's assumption that culture is an adaptive response to environmental conditions,
Lewis concluded that poor people's behavior is shaped by their relationship to
their society's mode of production; slum behavior is "both an adaptation and
a reaction of the poor to their marginal position in a class-stratified, highly-
individuated, capitalistic society."[59] With the globalization of capitalism, these
conditions become universal, and all slum dwellers become the same; the culture of poverty cuts "across regional, rural-urban, and even national boundaries."[60] Lewis also accepted Benedict's claim that culture is personality writ large.
For those in the culture of poverty, this personality is dysfunctional, a product
of class oppression and material deprivation.[61] The central paradox of Lewis's
theory is that the culture of poverty is not really a culture at all. It is a liminal state of culture—the condition that results when a people have had their
culture stripped away from them. Lewis characterized a Puerto Rican family
as "closer to the expression of an unbridled id than any other people I have
studied" and described the culture of poverty as a "thin culture," marked by
"pathos, suffering and emptiness." "The poverty of culture," he concluded, "is
one of the crucial aspects of the culture of poverty."[62] In synthesizing Benedict
and Marx, Lewis jettisoned Benedict's cultural relativism and Marx's distinction between superstructure and base. He replaced Benedict's multiplicity of
cultural archetypes with a simple binary distinction between healthy and pathological class cultures, and he replaced Marxist economic determinism with a
circular causality whereby poverty creates cultural dysfunctions which in turn
create more poverty.[63]

Although countercultural writers like Kerouac, Olson, and Baraka seemingly inverted Lewis's theory, viewing lower-class cultures as necessary anti-
dotes to the sickness of the American middle class, they conceived of the poor
in strikingly similar terms. Lewis recognized this proximity between his work
and that of the American counterculture, writing that the poor have a unique
"capacity for spontaneity and adventure, for the enjoyment of the sensual,
the indulgence of impulse, which is often blunted in the middle-class, future-
oriented man. Perhaps it is this reality of the moment which the existentialist
writers are so desperately trying to recapture but which the culture of poverty

experiences as a natural, everyday phenomenon."[64] Postwar writers developed their own versions of the culture of poverty thesis, imagining that the poor of various racial and ethnic backgrounds inhabited the stripped-down remains of once-functioning cultures. Kerouac's term for those who inhabited this liminal culture was the "Fellahin peoples of the world,"[65] a phrase that he used throughout his fiction to refer to anyone other than middle-class whites. Kerouac borrowed this term from Oswald Spengler's *Decline of the West* (1918), where it refers to various conquered peoples living on the margins of the West. They experience life as a "planless happening without goal . . . wherein occurrences are many, but, in the last analysis, devoid of signification."[66] Olson similarly described the Maya as "poor failures of the modern world, incompetent even to arrange that, in the month of June, when the rains have not come far enough forward to fill the wells, they have water to wash in or to drink. They have lost the capacity of their predecessors to do anything in common."[67] The Maya's proximity to their flesh, the quality of their life that brings them closest to Olson's poetics, results from this dissolution of the minimal traditions that allow a people to cope with their surroundings.

The culture of poverty thesis thus gave rise to competing responses by postwar intellectuals. As a culture, a distinct way of life, it could be appreciated or even preserved by writers seeking alternatives to middle-class routine. As both the effect and ongoing cause of poverty and oppression, it required intervention by welfare professionals. In both cases, the participatory professionalism that addressed this culture of poverty was both a technique for bringing experts closer to their clients and a technique for *processing* those clients. The differences and affinities between these competing literary and social scientific responses are allegorized in a scene from Thomas Pynchon's *The Crying of Lot 49* (1966), a novel set in 1964—the year that Johnson declared war on poverty. While searching for signs of the Tristero, the novel's underground mail network, in the streets of San Francisco, Oedipa Maas encounters an old sailor outside a rooming house with the Tristero post horn tattooed on his hand. The man, an alcoholic, suffers from delirium tremens and laments the loss of his wife, whom he abandoned in Fresno. Oedipa imagines helping him: "She might find the landlord of this place, and bring him to court, and buy the sailor a new suit at Roos/Atkins, and shirt, and shoes, and give him the bus fare to Fresno after all." However, she realizes that to reintegrate the sailor into middle-class society would destroy the distinctive experience he embodies. This experience depends on the disease responsible for his destitution; the delirium tremens (DTs), she reflects,

> also meant a time differential, a vanishingly small instant in which change had to be confronted at last for what it was, where it could no longer disguise itself as something innocuous like an average rate; where velocity dwelled in the projectile though the projectile be frozen in midflight, where death dwelled in the cell though the cell be looked in on at its most quick. She knew that the sailor had seen worlds no other man had seen if only because there was that high magic to low puns, because DT's must give access to dt's of spectra beyond the known sun, music made purely of Antarctic loneliness and fright.

The sailor is one of many figures in the novel who offers an alternative to the closed system that America, in Pynchon's analysis, has become. He prefigures the alternative America of squatters and drifters that Pynchon elegiacally evokes in the novel's conclusion, an America "invisible yet congruent with the cheered land she [Oedipa] lived in." He also embodies the aesthetic that Pynchon tries to achieve in his novel, an aesthetic that recovers the "excluded middles" pushed out by a culture in the midst of becoming a "great digital computer."[68]

Through this encounter with the sailor, Pynchon comments on mid-1960s antipoverty efforts. As J. Kerry Grant notes, Oedipa's visit to San Francisco puts her in contact with Michael Harrington's "other America,"[69] a world of juvenile delinquents, black and Latino/Latina workers, alcoholics, and abandoned elderly generally invisible to middle-class whites. Oedipa's first response to the sailor is to cradle him in her arms "as if he were her own child,"[70] replicating the maternal concern for the poor and infirm that supposedly defined the welfare state. She then envisages her transformation into a community organizer who will encourage her client to challenge her landlord, as many welfare activists did throughout the 1960s. However, in a gesture that Sean McCann and Michael Szalay identify as typical of postwar literature, Oedipa dismisses pragmatic social reform in favor of "a new political vision built in large part on the appeal of the spontaneous, the symbolic, and ultimately, the magical."[71] Once she abandons her reformist ambitions, she can appreciate the sailor's unique perception of the world, which allows her to finally break free from the rut of middle-class routine she has been trying to escape since the novel's opening: the "safe furrow the bulk of this city's waking each sunrise again set virtuously to plowing."[72] As Pynchon underscores, however, Oedipa's appreciation of the sailor is just as rooted in middle-class subjectivity as her social work fantasy. Oedipa's interpretation of the DTs begins with a memory of one of her college boyfriends complaining about calculus and concludes—appropriately, since she is a former English major—with an allusion to Coleridge's ancient mariner. Oedipa, in other words, can access the sailor's visionary experience only with the help of the educational capital she acquired in college. Indeed, given that the sailor's "high magic" resides in the "low pun" between medical and mathematical terminology, this visionary experience is embedded in that educational capital itself rather than in the laconic old man. The old man derives no benefit from his poverty and sickness, which are in the process of destroying him. Rather, his experience is valuable only insofar as it can be processed and assimilated by professionally trained readers like Oedipa.

Oedipa's abandonment of the sailor prefigures the War on Poverty's evolution into the War on Welfare of the 1980s and 1990s. From the late 1960s onward, the poor's cultural difference became a justification for neglecting them entirely. In particular, American conservatives appropriated the culture of poverty thesis, turning it into a powerful weapon to attack the very Johnson-era programs that the theory originally helped inspire. The first conservative text that drew on Lewis's research was *The Unheavenly City* (1970), written by Edward Banfield, a future adviser to Richard Nixon, Gerald Ford, and Ronald Reagan. Citing Lewis, Harrington, Moynihan, and others, Banfield constructed a scale of class cultures, each defined by "its distinctive orientation toward providing for a more or less distant future." Moving even further away than Lewis from Benedict's Culture and Personality model, Banfield rejected any environmental origin or adaptive function for these class cultures. Present orientation, he argued, is immutably built into groups and individuals, and no government can intervene to change it; lower-class culture is a generative cause rather than an effect of poverty. Welfare is wasted on those who live in this culture; lacking impulse control, the lower class will squander whatever resources are given to them. In developing this argument, Banfield briefly distinguished his argument from biological racism:

> Strong correlations have been shown to exist between IQ score and socioeconomic status, and some investigators have claimed that these correlations are largely attributable to genetic factors. These considerations suggest the possibility that one's ability to take account of the future may depend mainly upon one's biologically inherited intelligence. The assumption being made here, however, is a contrary

one—namely that time horizon is a cultural (or subcultural) trait passed on to the individual in early childhood from his group.[73]

In practice, however, Banfield's theory is indistinguishable from genetic essentialism; present orientation is immutably built into cultures associated with specific racial and ethnic groups.

This essentialist adaptation of Lewis's theory was central to the invention of what later conservatives called the underclass: a group culturally defined by its failure to embody middle-class values, especially the Protestant work ethic.[74] This group, conservatives claimed, absorbed most welfare expenditures and was responsible for most criminal violence. For Banfield, the lower class was relatively small, consisting of "perhaps 10 to 20 percent" of all families with incomes below the poverty line.[75] As Adolph Reed documents, this statistic appeared again and again in essays about the underclass published between the 1970s and 1980s.[76] It has never been empirically verified; Banfield drew it from Lewis, who offered the "rough guess" that "only about 20 percent of the population below the poverty line (between six and ten million people) in the United States have characteristics which would justify classifying their way of life as that of a culture of poverty."[77] This statistical vagueness is intrinsic to the underclass concept; unlike income level or occupation, culture cannot be recorded in the census. Indeed, as its name implies, the underclass exists outside all typical conceptions of class and all of the metrics used to measure it. Not all poor people belong to the underclass; many who live in slums exhibit the same cultural traits as other Americans and will eventually escape their circumstances. Not all members of the underclass are poor; drug dealers and pimps can be affluent. Although conservatives generally use the term as shorthand to refer to inner-city blacks and Latinos/Latinas, the underclass is also not simply a racial category. Following the lead of Moynihan, who insisted in *The Negro Family* that "the Negro community is in fact dividing between a stable middle-class group that is steadily growing stronger and more successful, and an increasingly disorganized and disadvantaged lower-class group,"[78] virtually all conservatives distinguish between the underclass and the black bourgeoisie. The underclass is a malleable, abject category that absorbs all of the social animosity hitherto directed toward a variety of nonwhite and impoverished groups, while ostensibly liberating its user from charges of racism or class bias. Over the course of the 1970s, 1980s, and 1990s, this category became a pervasive feature of public discourse about the welfare state, invoked by both Republicans and Democrats. It featured centrally in the debate leading up to the Clinton-era Personal Responsibility and Work Opportunity Reconciliation Act (1996), which eradicated Aid to Families with Dependent Children (AFDC), one of the cornerstones of the New Deal.

The paradox of participatory professionalism, then, is that a paradigm oriented toward assimilating the poor drew on a conception of poverty that so readily lent itself to their abjection. The readings that follow trace multiple moments when the process impetus to dissolve boundaries between artists and the poor instead reinforces those boundaries. This abrupt turn to abjection is especially characteristic of writers who drew on a process aesthetic to help fashion the idea of the underclass. Tom Wolfe, discussed in Chapter 4, exemplifies this turn. His New Journalism, formally influenced by Beat prose, drew on his supposed capacity to channel the anarchic energies of juvenile delinquents, rural Southerners, and other plebeian figures into his reporting. In his satire of Great Society liberalism, *Radical Chic and Mau-Mauing the Flak Catchers* (1970), the minority recipients of Community Action largesse embody these same anarchic energies as they perform their racial difference in ways that overwhelm and terrify War on Poverty administrators. Wolfe mimics this performance with his style, which similarly explodes bureaucratic procedures meant to contain San Francisco's welfare recipients. However, Wolfe appropriates this style to expose liberal sympathy for the poor as a dangerous illusion that fosters underclass criminality. *Radical Chic* draws a sharp line between process art's aesthetic and political projects in ways that appealed to the conservative reviewers who lauded the book.

Juvenile Delinquents and Welfare Mothers

Throughout the postwar era, two figures alternately facilitated and interrupted the process identification between participatory professionals and the poor: juvenile delinquents and welfare mothers. These figures have been central to debates about welfare since the 1960s, and they play a key role in many of the readings that follow. For conservative critics like Banfield, they were the two gendered sides of the underclass, figures in need of tough discipline that liberals were incapable of providing. Appealing to the racial animosities of white working- and middle-class voters (usually in ways that worked against their economic interests), politicians from Richard Nixon to Bill Clinton presented delinquents and welfare mothers as people who had rejected the middle-class work ethic. These politicians created a post-welfare state in which tough dis-cipline became the norm for American social policy toward the poor, as crime laws targeted lower-class African American and Latino men and as workfare replaced welfare for single mothers. Loïc Wacquant describes the gendered ef-fects of these two institutional changes:

> The public aid bureaucracy, now reconverted into an administrative springboard into poverty-level employment, takes up the mission of inculcating the duty of working for work's sake among poor women (and indirectly their children): 90 per-cent of welfare recipients in the United States are mothers. The quartet formed by the police, the court, the prison, and the probation or parole officer assumes the task of taming their brothers, their boyfriends or husbands, and their sons: 93 percent of US inmates are male.

These complementary institutions reinforce an economy defined by "the ero-sion of stable and homogeneous wage work."[79] They ensure that those at the bottom of the occupational hierarchy pursue low-wage jobs, even when those jobs are not available.

This post-1968 abjection of juvenile delinquents and welfare mothers was partly a response to their perceived status as privileged objects of professional concern during the War on Poverty. Throughout the 1950s and 1960s, the juve-nile delinquent was the major figure that stood, in the eyes of most Americans, for the dangers of urban poverty.[80] As originally conceptualized by John F. Ken-nedy, the War on Poverty was a war on delinquency; the Community Action Program, in particular, originated in the Kennedy-era President's Committee on Juvenile Delinquency and Youth Crime. Most War on Poverty programs continued to focus on youth; Title I of the Economic Opportunity Act estab-lished the Job Corps "to increase the employability of young men and women aged sixteen through twenty-one,"[81] and one of the unstated aims of the War on Poverty was to prevent young black men from rioting. Much of the socio-logical theory that informed the War on Poverty also focused on the problem of delinquency—in particular, Cloward and Ohlin's *Delinquency and Oppor-tunity*. In the War on Poverty's later years, this focus on delinquency became a target for the program's conservative critics, who pointed to several instances where Community Action Agencies paid salaries to gang leaders.[82] Meanwhile, one of the most important effects of the War on Poverty was to expand AFDC, the primary New Deal program that helped single mothers. When President

Johnson signed the Economic Opportunity Act, he insisted, "We are not content to accept the endless growth of relief rolls or welfare rolls. We want to offer the forgotten fifth of our people opportunity and not doles."[83] However, welfare activists associated with the Community Action Program successfully challenged discriminatory eligibility criteria that prevented many black single mothers from applying for AFDC, leading to a dramatic rise in welfare rates, especially in New York City. Between 1960 and 1970, the percentage of the city's population receiving public assistance (mostly in the form of AFDC), rose from 4.9 to 14 percent.[84]

Of these two figures, the juvenile delinquent was more often adopted by participatory professionals as a synecdoche for the energies they associated with the poor. Juvenile delinquents were especially important for many postwar writers as mediating figures enabling their transition from product to process art. As I argue in Chapter 1, white delinquents played this role for Jack Kerouac. His novels depict them as class hybrids, caught between lower-class subcultures and a middle-class society. As such, they mirror Kerouac's own sense of split class identity. Other countercultural writers, like Norman Mailer, similarly used white delinquents to imaginatively bridge the gap between middle-class whites and lower-class minorities. In Greenwich Village in the 1940s, Mailer imagined, "a ménage-a-trois was completed—the bohemian and the juvenile delinquent came face-to-face with the Negro, and the hipster was a fact in American life." For both Kerouac and Mailer, the white delinquent embodied the present-oriented ontology that they wanted to capture in their work; in particular, both writers were fascinated by the delinquent's capacity for spontaneous violence and willingness to court danger. "It can be suggested," Mailer argued,

> that it takes little courage for two strong eighteen-year old hoodlums, let us say, to beat in the brains of a candy-store keeper. . . . Still, courage of a sort is necessary, for one murders not only a weak fifty-year old man but an institution as well, one violates private property, one enters into a new relation with the police and introduces a dangerous element into one's life. The hoodlum is therefore daring the unknown, and so no matter how brutal the act it is not altogether cowardly.[85]

For Mailer, the delinquent's ability to live with danger, if properly channeled by the white writer, could be used as a force to disrupt the bureaucratic stasis of the welfare state and the formal rigidity of product art. Baraka's version of the Black Arts similarly insisted that revolutionary artists can tap into the violent energies of juvenile delinquents; *The System of Dante's Hell* imagines delinquent violence as a medium through which the black artist must pass in order to escape from the deadening influence of white literature.

Kerouac, Mailer, and Baraka's romanticization of delinquent violence did not appeal to War on Poverty officials. However, activists associated with the Community Action Program similarly targeted delinquents as figures who best exemplified the need for more fluid forms of welfare work capable of reaching the urban poor. Chicago's largest Community Action Agency, the Woodlawn Organization, received $927,000 to provide education and training to two of the city's most violent street gangs, the Blackstone Rangers and Disciples. The program ran into problems almost immediately; the Rangers' leader, Jeff Fort, was arrested for murder shortly after being hired as a teacher, and "trainees falsely signed checks and routinely didn't show up to the programming."[86] Drawing on Cloward and Ohlin's *Delinquency and Opportunity*, supporters argued that gang membership was the product of black youths' inability to pursue social goals through legitimate means. Gangs were a sign of youths' self-esteem and desire for community, and they could be turned into legitimate political organizations once assimilated into established institutions like the black church. As Reverend John Fry, who promoted the venture to the OEO, explained, the Blackstone Rangers' "answer to the chaos and violence and banality of life in an antidemocracy has been to create a large organization capable of producing some genuine order and some safety from this exceedingly hostile environment."[87] The Woodlawn Organization's gang outreach project, Fry believed, would not just transform the Rangers; it would change Chicago's welfare establishment, making it more attentive to the legitimate concerns of the city's black youth.

In perceiving delinquents as a rejuvenating force for middle-class experts, postwar writers and welfare professionals drew on a rich tradition of literary and journalistic representations of youth criminality. As Keith Gandal points out, although Progressive-era writers and journalists demonized lower-class criminals as threats to social order, they also titillated their readers with representations of delinquent violence. Stephen Crane, in *Maggie, a Girl of the Streets* (1893), underscored the ruthlessness, empty bravado, and moral hypocrisy of Bowery toughs like Maggie's brother, Jimmie, and lover, Pete. At the same time, he imagined that they embodied an ethic of manly self-esteem that he counterpoised against the effete conformism of bourgeois society. The tough "has the proper relation to others: he is dedicated to defiance, immune to their opinions of him, and thus capable of resistance."[88] Slum violence, for Crane, was a sign of the ongoing energy of the lower class, an energy that he hoped to channel into his fiction and journalism and offer to the reader as an entertaining spectacle. Jacob Riis, in *How the Other Half Lives* (1890), was similarly fascinated by violent toughs. He distinguished between the toughs and thieves who preyed on the middle class and the paupers who depended on begging and charity: "The thief is infinitely easier to deal with than the pauper, because the very fact of his being a thief presupposes some bottom to the man. Granted that it is bad, there is still something, a possible handle by which to catch him."[89] As in the case of the Rangers, the very extremity of the thief's challenge to middle-class institutions was a sign of his adaptability to them.

The other figure most often associated with the War on Poverty, the welfare mother, has rarely functioned as a sympathetic object of identification, either in literature or social science. While Crane's Bowery toughs elicit his qualified admiration, destitute women like Maggie's alcoholic mother, Mary, are wholly abject. In *Maggie*, Mary embodies a grotesque, feminine agency, and the novel highlights the violence that she unleashes on her children and furniture. Contemporary texts and films that ostensibly elicit sympathy for welfare mothers, such as Sapphire's *Push* (1996) and its film adaptation, *Precious* (2009), often depict them in similar terms.[90] For several of the writers discussed in the chapters that follow, single mothers function as figures who interrupt, rather than enable, the process impetus to deconstruct received literary forms and dissolve boundaries between artist and audience. In Kerouac's *On the Road*, Dean Moriarty's wives and girlfriends threaten to halt his cross-country, delinquent flights, confining him in lower-middle-class domesticity and silencing his improvisational raps. In Oscar Zeta Acosta's autobiographical fiction, discussed in Chapter 3, Oscar's Legal Services work for welfare mothers leaves him trapped in the static bureaucracies of Oakland's poverty program; he becomes a radical lawyer and process artist when he begins to work for and write about male Chicano activists and delinquents in Los Angeles. In black nationalist dramas like *Madheart* (1966), Amiri Baraka chastens black women and seeks to reincorporate them into male-headed nuclear families; meanwhile, his poems celebrate black delinquents as potential revolutionaries.[91] In general, whereas postwar writers imagine male delinquency as an expression of admirable, if exaggerated masculinity, they depict welfare mothers as monstrously aberrant. At times, the welfare mother resembles Riis's pauper; she is a passive woman without character who loses her willpower when offered public charity. At other times, she is too willful—a domineering matriarch who castrates her male children and defrauds the state.[92] When postwar writers offer sympathetic portraits of welfare mothers, they usually do so by rejecting the participatory thrust of process art. Gwendolyn Brooks, discussed in Chapter 2, is a case in point; her long poem "In the Mecca" seeks to rethink black nationalist depictions of single black mothers by insisting on the critical distance that the poem opens between the artist and her subject matter.

This abjection of welfare mothers reflects gender inequities embedded in the welfare state since the 1930s. The New Deal established a two-track system of welfare entitlements. Social Security programs in the first track, like unemployment insurance and old-age pensions, largely benefited white working- and middle-class men. These programs excluded most women and minorities; they did not apply to agricultural and domestic workers or to those in female-dominated professions like teaching and nursing.[93] Programs in the second track, like AFDC (originally called Aid to Dependent Children, or ADC), specifically targeted poor women. Unlike programs in the first track, these programs were means tested; women had to prove that they had no other means of support. This division re-encoded a series of Victorian-era sentimental assumptions about women's place in the public and private spheres.[94] Unemployment insurance and old-age pensions were entitlements for working men, who were imagined as their families' primary breadwinners. AFDC provided charity for poor mothers who, through no fault of their own, could not rely on those men; the program was designed for widows.

Through the War on Poverty, Democrats attempted to redress the racial inequalities of New Deal welfare redistribution. However, they replicated the New Deal's treatment of single mothers as exceptional figures whose problems could be solved only by reintegrating them into families with fully employed male heads. Daniel Moynihan offered the most infamous version of this argument in *The Negro Family*. Drawing on earlier studies of the black family, especially E. Franklin Frazier's *The Negro Family in the United States* (1939), Moynihan argued that black men's exclusion from employment had damaged the African American family, creating a matriarchal pattern in which fathers "have unusually low power" or are altogether absent. Moynihan conceived of black women as both the victims and aggressors in this family structure. The high incidence of divorce and illegitimacy increases black women's poverty and welfare dependency. However, black women also perpetuate a sense of inferiority in their husbands and sons, in part due to their own comparative success in finding domestic and secretarial work: "Both as a husband and as a father the Negro male is made to feel inadequate. . . . To this situation he may react with withdrawal, bitterness toward society, aggression both within the family and racial group, self-hatred, or crime." Deprived of the example of strong working fathers, black sons in turn grow up to be weak or absent fathers, perpetuating the "tangle of pathology" for another generation.[95] For Moynihan, black matriarchy was a problem that could not be resolved through Community Action Programs aimed at politicizing the poor.[96] Instead, one of his chief recommendations was to enlist more black men in the army, "a world away from women, a world run by strong men of unquestioned authority."[97] In Moynihan's work, participatory professionalism gives way to disciplinary solutions to the problem of lower-class cultural difference.

In the 1980s and 1990s, the delinquent and the welfare mother presided over the Democratic Party's repudiation of the War on Poverty, dramatized by the emergence of the centrist Democratic Leadership Council and Bill Clinton's signing of the Personal Responsibility and Work Opportunity Reconciliation Act. With this legislation, Democrats largely abandoned their unfinished project of suturing the class divide between professionals and the underclass. They capitulated to Republican efforts to brand them as the party of liberal elitists invested in maintaining the nonwhite poor as a permanent welfare clientele. The perils and allure of process professionalism, however, continue to shape American political culture. This ongoing influence was evident in the presidency of Barack Obama, who began his career as a community organizer in Chicago, and by the white middle- and working-class backlash against that presidency, which culminated in the election of Donald Trump. America continues to work through the cultural debates provoked by the War on Poverty's unrealized promise of an expanded welfare state. *Maximum Feasible Participation* traces the evolution of these debates in postwar literature, exploring the possibilities and limitations of welfare politics at the moment of its apotheosis and disappointing failure.

Jack Kerouac's Delinquent Art

"They're always printing things about Jack that aren't true—
you know, about the Beat Generation and all that juvenile
delinquency. Everybody says, 'Beat Generation!—He's a juvenile
delinquent!' But he's a good boy—a good son. He was never any
juvenile delinquent. I know, I'm his mother."

"Yeah," he added, "We're middle class, we've always been
middle class. We're middle class just like you."

Gabrielle and Jack Kerouac, 1959 interview[1]

In interviews and essays published after *On the Road* transformed Jack Kerouac into a literary celebrity, he inveighed against journalists' equation of the Beat Generation with juvenile delinquency.[2] Beat, he complained, "never meant juvenile delinquents, it meant characters of a special spirituality who didn't gang up but were solitary Bartlebies staring out the dead wall window of our civilization."[3] Repeatedly in the late 1950s, highbrow and Hollywood interpreters of Kerouac's work read it through the lens of the Cold War fascination with youth criminality. Norman Podhoretz, for instance, argued, "The spirit of hipsterism and the Beat Generation strikes me as the same spirit which animates the young savages in leather jackets who have been running amok in the last few years with their switch-blades and zip guns."[4] Echoing this conflation, when 20th Century Fox attempted to purchase screenplay rights to *On the Road*, they hoped to reimagine Kerouac's novel as a synthesis of *The Wild One* and *Rebel without a Cause* (1955)—the two most celebrated juvenile delinquency films of the 1950s. Jerry Wald, who entered into failed negotiations with Kerouac, wanted to cast Marlon Brando as Dean Moriarty and conclude the film with his fiery automobile death in a nod toward James Dean's recent demise.[5]

These readings responded to obvious aspects of *On the Road*. Dean, the novel's central figure and archetypal Beat, is a former delinquent who spends time in a New Mexican reform school after a series of compulsive car thefts. He is a thinly fictionalized version of Neal Cassady, whose manic conversation and letter-writing style became the inspiration for Kerouac's version of process art—the spontaneous prose that he made famous with *On the Road*. Even more fundamentally than the black jazz musicians whom Kerouac admired, white delinquents embodied the energies that he hoped to capture in his fiction. In spite of his mother's insistence that he was a "good son," he often imagined himself and other hipsters as potential delinquents. At the same time, Kerouac depicted hipsterism and delinquency as tragic conditions. Indeed, one feature of Kerouac's work that distinguishes it from that of other Beat writers is his refusal to consistently depict hipsters as figures who embody the "special spirituality" that he described in his late-1950s interviews. His notion of the Beats as "solitary Bartlebies" encapsulates the mythos publicized in texts like Allen Ginsberg's "Howl" (1956) and Norman Mailer's "The White Negro" (1957). This mythos envisaged hipsters as doomed but heroic figures who, like Melville's Bartleby, refuse to fit into the white-collar workplace. However, Kerouac rarely affirmed this mythos in an unadulterated fashion. Rather, his work is an anxious inquiry into the psychological and cultural reasons behind certain American young men's failure to adapt to the US class structure. Rather than imagine this failure as an act of resistance, Kerouac depicted it as a tragic flaw—an inability to become, as he put it, "middle class just like you."

This focus on hipsters' alienation from America's class structure echoes the concerns of 1950s and early 1960s social scientists, who attempted to understand the proliferation of disaffected teenagers and young men in an affluent society. These theorists attributed this proliferation to the simultaneous breakdown of working-class cultures and the institutions that transmit middle-class habits and values. This twin breakdown left young lower-class men stranded in a cultural no-man's-land between two classes. Kerouac's fiction attempts to map out this no-man's-land; his autobiographical novels return again and again to young men who are alienated from the cultural attitudes of both the traditional working and new middle classes. Thus, Kerouac's fiction also maps out the location where future writers and social scientists would locate the underclass and the kind of literary and welfare activism that they would use to address its needs. As Carlo Rotella notes, the problem of juvenile delinquency, "which played such an important role in discussions of the inner city during the 1950s and early 1960s, was subsumed by the problem of race that defined the urban crisis during the 1960s."[6] This shift took place when President Johnson launched the War on Poverty, as OEO planners took ideas from delinquency theorists such as Richard Cloward and Lloyd Ohlin and applied them to the problems of inner-city black and Latino/Latina youth. As I argue in this chapter, Kerouac's fiction prefigures this shift. In his depictions of hipsters and white delinquents, he synthesizes two competing strands of postwar delinquency discourse: a strand that insists on delinquents' alienation from American class structures and a strand that insists on their Oedipal attachment to overbearing mothers. Kerouac's hipsters and delinquents, in other words, are white versions of the black and Latino/Latina underclass that would populate social scientific and literary texts about the inner city from the mid-1960s onward. At the same time, Kerouac also prefigures the tensions confronted by subsequent African American and Latino/Latina writers who drew on a process aesthetic to cross the cultural gap between middle-class professionals and the underclass. A potential delinquent himself, Kerouac experiences this gap as an internal division that he tries and fails to suture with his improvisatory art.

Hipster Anomie

Although delinquency discourse in the 1940s and 1950s articulated many of the same themes as poverty discourse in the 1960s, each defined its object in different terms. As Rotella notes, delinquency theory marked the beginning of postwar sociologists' recognition of the existence of structural poverty in the United States. Attempting to understand juvenile violence, sociologists became aware of "the prospect of a permanent ghetto underclass drastically and lastingly cut off from opportunity and the rest of the metropolis by lines of racial difference and class conflict."[7] However, the 1950s delinquent was not always a lower-class ethnic or racial minority. Post–World War II social scientists distinguished between two species of delinquent, each distinct in its class origins and in its potential threat to society. The first was the anomic delinquent, who frequently belonged to an ethnic or racial minority and deviated from middle-class behavior because he lacked occupational opportunities. The second was the psychopathological delinquent, born to a middle-class family but psychologically stunted due to the influence of a weak father and domineering mother.[8] Both theories were efforts to chart out the delinquent's cultural distance from the white middle class, explaining the circumstances under which outsiders and certain insiders fail to assimilate middle-class values and work habits. Crossing this cultural divide became the motivation for the participatory professionalism institutionalized in the War on Poverty.

The first type of delinquent was the product of 1950s sociologists' application of Émile Durkheim's notion of anomie to the behavior of rebellious male youth. Durkheim developed this concept in *Suicide* (1897) in an effort to explain why the suicide rate spiked during economic depressions and times of sudden, widespread affluence. Every society, he argued, is governed by a system of expectations about the economic rewards that accrue to people from different socioeconomic backgrounds. In a well-governed society, "each in his sphere vaguely realizes the extreme limit set to his ambitions and aspires to nothing beyond." In times of sudden socioeconomic change, however, this system is thrown into disarray. Anomie refers to this state of unregulated expectations: either people are forced to come to terms with diminished opportunities, or their desires expand beyond the viable limits of these opportunities. When either happens, people are prone to frustrated outbursts of violence against themselves and others. For Durkheim, this mismatch between ambition and opportunity was something that afflicted the well-to-do, especially people involved in industry and finance. The poor, he argued, were shielded from it: "The less one has the less he is tempted to extend the range of his needs indefinitely."[9] In the 1950s, delinquency theorists revised this assumption, arguing that the specific conditions of American society make poor people particularly prone to anomie. According to their theory, first developed by Robert Merton and later elaborated by A. K. Cohen, Lloyd Ohlin, and Richard Cloward, the United States is an unusually anomic society. It is a nation that emphasizes the accumulation of wealth, power, and fame as social goals above all others. However, this emphasis is not accompanied by a well-elaborated system of norms governing how these goals should be achieved and what groups can reasonably hope to do so. As a result, all Americans' desires outstrip their opportunities; everyone is like the suicidal financiers described in Durkheim's study. This condition is especially acute among impoverished young men. Impelled by a consumeristic mass media, they share the same desire for wealth, power, and fame as all other Americans. However, they lack the practical skills and opportunities to pursue those goals. Instead, lower-class youth turn to illegitimate means at their disposal; they join youth gangs, hoping to achieve wealth and notoriety through theft, violence, and other criminal activities. As a result, the subcultures established by anomic delinquents seem like parodies of straight, middle-class society. As Paul Goodman put it in *Growing Up Absurd*, "There have now been numerous reported cases of criminal delinquent acts performed to get a picture in the paper, just as a young man on Madison Avenue may work hard for a year to get two five-second plugs on TV. The delinquents, perforce, take short cuts to glamour."[10]

Sociologists in the 1920s, 1930s, and 1940s had already explored the idea that lower-class youth were ambivalently attached to middle-class values. In particular, Chicago school urban ecologists had argued that lower-class delinquency resulted from the cultural dislocation experienced by immigrant youth. Frederic Thrasher, in a 1927 study of Chicago gangs, described juvenile delinquency as an "interstitial" phenomenon, one that emerged within "fissures and breaks in the structure of social organization." These fissures were both geographical and cultural; delinquency emerged in unstable slums that lie between the industrial core and surrounding residential neighborhoods, and it thrived on the "cultural frontier" between traditionalist immigrant communities and mainstream US society.[11] For Thrasher and other pre–World War II sociologists, however, this phenomenon was temporary, a generational aberration before ethnic assimilation into the middle class. Moreover, even within the frontier neighborhoods, most youth fell into stable patterns of behavior. In terms that William F. Whyte used in a 1943 study of young Italian Americans, most immigrant youth were either "corner boys" or "college boys." The former lacked ambition, were "primarily interested in their local community," and eventually settled into working-class trades. The latter were "primarily interested in social advancement,"[12] acquired the work habits of the American middle class, and eventually gravitated toward professional careers.

For post–World War II observers, in contrast, these behavior patterns were disappearing. Traditional corner boys had vanished; the ethnic institutions that once sustained them—such as community social clubs and the urban political machines—no longer existed.[13] Similarly, it was increasingly difficult to be a college boy. With the middle classes fleeing to the suburbs, lower-class neighborhoods became isolated and underserviced. The poor were concentrated in what John Kenneth Galbraith called "islands of poverty" cut off from the affluent society.[14] This concentration was especially true for African Americans and other racial minorities, who were trapped in their neighborhoods by housing discrimination. Instead of becoming corner boys or college boys, impoverished young men became disturbed hybrids of the two: they combined the corner boy's resistance to middle-class advancement with the college boy's boundless dissatisfaction.

Kerouac's 1950s fiction explored this troubled frontier between lower- and middle-class behavior, imagining it as the terrain occupied by hipsters and white delinquents. For Kerouac, this frontier was both the condition of possibility for his own delinquent art and a debilitating internal division that he tried and failed to overcome. Kerouac consistently drew on a racist romanticism to describe the groups most afflicted by poverty in the 1950s, especially African Americans and Latinos/Latinas. This racist romanticism is exemplified by Sal Paradise's desire in *On the Road* to become a "Negro," "Denver Mexican," or "poor overworked Jap" while visiting Denver (*OR*, 169–170). Sal conflates all of the US racial minorities into a common culture of joy and kicks and juxtaposes them against the "white sorrows" of the middle-class majority (*OR*, 171). As Robert Holton, among others, has shown, this tendency to lump together nonwhites is a consequence of Kerouac's primitivist notion of the Fellahin, which he shared with other Beat writers such as William S. Burroughs.[15] The "Fellahin Indians of the world," Sal comments, are "the essential strain of the basic primitive, wailing humanity that stretches in a belt around the equatorial belly of the world between Malaya (the long fingernail of China) to India the great subcontinent to Arabia to Morocco to the self same deserts and jungles of Mexico and over the waves to Polynesia" (*OR*, 268). In Oswald Spengler's *The Decline of the West*, the term "Fellahin" describes cultural groups left behind after the collapse of a world civilization. In the modern world, it describes remnants of older cultures that survive on the margins of the modern West. Westerners are animated by their culture's Faustian spirit, which endows them with a sense of their place in world history and leads them to conquer ever-new conceptual and geographical territories. The Fellahin, in contrast, consist of people who no longer occupy a meaningful historical trajectory: "Life as experienced by primitive and by Fellahin peoples is just the zoological up-and-down, a planless happening without goal or cadenced march in time, wherein occurrences are many, but, in the last analysis, devoid of significance."[16] To extend Spengler's pervasive organic metaphors, the Fellahin are a civilization's dead husk, gradually returning to the soil out of which that civilization was born. They are at one and the same time pre- and posthistorical. Describing them as "the source of mankind and the fathers of it," Sal states that they will remain on the earth long after the "Fellahin apocalypse" sweeps Western civilization away (*OR*, 286).

Most of Kerouac's fiction reversed Spengler's negative valuation of the Fellahin. In particular, he affirmed African Americans and Latinos/Latinas' spontaneity and planlessness, drawing on it as an alternative to the product aesthetic instilled in him by his English professors at Columbia University. In his 1957 manifesto, "Essentials of Spontaneous Prose," Kerouac outlined his version of the antiformalist aesthetic theorized by Black Mountain poets like Charles Olson.

For both Kerouac and Olson, this aesthetic was rooted in the author's body, especially in the physical rhythms of his or her breath.[17] Spontaneous prose no longer seeks to fashion a New Critical well-wrought urn, separable from both author and reader and the world they inhabit. Rather, it creates a this-worldly rapport between author and reader based on their respective bodily sensations. For Kerouac, one possible model for this spontaneous bodily aesthetic was jazz music—for him, as for other Beats, the quintessential Fellahin art. Describing spontaneous writing as "blowing (as per jazz musician)," he imagined that it creates telepathic communities: "Fish as far down as you want, satisfy yourself first, then the reader cannot fail to receive telepathic shock and meaning-excitement by the same laws operating in his own human mind."[18] By entering into this community, author and reader step outside the future-oriented temporality of Faustian civilization into the timeless present that Spengler attributed to the Fellahin. Sal evokes this alternative temporality when describing an alto saxophonist's performance in *On the Road*: "All of the sudden somewhere in the middle he *gets* it—everybody looks up and knows; they listen; he picks it up and carries. Time stops. He's filling empty space with the substance of our lives" (*OR*, 195).

However, Kerouac also revised Spengler's concept of the Fellahin in ways that complicated his version of process art, distancing it from the artistic productions of African Americans and Latinos/Latinas and instead aligning it with the anxious inquiry into the health of the middle-class work ethic characteristic of 1950s delinquency discourse. For Spengler, the Fellahin cut across class lines. The term encompasses non-Western remnants of older civilizations. However, it also encompasses groups and individuals within the West that prefigure that civilization's demise. In particular, Spengler believed that overly sophisticated, urban intellectuals are the harbingers of the West's inevitable decline into Fellahin existence; he described them as the "waste products" of modern civilization.[19] For Kerouac, in contrast, the term "Fellahin" hews more closely to class distinctions in the United States. It does not include modern intellectuals, whom Kerouac lumps in with the deracinated, white middle class. In *Vanity of Duluoz* (1968), his alter ego reflects that "the city intellectuals of the world were divorced from the folkbody blood of the land and were just rootless fools."[20] The Fellahin does, however, encompass all lower-class Americans, including ethnic and non-ethnic whites. For instance, when Kerouac visits Morocco, he predictably comments that it is "exactly like Mexico, the Fellahin world." However, Tangiers is also just like the working-class, francophone neighborhood where he grew up:

"We walk almost running down a steep hill of grass and boulders, with a path, to a magical little street with African tenements and again I'm hit in the eye by an old magic dream: 'I was born here: This is the street where I was born.'"[21] Similarly, in his Lowell books, Kerouac uses the term to describe working-class residents of his Massachusetts hometown who resist assimilation into the US middle class. The category of the Fellahin, in other words, allows Kerouac to think of intransigently lower-class Americans as being culturally different from middle-class Americans in the same way that (according to Kerouac's racist logic) African Americans, Mexicans, and Moroccans are different from whites. Kerouac thus uses the term "Fellahin" to refer to lower-class cultural proclivities that cut across racial and ethnic lines. The term "Faustian" works in similar ways: it refers to individualist strivers who resist the stasis of the Fellahin. Kerouac, in other words, uses the terms "Fellahin" and "Faustian" in a fashion that resembles the corner boy / college boy dichotomy established by Whyte; they designate a contrasting set of attitudes toward middle-class assimilation.

Like many post–World War II delinquency theorists, moreover, Kerouac was not principally interested in representatives from either group. Rather, Kerouac's Duluoz Legend (the interlinked series of confessional novels that forms the core of his work) focuses on transitional figures who are caught midway between the stasis of the Fellahin and the Faustian ambitions of middle-class America—the same conflict that, according to delinquency theorists, was responsible for the behavior of delinquent youth. The tension between these two modes of being is especially important in Kerouac's Lowell novels, which detail his adolescence as a budding football hero destined for college and a professional career. Kerouac documents this autobiographical period in *Maggie Cassidy* (1959), the story of his teenage relationship with a working-class, Irish Catholic girl.[22] In this novel, Jackie Duluoz is torn between his attraction to Maggie and his sense that he must become "an incarnation of the American Super Dream Winner, Go Getter" (*MC*, 166). As Nancy Grace notes, Kerouac codes Maggie as being akin to the women of color whom he fetishizes in his novels about interracial relationships, such as *The Subterraneans* (1958) and *Tristessa* (1960).[23] The narrator describes Maggie as "forlorn, dissatisfied, dark, unpleasantly strange" (*MC*, 28) and later comments that she leans "on one leg with the laze of a Spanish cat, a Spanish Carmen" (*MC*, 29). Thus, Maggie resembles Jackie himself, a dark-complexioned, "Canuck, half-Indian" from a working-class family (*MC*, 30). Both of them live amid the "brown Fellahin lights of life" (*MC*, 152), a phrase that Kerouac associates with Lowell throughout the novel. The two characters, however, are separated by their divergent class ambitions. Jackie is a college boy, a talented youth whose social trajectory will take him out of the town. He is a "little angel of pure future" (*MC*, 169), a Faustian man ready to cut all ties with his community. Maggie, in contrast, is an unrepentant corner girl, a high school dropout whose ambitions amount to nothing more than to "live in a little house by the tracks, play the 920 Club, have babies" (*MC*, 75). She lives in the perpetual, zoological present that Spengler associates with the Fellahin. This cultural difference facilitates the narrator's construction of the light-complexioned Cassidys as figuratively darker than the dark-complexioned Jackie. Maggie's brother, a brakeman, is "black-in with grime of his job, his teeth pearly white" (*MC*, 87). Maggie insists that if Jackie wants to marry her, he will "have to take me at home and as I yam" (*MC*, 185). The phrase echoes the famous scene from Ralph Ellison's recently published *Invisible Man* (1952), in which the unnamed narrator similarly declares, "I yam what I yam" in a deliberate reductio ad absurdum of black identity politics.[24]

Jackie, however, ends the novel as neither a college nor a corner boy. Rather, three years after his breakup with Maggie, he drops out of school and returns to Lowell as a disturbed hybrid of the two. When Jackie first reenters the narrative, he seems to have renounced a professional career in favor of a working-class trade; the narrator introduces him as an anonymous "garageman" (*MC*, 190). Jackie has been reabsorbed into Fellahin Lowell, a world of tradesmen and blue-collar workers such as Maggie's brother. However, he has been warped by his middle-class ambitions. Driving to a rendezvous with Maggie, Jackie imagines a boastful conversation with her in which he highlights his new hipster identity and asserts his sexual prowess:

> Baby . . . I'm sure gonna get you tonight—aint gonna be like it used to be with you—I'm gonna find out about you at last—I've had women since you, and traveled, and been far—the stories I could tell you'd make your little Massachusetts Street sit pale in *this* star—about railroads, and bottles I throwed, and women brought me gin for supper, and old bo's I followed across fields to hear them sing the blues—and moons over Virginia . . . Books I've read, new philosophies I've made—Thorstein Veblen, my dear—Sherwood Anderson, sweet—and some man they call Dostoevsky—and North Pole mountains I've climbed—So dont manage me off tonight, I'll slap your wrist, I'll drive you inta rivers, I'll show ya. (*MC*, 192)

This boast combines, in a schizoid fashion, Jackie's Faustian desire to transcend the actual (reading Dostoevsky, climbing North Pole mountains) with a Fellahin insistence that he is a working-class tough. In particular, the cavalier name-dropping of figures as heterogeneous as Veblen, Anderson, and Dostoevsky signals that he has not fully assimilated his college reading, that his intellectualism is mostly pretense. His divided, middle-class / lower-class cultural inclinations have transformed Jackie into a disreputable criminal type. He shows up at Maggie's house driving a Buick that he steals from work, bearing "the wild look of a man emancipated into the redbrick heap of night from some bank jail" (*MC*, 191). "Redbrick" in Kerouac's prose is usually shorthand for working-class communities. Jackie is a criminal intruder from the white-collar world, let loose to pillage and exploit the lower class. The date ends in an attempted rape thwarted by Jackie's drunkenness and Maggie's girdle.

In the context of the Kerouac's Duluoz Legend, this transformation of Jackie from would-be college boy to self-divided hipster coincides with his birth as a writer.[25] Indeed, Kerouac often depicts Jackie's literary career as a species of delinquency—a case of a working-class boy whose aspirations are out of tune with his abilities. This depiction is especially evident in *Vanity of Duluoz*, which encompasses the same autobiographical period as *Maggie Cassidy* and was written in the last stages of Kerouac's alcoholic self-destruction. Addressed by an aging Jackie to his third wife, Stella, the novel tells the story of how he became a "W R I T E R whose very 'success,' far from being a happy triumph as of old, was the sign of doom Himself" (*VD*, 7). As the novel's title suggests, it traces the various kinds of vanity to which Jackie is subject, starting with his teenage efforts to escape from Lowell. He imagines football as a shortcut to middle-class prosperity: it will help him "graduate from college and become a big insurance salesman" (*VD*, 15). Literature fulfills a similar function. Jackie identifies his literary aspirations with the figurative center of US white-collar culture; he will "become the greatest writer that ever lived and write a book so golden and so purchased with magic that everybody smacks their brows on Madison Avenue" (*VD*, 87). Jackie's vanity, in other words, consists of seeking fantasy alternatives to the hard work it takes to enter the middle class. These fantasies lead him to drop out of Columbia University—the institution that might actually help him achieve a middling degree of affluence. For Kerouac in *Vanity of Duluoz*, the only salvation for working-class writers is to abandon their unrealizable Faustian ambitions. The now mature Jackie thus returns to the dogmatic Catholicism of his youth and marries the working-class sister of one of his boyhood friends.

In his 1957 manifesto, Kerouac similarly envisaged his process writing as a delinquent art, caught somewhere between Fellahin and Faustian cultures. Although Kerouac compared his fiction to jazz performance, he insisted that it was not popular fiction of the kind consumed by working-class readers. He was not writing "science fiction," a "bizarre" form that arises "from language being dead." He instead situated his work within the Western literary tradition, which he described using the same pseudo-intellectual rhetoric that young Jackie uses in his boast to Maggie. The prose writer must be governed by no grammatical rule but the "time-Shakespearian stress of dramatic need." His or her work should resemble "Yeats's later 'trance writing'" and "Reich's 'beclouding of consciousness,'" and it should express "the song of yourself."[26] These formulations capture Kerouac's position in the literary field, which has remained remarkably constant since the publication of *On the Road*. His fiction lacks the eccentric but extensive erudition that informs the work of other 1950s avant-garde writers, such as William S. Burroughs, Charles Olson, and John Ashbery. Unlike those writers' work, it has rarely been seen as a precursor to the high postmodernism of the 1960s and 1970s. Instead, Kerouac's aesthetic paradoxically synthesizes the middlebrow and avant-garde. The middlebrow that first emerged in the 1920s was an aspirational art generally aimed at upwardly mobile audiences with limited education. In Christina Klein's terms, it "offered its consumers the cultural capital that would make them feel more secure in their new class identity," promising them "that if they read certain books or listened to certain radio shows, they could learn to understand the ideas and aesthetic forms that defined middle-class and international respectability."[27] The historical avant-garde was the enemy of the middlebrow; it travestied the respectable cultural capital that middlebrow entertainers offered their audiences. Drawing on the strange logic of the literary field outlined by Pierre Bourdieu, the avant-garde did so from a perspective of superior mastery of that capital, refusing "pedantic taste" for its "prudence and backwardness."[28] Kerouac's work affirms both of these competing impulses; it travesties cultural forms that it has not yet fully assimilated, offering its readers an easily digestible version of the avant-garde. In so doing, it replicates within the literary field the contradictory class longings that postwar sociologists attributed to anomic juvenile delinquents; Kerouac's fiction at once attacks and seeks to emulate a high literary aesthetic that lies beyond its grasp.[29]

Kerouac eventually decides, in *Vanity of Duluoz*, that this aesthetic reflects his doomed efforts to escape from his class origins. Elsewhere in his fiction, however, Kerouac tries to find delinquent role models who mediate between working-class roots and middle-class ambitions in a way that his authorial personas cannot and who embody his process aesthetic more fully than Kerouac can in his own fiction. The most famous of these characters is *On the Road*'s Dean Moriarty, modeled after Neal Cassady, who inspired Kerouac's turn to spontaneous prose. When Sal Paradise first encounters Dean, he comments that Dean stands out amid his New York intellectual friends. In an instance of Proustian involuntary memory, Dean's sweaty neck evokes the Fellahin rootedness of Sal's small-town, ethnic-American upbringing:

> His suffering bony face with the long sideburns and his straining muscular sweating neck made me remember my boyhood in those dye-dumps and swim-holes and riversides of Paterson and the Passaic . . . in his excited way of speaking I heard again the voices of old companions and brothers under the bridge, among the motorcycles, along the wash-lined neighborhood and drowsy doorsteps of afternoon where boys played guitars while their older brothers worked in the mills. (*OR*, 7)

At the same time, Dean also embodies Sal's Faustian ambitions; like Sal, he is a working-class kid with writerly pretensions, a "young jailkid all hung-up on the wonderful possibilities of becoming a real intellectual" (*OR*, 3). Neither a corner nor a college boy, Dean, like Jackie Duluoz, is instead an idiosyncratic hybrid of both. These conflicting cultural impulses lead him to take criminal shortcuts; Dean turns his Faustian energies toward automobile theft, reckless driving, and petty hustling. "I used to be in reform school all the time," he explains to Sal. "I was a young punk, asserting myself, stealing cars a psychological expression of my position, hincty to show" (*OR*, 111). Throughout the novel, he is driven by a perverse distortion of the middle-class work ethic. In Denver, when Sal meets up with him during his first road trip, Dean's life is governed by a strict schedule, timed to the minute, which he uses to arrange his rendezvous with various friends and mistresses. Dean thus parodies the throngs of businessmen that Sal imagines in New York: "millions and millions hustling forever for a buck among themselves" (*OR*, 98). Unlike them, Dean's schedule precludes economically productive activity: "I haven't had time to work in weeks," he complains (*OR*, 40).

In contrast to his representation of the self-tortured Jackie Duluoz, however, Kerouac tries to imagine Dean as a viable alternative to middle-class ambition and Fellahin stasis. His delinquency, for instance, seems qualitatively different from the criminality that Sal encounters in New York. Unlike the junkies and thieves with whom Sal and Carlo Marx (Allen Ginsberg) associate in Times Square, Dean's "'criminality' was not something that sulked and sneered; it was a wild yea-saying overburst of American joy; it was Western, the west wind, an ode from the Plains, something new, long prophesied, long a-coming" (*OR*, 7). Sal sees Dean as a frontier individualist, one who challenges the conformism of middle-class America. Dean also embodies a different kind of postwar poverty, one that is active and affirmative rather than static and pessimistic. According to Cloward and Ohlin, one of the distinguishing features of delinquents' anomie is the sense of despair engendered by their permanent exclusion from middle-class affluence: "Many lower-class male adolescents experience desperation born of the certainty that their position in the economic structure is relatively fixed and immutable—a desperation made all the more poignant by their exposure to a cultural ideology in which failure to orient oneself upward is regarded as a moral defect."[30] Dean shares the delinquent's infinite desire for things that exceed his grasp; he is one of "the mad ones, the ones who are mad to live, mad to talk, mad to be saved, desirous of everything at the same time" (*OR*, 5). These desires do not make him, unlike the delinquent, resent his poverty. Rather, Dean is perpetually enthusiastic about the prospect of scrabbling for the basic necessities of life: he "just raced in society, eager for bread and love; he didn't care one way or the other, 'so long as I can get that lil ole gal with that lil sumpin down there between her legs, boy,' and 'so long's we can *eat*'" (*OR*, 7).

Above all else, Sal values Dean as a model for the kind of working-class intellectual that Sal would like to become, one who holds in balance all of the tensions that tear Sal and Jackie apart. Unlike Sal, who begins the novel "hanging around the campus" that he attended as a younger man (*OR*, 1), Dean's education takes place outside postsecondary institutions. As a youth, he spends "a third of his time in the poolhall, a third in jail, and a third in the public library" (*OR*, 4). He reads Nietzsche in reform school and arrives in New York hoping to become a writer. At first, he replicates the mock-erudite rhetoric that characterizes Jackie after his return from college: "He liked to talk in the tone and using the words, but in a jumbled way, that he had heard from 'real intellectuals.'" However, he quickly masters the lingo and concepts of the New York intellectual scene; after "a few months with Carlo Marx," he became "completely *in there* with all the terms and jargon" (*OR*, 3). This autodidact genius turns Dean into an embodiment of the process aesthetic that Sal tries to channel in his narrative. Reading over Sal's shoulder as he writes a story, Dean articulates the basic principles of spontaneous prose that Sal has not yet mastered: "There's so many things to do, so many to write! How to even *begin* to get it all down and without modified restraints and all hung-up on like literary inhibitions and grammatical fears" (*OR*, 4). Similarly, Dean fashions the telepathic community that Kerouac elsewhere attributes to jazz musicians; he insists that he and his friends "communicate with absolute honesty and absolute completeness every-thing on our minds" (*OR*, 37). This pure process art is oral, and the novel's Beat intellectuals can achieve imperfect renditions of that art only by writing it down. Carlo develops his poetry by writing a journal in which he keeps "track of everything that happened every day—everything Dean did and said" (*OR*, 42), and Sal's narrative similarly tries to replicate Dean's conversation.

However, Sal's idealization of Dean as a "saint" and "holy goof" capable of synthesizing the tensions that mark Sal's writerly profession ultimately falters (*OR*, 183). Throughout the novel, Sal is aware that Dean is a scam artist who abuses his conversational prowess and the illusion of telepathic community it fosters. Among the characters whom Sal and Dean encounter in their travels are figures who have been duped by Dean too often and denounce him as a "very interesting and even amusing con-man" (*OR*, 185). At such moments, Dean seems like an underworld version of the white-collar workers described by C. Wright Mills. According to Mills, such workers are dependent on selling "not only their time and energy but their personalities as well."[31] Dean, the small-time hustler, similarly has no capital other than his personality, which he uses to hypnotize his listeners. This capacity wanes as Dean ages, as does Sal's ability to sustain the mystique that he fashions around his friend. There are moments when Sal equates the two men's travels with the tawdriest kinds of middle-class labor. "I realized I was beginning to cross and recross towns in America as though I were a traveling salesman," Sal comments, "raggedy travelings, bad stock, rotten beans in the bottom of my bag of tricks, nobody buying" (*OR*, 234). Dean's own bag of tricks is exhausted by the novel's end. When Sal last sees him in New York, Dean's verbal improvisations lapse into aphasia and silence:

> He couldn't talk any more. He hopped and laughed, he stuttered and fluttered his hands and said, "Ah—ah—you must listen to hear." We listened, all ears. But he forgot what he wanted to say. "Really listen—ahem. Look, dear Sal—sweet Laura—

I've come—I'm gone—but wait—ah yes." And he stared with rocky sorrow into his hands. "Can't talk no more." (*OR*, 290)

Ultimately, *On the Road* has difficulty sustaining its own class mythology. Like Kerouac's Lowell novels, it presents its transitional hipsters and delinquents as would-be middle-class subjects out of touch with the zoological mode of being that Kerouac associates with the Fellahin. Both Sal and Dean have been infected by "white ambitions" (*OR*, 170) that prevent them from fully participating in the ecstatic culture of "life, joy, kicks, darkness, music" (*OR*, 169) experienced by the novel's African American musicians and Latino/Latina migrant workers. Insofar as white men do become temporarily assimilated into the culture of the poor, it is as economically privileged outsiders, on whom poor people of color attach their own hopes of assimilation into the white middle class. For instance, probably the most frequently discussed scene of racial masquerade in *On the Road* is the "Mexican Girl" section, in which Sal describes a two-week affair with Terry, a Mexican American mother fleeing from her abusive husband. The scene culminates in Sal's make-believe absorption into the Southern Californian subculture of Latino/Latina migrant workers. Sal comments that racist Okies "thought I was a Mexican, of course, and in a way I am" (*OR*, 90). This identification is only temporary: after experiencing the economic hopelessness of migrant life, he wires his aunt for fifty dollars to return back East. However, if Sal fantasizes that he can forget his economic and cultural privilege, Terry is always aware of these advantages. Her attraction to him hinges on her identification of him as a "nice college boy" (*OR*, 76) who will help her escape her impoverished existence. Terry's only fear about the relationship is that Sal might be a covert delinquent, "a goddam pimp like all of them" (*OR*, 77). While Sal may romanticize the zoological life of the Fellahin, Terry harbors her own Faustian ambitions. No one in *On the Road* escapes the lure of middle-class prosperity.

Oedipal Delinquents

Durkheim's theory of anomie was only one of several frameworks applied to juvenile delinquency in the 1950s. Other researchers applied psychoanalytic theory, attributing delinquent behavior to dysfunctions within the nuclear family. The pioneering theorist in this regard was Talcott Parsons, a prominent 1950s sociologist whose work ranged across various social scientific disciplines. In a 1947 article on the causes of aggressive behavior in Western societies, Parsons related male delinquency to boys' efforts to break free from their mothers' psychological influence. Echoing Philip Wylie's critique of "momism" in *Generation of Vipers* (1943), Parsons described the typical modern household as one in which the mother acts as chief agent of socialization, administering discipline and focusing in herself "the symbols of what is 'good' behavior, of conformity with the expectations of the respectable adult world." The father, in contrast, conducts his economic activities outside the home, playing a subservient role in household routines and thus providing a weak model for male identification. This situation poses a problem for boys, who must disidentify with their mothers and flee the feminine domestic sphere to conform to their adult roles as masculine breadwinners. As a result, many boys cultivate deviant, hypermasculine behavior in an effort to break their Oedipal attachments: "When he revolts against identification with his mother in the name of masculinity, it is not surprising that a boy unconsciously identifies 'goodness' with femininity and that being a 'bad boy' becomes a positive goal."[32] Typically, this rebellion is temporary; Parsons associated it with Freud's latency stage, the period of development after the Oedipus complex dissolves. Eventually, most boys learn to identify with their fathers and accept a disciplined, economically productive role in society. However, boys with dominating mothers and weak or absent fathers can become stuck in this hypermasculine stage, developing into criminal adolescents.

For many 1950s sociologists, Parsons's theory did not seem like an effective model of delinquency. It implied that delinquency was a predominantly middle-class phenomenon.[33] According to Albert Cohen, if Parsons's theory were true, crime rates should be lower among the poor, since "the working-class child is more likely to see within the area of his normal daily movements the distinctive activities of men and women, and therefore to build up definitions of masculinity which are positive and independent and not merely negations of femininity."[34] However, if the idea of the middle-class, psychopathological delinquent never found much purchase beyond the 1950s, an important component of Parsons's theory did: the notion that weak and especially absent fathers produce problem sons. In the 1960s, this explanation migrated from studies of white, middle-class families and became overwhelmingly associated with the black urban poor. Most infamously, this idea was the cornerstone of Moynihan's *The Negro Family*, which argued that black communities are caught up in a "tangle of pathology" generated by their matriarchal family structure—one in which mothers act as primary providers and fathers are unemployed and/or absent. As Moynihan put it, "White children without fathers at least perceive all about them the pattern of men working. Negro children without fathers flounder—and fail."[35] Implicitly synthesizing the psychopathological and anomic theories of the 1950s, Moynihan cited studies that show that ghetto children who lack strong father figures never learn how to delay gratification of their desires. As a result, male youth cannot acquire the discipline needed to launch a middle-class career and thus turn to delinquency. These youth in turn become the next generation of absent or unemployable fathers, perpetuating the cycle of poverty and delinquency within the black community.

Kerouac's Duluoz Legend prefigured this 1960s effort to link family dysfunction with intergenerational poverty. His novels are filled with weak and/ or absent fathers who are responsible for perpetuating the failed Faustianism that afflicts Kerouac's countercultural protagonists. In particular, this motif is at the core of *On the Road*, which consistently pathologizes its hipster characters, presenting them as damaged sons who have inherited their fathers' failure to embody the middle-class work ethic. This failure is most obvious in the case of Dean Moriarty's missing father. Once a "respectable and hardworking tinsmith" (*OR*, 34), he becomes an alcoholic and disappears into America's hobo population. At various points, Dean recounts how, when he was a child, his father lost him in a boxcar, exposed him to sexual molestation by a legless transient, and sent him into the streets to beg for liquor money. In spite of Sal's claim that Dean's criminality is based on an affirmative thirst for experience rather than the usual "tired bookish or political or psychoanalytical reasons" (*OR*, 7), it is also a traumatic reaction to this paternal neglect. For instance, in one of Dean and Sal's visits to Denver, Colorado, they meet Dean's cousin Sam, "the one man in the family who took tender concern for me" (*OR*, 204). When Sam, a father substitute, asks Dean to sign a paper breaking off all family ties, Dean reverts to an adolescent state, recklessly stealing a series of cars—the same behavior that landed him in juvenile detention years earlier. This pattern of paternal abandonment resonates throughout the novel; as James Jones details, dysfunctional father-son relationships recur in the backstories of most of the novel's minor characters.[36] America, for Kerouac, is a nation of absent fathers who have bred a generation of delinquent sons.

These sons themselves turn out to be inadequate fathers. Dean moves from one wife to another, eventually fathering four children, whose care and support devolve on their mothers. Sal's aunt comments on the family dysfunction that Dean leaves in his wake: "You can't go all over the country having babies like that. The poor little things'll grow up helpless. You've got to offer them a chance to live" (*OR*, 241). Like his automobile thefts, this repeated abandonment seems like a traumatic reaction to his own paternal neglect; he is condemned to imitate his father by establishing families he cannot sustain. As is typical in the novel, this behavior mirrors, in an exaggerated fashion, Sal's own inadequacies. Sal also mimics a paternal role that he cannot inhabit. He begins his narrative after the conclusion of one marriage and ends it with the beginning of another. In between, he is obsessed with his failure to be a breadwinner. "What kind of old man was I that couldn't support his own ass, let alone theirs?" (*OR*, 89), he reflects after recognizing that he cannot pick enough cotton to feed and shelter Terry and her child. Later, his experience with Terry is repeated with the Italian American Lucille, a working-class single mother, whom he similarly fails to support and eventually abandons.

Both Dean and Sal are therefore like the African American children whom Moynihan describes in *The Negro Family*. Born to weak or absent fathers, they inherit a disabled work ethic that they pass on to their sons, thereby perpetuating the "tangle of pathology" for another generation. The unstated, biographical subtext of this concern with failed or absent fathers is Kerouac's relationship with his real-life father, Leo Kerouac. Leo died shortly before the autobiographical events that inspired *On the Road*.[37] This death was preceded by a long period in which Leo was demoted from his position as the family's breadwinner. Like Dean's father in *On the Road*, Leo was an independent artisan who fell on hard times. After losing his printing business due to a combination of gambling debts and bad luck, he became a contract laborer forced to work far away from his family. Jack Kerouac's mother, meanwhile, helped support the family by working in a shoe factory. Throughout the Duluoz Legend, in particular the Lowell books that describe Kerouac's childhood and adolescence, he often returns to this occupational failure, linking it to Jackie Duluoz's conflicted, lower- and middle-class cultural inclinations and to his eventual career as a writer. Prefiguring Moynihan's version of the culture of poverty thesis, Kerouac synthesizes a psychopathological with an anomic account of his own difficulties in becoming a middle-class subject: he suggests that Jackie's failed Faustianism is inherited from his similarly self-divided father.

This link is explicit in *Dr. Sax: Faust Part III* (1959), the Lowell novel that details the end of Jackie Duluoz's latency period—the moment when, according to Parsons, healthy boys identify with their fathers and adopt mature economic roles.[38] As the novel's subtitle indicates, Kerouac conceived of it as a sequel to Goethe's *Faust* and as an exploration of Spengler's notion of the Western, Faustian soul. The novel describes the events surrounding Jackie's puberty, interwoven with preadolescent fantasies about a figure named Dr. Sax who battles a giant, world-devouring snake. The Oedipal connotations of this story are heavy-handed and have been explicated by other critics.[39] As in the case of *On the Road*, what interests me is the way that Kerouac mobilizes these psychoanalytic themes to explore issues of failed class mobility that inform his concept of process art. In terms of the Duluoz family's downward economic trajectory, *Dr. Sax* documents a crucial moment in Emil Duluoz's (Leo Kerouac's) career—the 1936 Merrimack flood, which destroys his uninsured printing business and forces him into bankruptcy. The novel establishes a series of parallels between this economic catastrophe and Jackie's psychological development. At the moment when Jackie must learn to identify with his father, Emil undergoes a personal crisis that makes him a less-than-desirable role model.

Much of the psychological drama of *Dr. Sax* concerns Jackie's efforts to sever his Oedipal connection to his mother, Ange. He refers to his earliest childhood memory as the "Great Bathrobe Vision," a recurring image of himself as an infant, "sitting in my mother's arms in a brown aura of gloom sent up by her bathrobe" (*DS*, 18). Jackie's attempts to assert his independence take the form of various delinquent acts inspired by the pulp fiction magazines that he reads. Donning a black and red cape and the identity of the "Black Thief," he steals various objects from neighborhood children and engages in acts of petty vandalism. This alter ego is at once an expression of Jackie's fascination with his father's economic role as family breadwinner and an early manifestation of his desire to become a writer. Disguised as the Black Thief, Jackie prints threatening notes to his victims "on beautiful scraps of glazed paper I got from my father's printing shop" (*DS*, 50). The Black Thief later morphs into the fantasy figure of Dr. Sax, who appears throughout Jackie's memories, especially his recollections of pubescent, homoerotic play. Dr. Sax haunts the room where Jackie and his friends host a "juvenile homosexual ball" (*DS*, 68), and he later takes notes as a local idiot entertains the boys with marathon masturbation sessions and acts of bestiality. This immature sexuality, the narrator reflects, will disappear as the boys grow older and discover women: "Later we simply forgot dark Saxes and hung ourselves on the kick of sex and adolescent lacerated love." In future years, the same group of boys finds a new sexual exhibitionist to entertain them: a local whore who reminds Jackie "that I had a father (who visited her in purple doorways) and a real world to face in the future" (*DS*, 70).

Jackie's problem, then, in moving beyond the transitional stage represented by Dr. Sax lies in forging a sense of identification with his father. This effort lies at the center of the novel's second book. The narrative of this section takes place amid a torrential rainstorm that keeps Jackie away from school. Mirroring the structure of the entire novel, the section opens with a description of Jackie's close connection to his mother: the two sit watching the storm, framed by the window "like a Madonna and a son" (*DS*, 83). However, the section soon shifts to the elaborate games that Jackie plays alone in his bedroom, all of which mimic his father's occupations. Jackie, for instance, pretends that his marbles are race horses and publishes the results in a homemade newspaper. Watching from the stands, an imaginary father and son bet on the races, hoping to improve their finances. In attempting to fold his father into his private fantasy world, Jackie imitates the compulsive gambling responsible for his family's downward trajectory; after the races, he imagines, "you see me . . . marching out of the grandstand but also shaking my head quizzically from side to side like a disgruntled bettor, tearing up my tickets, a poor child pantomime of what sometimes I'd seen my father do after the races" (*DS*, 92). In terms of the Fellahin-Faustian binary at the center of Kerouac's work, the middle-class father is the figure who embodies his family's Faustian spirit, its drive to transcend its current conditions through hard work and self-improvement. In Emil's case, this Faustian drive takes the deviant form of a search for economic shortcuts, for the quick win that will instantly propel the family into affluence. This is the same deviant Faustianism that influences Jackie's transformation from college boy to bohemian writer and Times Square hipster. Jackie's self-divided hipsterism is a direct inheritance from his would-be middle-class father.

Jackie's game gains poignancy from the fact that it unfolds during a family crisis, generated by his father, which will soon upend the Duluoz's fortunes. While Jackie is playing marbles, Emil is trying to recoup his gambling losses by working a second job as a bowling alley manager at the Pawtucketville Social Club. This institution is typical of ethnic, working-class social clubs from the 1930s. Intended as a genteel "meeting place for speeches about Franco-American matters," it is in fact a "roaring saloon and bowling alley and pool table with a meeting room always locked" (*DS*, 40). The club thus satisfies both the community's middle-class aspirations and its working-class pleasures. Emil's presence there as salaried manager prefigures his gradual loss of independence: his transformation from independent artisan to itinerant employee. Indeed, the spring storm that keeps Jackie away from the school and leaks through the club's bathroom ceiling is the beginning of the great flood that destroys Emil's printing shop (*DS*, 174). The novel equates this flood with the decline of Emil's virility: the club patrons joke that "Emil's starting to have holes in his pissery" and suggest that he plug them up with a medical book about syphilis (*DS*, 94). The most direct sign of this decline is the fact that Mrs. Duluoz must now help rescue the family's finances. Book Two concludes with Ange leaving the domestic scene with which it opens, entering instead into her husband's workplace to sew the pool table's torn cloth.

Much of the novel's phantasmagoria about Dr. Sax and the giant snake similarly comments on Jackie's inability to find a father figure who will help him break free from his latency stage and settle into a mature economic role in middle-class society. Dr. Sax, the narrator explains, is a "Faustian man" (*DS*, 43). Like the figure represented in Part Two of Goethe's *Faust*, he plumbs the depths of human knowledge, mastering black magic and advanced science in hopes of conquering the ills that plague humankind. According to James Jones, his name derives "from Saxon, suggesting that he is charged with helping Jackie make the linguistic transition from his French-speaking neighborhood . . . to a polyglot Pawtucketville."[40] For Kerouac, Anglo-Saxon civilization is the American repository of the Faustian culture at odds with his peasant-based, French-Canadian heritage. Sax thus seems like he might function as a substitute father for Jackie—one who will mediate his passage into middle-class America in a way that his real father cannot. Sax, for instance, outlines Jackie's future as a 1950s organization man, ruled by the clock: "You'll come to angular rages and lonely romages among Beast of Day in hot glary circumstances made grit by the hour of the clock—that is known as Civilization" (*DS*, 202).

However, Dr. Sax is a pubescent, fantasy version of Faust—a vigilante superhero with hypnotic powers. As his jazz-inspired name suggests, he is a hipster, partially modeled after William S. Burroughs, with whom Kerouac was living when he wrote the book. William S. Burroughs acted as a mentor for younger Beat writers like Kerouac and Ginsberg, and Sax represents the writer whom Jackie will someday become. Sax, in other words, is a figure for the Faustian soul caught in a transitional state of development—much like Emil Duluoz and all of the other hybrid Fellahin/Faustians who populate Kerouac's books.

In Goethe's *Faust*, the point of Faust's wager with Mephistopheles is that Faust will be damned if he becomes so satiated by the devil's gifts that he would like to preserve his happiness forever. In Kerouac's version of the myth, this moment of satiation has always already happened. When Dr. Sax lays out Jackie's white-collar future, he warns him, "You'll never be as happy as you are now in your quiltish innocent book-devouring boyhood immortal night" (*DS*, 203). The failed Faustian remains trapped in superhero delusions of preadolescent fantasy, never wanting to move beyond them. As the denouement of Kerouac's novel suggests, this immature Faustianism cannot, by itself, mediate the individual's entry into middle-class adulthood. Dr. Sax's magic herbs, which are supposed to kill the snake, do not work. Denuded of his cape and hood, Dr. Sax changes into an impoverished old man wearing "poor old beatup trousers, . . . and regular brown shoes, and regular socks" (*DS*, 240). He becomes another version of Emil Duluoz, a weakened father stripped of the accoutrements that make him seem bigger than life.

This failed Faustianism at once enables and limits the process aesthetic that Kerouac tries to realize in his books. As Kerouac insists throughout his fiction, this aesthetic is realizable only by juvenile men like Jackie, Sal, and Dean, who are in flight from domestic responsibility and postwar forms of middle-class work. Indeed, Kerouac defined his aesthetic against the middle-class institutionalization that increasingly shaped American fiction after World War II. Malcolm Cowley outlined the effects of this institutionalization in *The Literary Situation* (1954). Describing the late modernist "new fiction" of writers like Carson McCullers, Jean Stafford, Truman Capote, Peter Taylor, and Paul Bowles, Cowley criticized their obsessive formalism and limited experiential scope. Written "to be admired by the critics who write for *Kenyon, Sewanee, Hudson*, and other quarterly reviews," the fiction dealt with "private lives," rarely addressing "any human institution larger than the separate family." These features derived from the new fiction's institutional conditions, which were the same as those which fashioned the New Criticism and New Poetry: "The typical authors of 'new' novels are university men and women. They start by taking advanced courses in writing fiction, then they apply the lessons in their own books, under critical supervision, and meanwhile they support themselves by working as part-time instructors, preferably in fiction courses."[41] Cowley outlined the autotelic structure of what Mark McGurl calls the Program Era. It is a structure that facilitates product art by creating the institutional illusion that writers, readers, and texts exist in a sealed-off world of their own. At the same time, it is a structure that requires writers to grow up, to become responsible middle-class women and men. Although Kerouac began his writing career as an English undergraduate, he fashioned his process aesthetic by breaking away from that structure. While the new novelists benefited from university jobs that allowed them to develop their writing skills while supporting a family, Kerouac created an antiformalist, peripatetic literature about institutionally adrift male loners. In the immediate postwar context, this rejection meant that Kerouac could never be, as he puts it, "middle-class just like you." Instead, his aesthetic gestured toward a synthesis of working-class ethnic roots and professional ambition that it could never achieve. In so doing, Kerouac outlined the central problem that process artists would confront in the 1960s and beyond.

Black Arts and the Great Society

In 1967, Gwendolyn Brooks declared her allegiance to the Black Arts movement, heralding a shift in her poetry away from the late modernism of her early work. This shift was provoked by two events that year. First, she attended the second Fisk Black Writers' Conference, where she observed the audience's enthusiastic response to Amiri Baraka. Second, she ran a poetry workshop for the Blackstone Rangers, one of Chicago's most notorious youth gangs. In running this workshop, Brooks fulfilled one of the Black Arts movement's central imperatives: the need to bring art to the people. Brooks's workshop was also typical of the Black Arts in another sense. Like Baraka's BARTS, it was sponsored by the War on Poverty. Part of an initiative for rehabilitating black gang members, the poetry workshop fell under the umbrella of the Woodlawn Organization, a federally funded Community Action Agency. As I have been arguing, this convergence between the War on Poverty and the Black Arts movement points to a shared desire to cultivate a participatory professionalism that would involve lower-class African Americans in the production and consumption of professional expertise. For liberals, this participatory professionalism was evoked by the Economic Opportunity Act's emphasis on maximum feasible participation by the poor. For Baraka, it was central to the process aesthetic that he outlined in his theoretical writing and realized in his poetry, fiction, and drama.

Brooks's relationship with this participatory model of literary professionalism, however, remained problematic after her Black Arts turn, even as she engaged in activities that seemed to fulfill the demands of younger poets. Inspired by the example of writers like Haki Madhubuti (Don Lee), Brooks expressed her desire to write poems that would be "immediately enjoyable by black people who spend a great deal of their time in taverns or the streets, blacks who, perhaps, have dropped out of high school."[1] Like Baraka, she wanted to create an art that would find an audience among lower-class blacks who had not,

like her, attended postsecondary institutions and had no toehold in the expanding black professional class.[2] She hoped to do so by enabling pedagogical
encounters outside the campus courses where literature and creative writing
were typically taught. Also like Baraka, Brooks dramatically broke ties with the
white literary establishment that had promoted her work, publishing her post-
1967 writing with black-owned companies such as Dudley Randall's Broadside
Press and Madhubuti's Third World Press.[3] However, as most of Brooks's critics have noted, her Black Arts poetry rarely exhibits the didacticism of black
nationalist art; Raymond Malewitz, for instance, comments that Brooks's Black
Arts poems resist the "simplistic unitary rhetoric" of poets like Baraka, instead
situating "the black nationalist movement, and, concomitantly, the black community from which it sprung, as highly contested hermeneutical spaces of inquiry."[4] Because of this awareness of the black community's internal divisions,
Brooks could never fully accept Baraka's insistence that the black poet must "*be
the people himself, and not be any different.*"[5]

The differences between Baraka and Brooks's conceptions of art and audience are especially evident in the transitional works that they wrote during
their respective conversions to the Black Arts. Everything that Baraka published between his first poetry collection, *Preface to a Twenty-Volume Suicide
Note* (1961), and his relocation to Harlem in 1965 could be described as transitional. However, Baraka usually singled out his experimental novel, *The System
of Dante's Hell* (1965),[6] as marking the birth of his mature style. Baraka wrote
the book in the early 1960s when he was a Beat poet living in Greenwich Village, and it demonstrates his indebtedness to the work of white avant-garde
and countercultural writers like Charles Olson, Allen Ginsberg, and Jack Kerouac. At the same time, the novel points toward the cultural nationalism that
dominated Baraka's work from the mid-1960s to the mid-1970s, when he became a third-world Marxist. In particular, the novel allegorizes Baraka's turn
from a subjectivist aesthetic oriented toward dramatizing the author's divided
racial identity to a participatory aesthetic aimed at achieving synthesis between
the author and the black community. Especially in the novel's last chapter,
"Heretics," this synthesis is achieved through the narrator's traumatic immersion in lower-class African Americans' "culture of violence and foodsmells"
(104). Brooks, in contrast, refuses this immersive narrative, instead positing an
alternative model of literary professionalism. She first develops this model in
her 1967 collection, *In the Mecca*,[7] the last book that she published with Harper

& Row. Rejecting Baraka's conception of the artist as someone who must erase the distance between herself and her community, she presents a drama of "hot estrangement" (403), whereby the poet, through the medium of poetic form, achieves a self-reflexive distance from her community that allows her to serve it more effectively.

These two accounts of the author's relationship to her audience generate divergent representations of the black underclass that dominated welfare politics during and after the War on Poverty. Even as Baraka, in *The System of Dante's Hell*, searches for an alternative to the open-field, Beat, and New York School styles that influenced his early work, he appropriates an ontology of poverty from white avant-garde writers such as Olson and Kerouac. He envisages lower-class black culture as a present-oriented alternative to the rationalized worldview of the black bourgeoisie. In spite of his desire to affirm that culture, he echoes Oscar Lewis, Daniel Moynihan, and other social scientists' pathological conceptions of poverty. In so doing, Baraka encounters a paradox that would shape his future poetry and community activism: The culture of poverty, in Lewis and other theorists' work, is not a distinct culture at all. Rather, it is a deviant version of middle-class culture that must be disciplined by welfare professionals. In contrast, Brooks's refusal of Baraka's immersive narrative leads her to a more complex account of the kind of lower-class behavior that poverty theorists deemed pathological. *In the Mecca* offers vignettes of black single mothers and juvenile delinquents, two figures central to the version of underclass discourse outlined in Moynihan's *The Negro Family*. However, Brooks neither collapses her perspective with that of these figures nor pathologizes them from a clinical distance. Rather, she achieves an intermediate stance that allows her to perceive single mothers and delinquents as at once victims of an oppressive environment and agentive figures capable of negotiating it. Baraka and Brooks thus chart out the perils and possibilities of participatory art, showing how it can establish the artist's authority over lower-class audiences and how it can defamiliarize or disrupt that authority.

Pathologies of the Poor in *The System of Dante's Hell*

The System of Dante's Hell, like much of Baraka's early work, investigates the psychological effects of his black bourgeois upbringing, which Baraka tries to counter to fashion a participatory art capable of addressing a lower-class black audience. Its narrator, variously named Roi, LeRoi, and LeRoy, is a black bohemian living in Greenwich Village, who benefits from his role as a token black intellectual within a mostly white counterculture.[8] As he recollects his youth in Newark, New Jersey, and later as a would-be intellectual in the US Air Force, he realizes that he never escaped the double consciousness instilled in him by his parents, who cultivated black bourgeois aspirations for their son.[9] This double consciousness is the hell announced in the novel's title. Echoing Du Bois's *The Souls of Black Folk* (1903), Baraka explains that hell is "the torture of being the unseen object, and, the constantly observed subject. The flame of social dichotomy. Split open down the center, which is the early legacy of the black man unfocused on blackness" (125). Roi's transformation into a black bohemian is an early attempt to overcome this dichotomy by sidestepping the usual racial divisions of US society. Within Greenwich Village, Roi finds an alternative community that embraces racial intermixture, exemplified by his white wife. This community, however, merely reiterates his parents' complacent vision of the good life. "You've done everything you said you wdn't," Roi reflects in an early chapter. "Everything you said you despised. A fat mind, lying to itself. Unmoving like some lump in front of a window. Wife, child, house, city, clawing at your gentlest parts" (23). The true path out of hell into the "soft black light" of "home" (125) instead lies with Roi's ability to cultivate a sense of identification with the black urban poor—a project that remains unfinished at the novel's end. The novel thus prefigures Baraka's abandonment of his Jewish wife, Hettie Jones, and relocation from Greenwich Village to Harlem in 1965.

At the same time, the novel traces Baraka's search for a new style distinct from that of the white avant-garde. *The System of Dante's Hell*, Baraka explained in subsequent interviews, is "when I consciously stopped trying to write like people whose work I was around, people like Charles Olson and Allen Ginsberg."[10] Just as Greenwich Village bohemianism reinscribes black bourgeois double consciousness, the American avant-garde reinforces African Americans' subordination to a European literary tradition. *The System of Dante's Hell* aims at deconstructing this tradition, which it presents as an imprisoning system from which the black artist must break free. As its title suggests, Baraka patterns the novel after Dante's *Inferno*, with chapter headings corresponding to the various levels of hell. Within this framework, Baraka incorporates extensive references to the canonical high-modernist texts that form Roi's reading material, especially *Ulysses* and *The Waste Land*. The novel, in short, is a textual hell generated by the insidious influence of Western forms, which Roi must learn to penetrate.[11] This deconstruction of Western forms is ambiguous, however, for it is mediated by the process aesthetic developed by Olson and other experimental poets in the 1950s. *The System of Dante's Hell*'s assault on established forms and search for an individual style is consistent with Olson's emphasis on the creative process at the expense of the finished product. Indeed, the entire text obsessively undoes itself to highlight the act of writing: "I am myself. Insert the word disgust. A verb. Get rid of the 'am.' Break out. Kill it. Rip the thing to shreds. This thing, if you read it, will jam your face in my shit" (24). As in the case of Roi's effort to expunge his bourgeois double consciousness, his attempt to move beyond the white literary counterculture remains incomplete at the novel's end; the novel is a self-consciously arty text indebted to Beat, Black Mountain, and New York school poetics.[12]

This incomplete rejection of 1950s poetics is crucial, for *The System of Dante's Hell* also remains ambiguously attached to the ontology of nonwhite poverty that animated writers like Kerouac and Olson. This ontology imagined that the nonwhite poor of various cultures embody an alternative mode of being at odds with the capitalist rationalism of middle-class America. Kerouac, I argue in Chapter 1, appropriated this ontology as the basis for his improvisatory prose. In essays like "American Sexual Reference: Black Male" (1965), Baraka dissected white bohemians' fascination with African Americans as a form of racial fetishism.[13] At the same time, Baraka recapitulated the Beats' ontology of poverty in his polemics against the black middle class and attempts to imagine an alternative, authentically African American culture. This ontology is most explicit in *Blues People* (1963), Baraka's history of black music, which imagines lower-class African Americans as the bearers of an antirationalistic black soul imported into America by the earliest slaves and reinforced through centuries of poverty and discrimination. "Americans," he claimed, "brought slaves to their country who were not only physical and environmental aliens but products of a completely alien philosophical system."[14] This black soul manifests itself in the blues, a style of music directly expressive of the body and of the human voice, as opposed to the artifact-like polish of Western music. The blues, in other words, is the chief repository of the process aesthetic that Olson similarly identified with impoverished nonwhites. In Baraka's account, this tendency in black music is continually at risk of being diluted by the self-hating black middle class, who want to assimilate into white America and destroy all traces of black cultural particularity. However, because of lower-class African Americans' material deprivation and enforced separation from Protestant America, the blues always survives. Baraka, like the Beats, thus abstracted American class and race relations into a Manichean struggle between two modes of being. Moreover, he identified the cultural effects of black poverty with the same energies that he hoped to capture in his writing; in his essays and poems from the early to mid-1960s, he aligned the mood of rebellion growing in the ghettoes with experimental art. The best political strategy for destroying America's institutionalized racism, he argued, is for African Americans to "turn crazy, to bring out a little American dada, Ornette Coleman style, and chase these perverts into the ocean, where they belong."[15]

Baraka's claim that authentic black culture is exclusive to lower-class African Americans, however, led him to replicate many of the paradoxes that troubled Oscar Lewis and other liberal social scientists' conceptions of poverty. In particular, he replicated the conflation of class and culture that characterized Lewis's culture of poverty thesis. This conflation is especially evident in "Heretics," the relatively accessible final chapter, which explores Roi's sense of disconnection from lower-class African Americans. In placing this section at the conclusion of his book, Baraka rearranges Dante's hell to make heresy, redefined as racial self-betrayal, its deepest sin: "It is heresy," he explains in his introduction, "against one's own sources, running in terror, from one's deepest responses and insights . . . the denial of being . . . that I see as basest evil" (17). The chapter focuses on Roi's experiences while stationed at an air force base near Shreveport, Louisiana. At this point in his life, Roi has reached the apex of his bourgeois ambitions, figured by his status as an air force cadet—literally soaring, like Ralph Ellison's protagonist in his short story "Flying Home" (1944), above the socioeconomic conditions that afflict African Americans. At the same time, he is in the process of becoming a modernist intellectual, a masturbatory enterprise that has made him effete and, according to the novel's heterosexist logic, potentially homosexual: "Thomas, Joyce, Eliot, Pound," Roi reflects, "all gone by & I thot agony at how beautiful I was. And sat sad many times in latrines fingering my joint" (101). On an evening pass, Roi ventures with a friend into the city's black slum, named "Bottom," for an evening of fornication and drunken carousing. Here, Baraka makes explicit the intertextual connections between his novel and Dante's *Inferno*. Bottom is the infernal city of Dis, approached by bus down a steep, misty slope. Like Dante's Dis, it is guarded by rebel angels: a group of angry black men who attack Roi when he tries to flee back to his air force base at the chapter's end.

When Roi ventures into Bottom, he perceives it in pathological terms that echo Lewis's depictions of Mexican and Puerto Rican slums. The residents of Bottom live in a "culture of violence and foodsmells" (104) that reminds Roi of the worst neighborhoods of Newark. They exemplify the death of social aspiration that, according to Michael Harrington's *The Other America*, was typical of post–World War II slums: "Tough black men . . . weak black men. Filthy drunk women whose perfume was cheap unnatural flowers. Quiet thin ladies whose lives had ended and whose teeth hung stupidly in their silent mouths . . [sic] rotted by thousands of nickel wines. A smell of despair and drunkenness" (107). Bottom is the hell imagined by War on Poverty theorists, peopled by those who have turned their backs on the middle-class values that supposedly permeate the rest of American society. In terms of the Dantean allegory on which the section draws, it is the hell reserved for those who have committed willful sin—an unapologetic embrace of lower-class cultural pathologies. The bus driver, watching his black passengers disembark, reflects on their essential perversity: "They live in darkness. No thought runs out. They kill each other & hate the sun. They have no God save who they are. Their black selves. Their lust. Their insensible animal eyes" (103). The point of Baraka's chapter is to reject this middle-class appraisal of Bottom as cultural hell. In spite of Bottom's violence, hopelessness, and promiscuity, it is the "soft black light" (125) within which Roi must bathe if he is to become whole. Hence, the chapter suggests that Roi's relationship with Peaches, an obese, seventeen-year-old black prostitute whom he picks up in Bottom, will redeem him from the effeteness he has absorbed from white society and modernist literature. He undergoes a symbolic baptism in her squalid apartment, dunking his head in her dirty dishwater, and eventually agrees to become her man. After this conversion, he reflects that his life was "All lies before. . . . All fraud and sickness. This was the world. It leaned under its own suns, and people moved on it. A real world of flesh, of smells, of soft black harmonies and color" (120). The true heretics, for whom Bottom is hell, are black bourgeois like Roi himself. Hence, when the bus driver drops off the passengers in Bottom, Roi announces his disconnection from his people. "You gon pay for that ol coon?" the driver asks after one of the passengers runs to avoid the fare. "No," Roi responds. "Fuck, man, I hate coons" (104). Roi later repeats this betrayal when he finally abandons Peaches, and the story ends where it begins, with Roi an effete intellectual detached from lower-class African Americans.

However, Baraka struggles to depict Bottom in affirmative terms; in the chapter, the city embodies few of the traditions generally affirmed in liberal pluralist celebrations of black cultural heritage. The actual St. Paul's Bottom of Shreveport, Louisiana, was a key location in the history of black music; it was the neighborhood where Huddie William Ledbetter (a.k.a. "Lead Belly") consolidated his blues style in the early twentieth century. Given Baraka's extensive knowledge of blues history, the choice of locale cannot be accidental. However, apart from the music coming out of the jukebox at the bar, there is little evidence of this blues heritage. Instead, "Heretics" focuses on Roi's fascinated/ repelled reaction to Bottom's violence and promiscuity. At the story's center is the casual brutality inflicted on outsiders like Roi and the hustling of Peaches and other prostitutes. Indeed, Peaches's apartment—the site of Roi's reconnection with black authenticity—seems to exemplify poverty theorists' claim that the culture of poverty is a distorted development of middle-class culture. Although her radio plays the blues, her walls are decorated with photographs of "Rheingold women" (111). In Eliotic fashion, this reference juxtaposes the Rhine maidens from Wagner's Ring cycle with their debased mass cultural counterparts—the white beauty pageant models used to advertise Rheingold beer in the 1940s and 1950s. Peaches, meanwhile, is reading a book about white Hollywood actress Linda Darnell (118). She seems just as fascinated by white culture as Roi himself. Moreover, she idealizes that aspect of white culture—mass cultural representations of white femininity—most often used to denigrate lowerclass black women. Like Roi, she suffers from an inferiority complex that makes her perpetually aware of her departures from imagined white cultural norms— her skin color, obesity, and promiscuity.

Hence, it is difficult to sustain the reading, affirmed by most of Baraka's critics, of Peaches as a redemptive figure "whose crude self-acceptance is superior to [Roi's] racial self hatred."[16] Rather, Peaches's characterization highlights an ambiguity in Baraka's efforts to associate African American authenticity with the culture of lower-class blacks in texts like *Blues People*. Peaches's relationship to white culture is not altogether different from the double consciousness that afflicts the upwardly striving black bourgeoisie. As depicted by Baraka, the young Roi's relationship to modernist literature is one of half-comprehending submissiveness; he is trying to embrace a set of texts and attitudes that he does not yet understand. He intersperses his dialogue and thoughts with showy allusions to literary modernism often out of touch with his immediate circumstances. In the bar, Roi compares Peaches's conversation to the neurotic dialogue from T. S. Eliot's "A Game of Chess": "Talk to me. Goddamnit. Say something. You never talk, just sit there, impossible to love. Say something" (111). Later, while she is raping him, he cries out, "I'm beautiful. Stephen Dedalus" (114). For Peaches, this desire to emulate white middle-class culture is short-circuited by her straitened social circumstances; she knows that she cannot actually become like Linda Darnell and does not try to do so. However, she is aware that this culture is more valued than her own lower-class manners, and she feels a sense of deference toward those who can effectively lay claim to it. According to Lewis, "People with a culture of poverty are aware of middle-class values, talk about them and even claim some of them as their own, but on the whole they do not live by them."[17] Part of Peaches's attraction to Roi, once she gets beyond his arty pretensions, lies in the fact that he is more educated than the other Bottom men, closer to the middle-class ideals she cannot herself live up to. Hence, while Peaches eats her watermelon with bare hands, she serves Roi his "on a plate, with a fork (since I was 'smart' and could be a lawyer maybe)" (119).

Conversely, the pathologies that supposedly characterize lower-class black culture also beset the black bourgeoisie. This insight informs "The Rape," another of the more cohesive narratives that comes near the novel's end. This chapter, which corresponds to the first round of the ninth circle of Dante's hell ("Treachery to Kindred"), describes Roi's triumphant return to New Jersey after a year at university. For his neighbors, Roi embodies the promise of black bourgeois uplift: "THE BEAUTIFUL MIDDLECLASS HAD FORMED," the narrator declares, "AND I WAS TO BE A GREAT FIGURE, A GIANT AMONG THEM. THEY FOLLOWED WITH THEIR EYES, OR LISTENED TO SOFT MOUTHS SPILL MY STORY OUT TO GIVE THEIR WIVES" (93). At a party with other college boys, all of them dressed in suits and ties, Roi sees a drunken prostitute who has stumbled out of Newark's slums into a black bourgeois neighborhood in East Orange. Promising to drive her home, Roi and his friends lure her into their car and sexually assault her in the back seat. At first glance, the prostitute seems utterly different from her assailants; her foul breath smells of the slum, which Roi associates with "dead minds, dead fingers flapping empty in inhuman cold" (96). She suffers from a venereal disease, which she claims will infect the college boys if they go through with the rape: "I'm sick . . . and you boys ketch what I got you'll never have no kids" (99). However, as the story's Dantean intertext suggests, she is the young men's kindred. Her position neatly mirrors

Roi's in "Heretics": She is a class outsider who has ventured out of her territory, and she is punished for her transgression. In a pun on Baraka's original name (LeRoi Jones), she is trying to find her way back home to "Jones St." (95). More fundamentally, the sexual assault is the young men's attempt to embody a virile model of masculinity that they associate with the ghetto. As teenagers, Roi and his friends belonged to middle-class gangs that mimicked the behavior and attitudes of the slums, and the attempted rape allows them to relive this juvenile delinquent fantasy. The assault takes place as the men drive through the wealthy white city of Montclair, where all of them aspire to live eventually, and the woman's screams raise the prospect that their crime will, in fact, reduce them to the status of the black underclass: "Someone would hear and we would die in jail, dead niggers who couldn't be invited to parties" (99). Indeed, from the perspective of those who live in Montclair, East Orange is little different from Newark; "the Negro rich," Roi reflects, "were lovely in their nonimportance in the world" (93).

This insistence that lower- and middle-class black pathologies mirror each other echoes E. Franklin Frazier, the foremost black sociologist of the 1940s and 1950s and a key influence on Baraka's intellectual development.[18] In *The Negro Family in the United States* (1939), Frazier outlined the argument about lower-class black family pathology that Moynihan later reiterated in his similarly titled 1965 government study, *The Negro Family*. He argued that male unemployment had damaged African American families, creating dysfunctional, female-headed households. In *Black Bourgeoisie* (1957), he similarly outlined the pathologies of the black middle class: a class obsessed with the pursuit of status without the economic means to sustain this pursuit. The black bourgeoisie, Frazier claimed, live in a "world of make-believe" characterized by improvident consumerism, self-hatred, and slavish imitation of white standards. Each of Frazier's two studies, however, imagined how lower- and middle-class African Americans might escape from their respective pathologies. *The Negro Family in the United States* predicted that black familial pathologies would disappear with lower-class black men's absorption into an interracial labor movement. *Black Bourgeoisie* envisaged a saving remnant of critical black intellectuals like Frazier himself. These intellectuals "have nothing to do with Negro 'society' and refuse to waste their time in frivolities. They take their work seriously and live in relative obscurity so far as the Negro world is concerned."[19] Baraka erased these class exceptions in his early 1960s work; he had no interest in the labor movement, and he singled out black intellectuals as embodying in an extreme fashion the middle-class pathologies identified by Frazier.

In spite of Baraka's increasing calls in the early to mid-1960s for black artists to return home to the black community—advice that he would follow in 1965—the way out of Roi's personal hell does not lie in his assimilation into the black urban poor. Baraka highlights this impossibility in the novel's final moments, after Roi abandons Peaches and tries to return to his air force base. He is set on by a group of young black men, who attack him because of his class pretensions and beat him into unconsciousness. His subsequent hallucination sums up his political and aesthetic ambitions at this point:

> It was in a cave this went on. With music and whores danced on the tables. I sat reading from a book aloud and they danced to my reading. When I finished reading I got up from the table and for some reason, fell forward weeping on the floor. The negroes danced around my body and spilled whisky on my clothes. I woke up 2 days later, with white men, screaming for God to help me. (123)

Kimberly Benston reads this scene as an adumbration of Baraka's cultural nationalism: "He is fractured yet he is one, and through his ordeal he guarantees the possibility of later assuming the Orphic role of shaman, the singer-prophet capable of establishing harmony and unity out of the shattered fragments of black civilization."[20] With Roi's immersion in the lower-class community of Bottom, he sheds his tortured self-consciousness and moves toward the community-centered aesthetic that Baraka would cultivate in his later work. In particular, the whores' response to Roi's reading exemplifies the synthesis between avant-garde literature and the blues that Baraka believed to be the goal of process-oriented black art. His dousing with whisky, like his baptism in Peaches's sink, suggests the whores' ritualistic acceptance of him. However, the fact that this ritual occurs in a dream implies that this desired synthesis between black artist and lower-class community is a wish-fulfillment fantasy, rendered impossible because of the ongoing differences between them. In Roi's waking reality, the black youth violently eject Roi from Bottom, sending him back to his white army and white God.

Baraka thus reaches an impasse in the conclusion to *The System of Dante's Hell*, one that he attempted to resolve with his turn to cultural nationalism. In the community drama that he produced after his relocation to Harlem and Newark, Baraka continued to present blackness as an ontological category at odds with the rationalism of the white and black middle class. This ontology is explicit in "A Black Mass" (1966), Baraka's dramatization of the Nation of Islam's myth of Jacoub—the evil scientist who creates the white man. In creating the "white beast," a devouring creature with the ability to transform nonwhite men and women into replicas of itself, Jacoub simultaneously invents time—a rationalized awareness of the passing of human history. Time is deadly, one of his fellow magicians explains. "It turns us into running animals. Forced across the planet. With demon time in mad pursuit. What good is that? What does it bring us that we need?"[21] Like Kerouac's Fellahin, Baraka's African American nation is pre- or posthistorical, existing in a perpetual present outside modern civilization. However, Baraka increasingly detached this timeless nation from the actually existing culture of lower-class black communities. Those communities, he imagined, are reflections of the white society that oppresses them. In "Columbia, the Gem of the Ocean" (1972), a godlike Uncle Sam stands before a crowd of black drunks, junkies, prostitutes, pimps, and gang bangers and proclaims, "I create all these things. I recreate my image all over this planet as the great thing I am. Look how they worship me. Look!"[22] Instead, as a devotee of Kawaida, Baraka envisaged preconquest African values and beliefs as a substitute for rather than amplification of the culture of the poor. "We need a value system to be predictable in our behavior," he explained in his Kawaida manifesto; "a value system is the spine of all cultures."[23] In spite of the participatory aesthetic that he embraced after 1965, he envisaged his role as a purveyor of this value system in paternalistic terms, as a top-down project managed by the professional artist. Although he insisted that artists are humble workers whose purpose is "to channel people's normal desires to see beautiful things and to make beautiful things,"[24] he imagined that he was a prophet capable of voicing the will of the African American nation: "I am a / vessel," one poem reads, "a black priest interpreting / the present and future for my people."[25] The avant-garde impulse to break down the barrier between art and life, between artist and nonartist, becomes an authoritarian gesture aimed at folding the black community into the artist's professional lifework.

Interrogating Process in *In the Mecca*

When Brooks reinvented herself as a Black Arts poet, she was one of the most recognizable members of an older generation of writers rejected by Baraka and other cultural nationalists. Like Ralph Ellison, she was the first African American in her field to win a major US literary prize: the Pulitzer for *Annie*

Allen (1949). This recognition was enabled by the racial universalism that early critics saw in her work. Paul Engle, in a review of her first book, *A Street in Bronzeville* (1945), summed up the terms that black and white critics used to praise Brooks's poetry until the mid-1960s: "Miss Brooks is the first Negro poet to write wholly out of a deep and imaginative talent, without relying on the fact of color to draw sympathy and interest." Her work, he continued, is no more "Negro poetry" than Robert Frost's work is "white poetry."[26] Brooks's early literary prestige was also enabled by her formalism. Writing poetry about black experience without polished technique, Brooks explained in 1950, "is like throwing dough to the not-so-hungry mob. . . . You have to cook that dough, alter it, until it is unrecognizable."[27] Unlike Baraka, Brooks insisted on the priority of product over process. This priority was reflected in her use of traditional forms—most famously, the sonnet, which she exploited in sequences like "Gay Chaps at the Bar" and "Children of the Poor." Because of her universalism and formalism, Brooks's early work resonated with the version of literary modernism that was being canonized in the 1940s university—the "New Poetry" championed by academic critics.[28] Although *A Street in Bronzeville* drew themes and techniques from Harlem Renaissance predecessors like Langston Hughes, the volume underscored Brooks's awareness that some of her audience were white, academically trained readers for whom a narrow range of high-modernist classics constituted the epitome of literary cultural capital. In this way, Brooks's poetry was typical of the work of her generation of post–World War II African American poets, including Robert Hayden and Melvin Tolson.

For Baraka, this alignment of Brooks's poetry with late modernism put her in the enemy camp of the various wars that he waged on behalf of black avant-garde aesthetics in the 1960s. She represented, for him, an older model of black literary careership that the Black Arts movement wished to set aside by speaking, as Larry Neal put it, "directly to the needs and aspirations of Black America."[29] Although Baraka didn't specifically name Brooks in his 1962 polemic, "The Myth of a 'Negro Literature,'" the essay took aim at her post–Harlem Renaissance generation of black writers. Taking his cue from Frazier's *Black Bourgeoisie*, Baraka complained, "In most cases the Negroes who found themselves in a position to pursue some art, especially the art of literature, have been members of the Negro middle class." This class's "mediocrity" consists of its need to display its familiarity with literature and art "that could be socially acceptable to the white middle class." After World War II, this need pushed black writers "headlong into the groves of the Academy, perhaps the most insidious and clever dispenser of middlebrow standards of excellence under the guise of a 'recognizable tradition.'"[30] For Baraka, postwar black poets like Brooks venerated high-modernist texts already in the process of becoming outdated. In so doing, they embodied the double consciousness that Baraka himself tried to shed in his work from the early to mid-1960s.

Baraka's polemic reductively simplified Brooks's and other postwar black poets' relationship to literary modernism; Brooks's early poem "The Sundays of Satin-Legs Smith" is just as subversive as *The System of Dante's Hell* in its appropriation of T. S. Eliot.[31] Nevertheless, Brooks took Baraka and other black poets' critiques of her early work to heart and began, in the late 1960s, to subject her universalism and formalism to a searching critique. In moving away from Harper & Row to Broadside Press, she distanced herself from the white literary establishment that had enabled her early career. She became involved in Chicago-area Black Arts collectives such as the Organization of Black American Culture.[32] At the same time, she emphasized that she would no longer write sonnets or other traditional poems; the black nationalist era, she commented, "does not seem to me to be a sonnet time. It seems to be a free verse time, because this is a raw, ragged uneven time, with rhymes, if there are rhymes, incidental and random."[33] In committing herself to the Black Arts movement, however, Brooks did not capitulate to Baraka's version of process art and participatory model of literary professionalism. Rather, she engaged process aesthetics in critical dialogue to reassert the artist's necessary reliance on a cooked aesthetic that maintains space between herself and her black urban subjects.

This dialogue with process art began shortly after the 1967 writing workshop that she ran for the Blackstone Rangers under the aegis of the Community Action Program. At this point, Brooks was a veteran workshop instructor, having taught courses at universities and colleges throughout the United States. In most of these courses, she assigned three books: Edmund Wilson's *Axel's Castle* (1931), a classic study of the origins of modernism; Elizabeth Drew's *Poetry: A Modern Guide to Its Understanding and Enjoyment* (1959), a textbook influenced by the New Critics; and Oscar Williams's *A Pocket Book of Modern Verse* (1960), one of the era's most popular poetry anthologies.[34] Brooks exposed her students to the African American poets entirely excluded from all three books by playing, near the end of her courses, a 1956 LP titled *Poetry of the*

Negro, which featured Sidney Poitier reading poems by Paul Laurence Dunbar, Langston Hughes, and Brooks herself. The course reflected the late-modernist paradigm that informed Brooks's pre-1967 work. Its structure, divided between white writing and supplemental black oral performance, evoked Brooks's respected yet marginal position in the American literary field. At the same time, the course highlighted Brooks's formalism; she organized the writing component of the course around a series of units that required students to try out different traditional forms: ballad verse, blank verse, heroic couplets, and the Shakespearean sonnet. This was the course that she adapted for the Blackstone Rangers. She did not assign the three textbooks, which the Rangers could not afford. However, she read many of the same poems and required her students to experiment with the same forms.[35] The course was a failure; the Rangers rebelled when she asked them to write sonnets, and, she later commented, "I quit and we just became friends."[36]

The Blackstone Rangers workshop marked a crisis in Brooks's conception of her role as a poet; after the course, she realized that her pedagogy and poetics were not ideally suited for the black urban audience she hoped to reach. In future workshops, she changed her course format, replacing Williams's textbook with Amiri Baraka and Larry Neal's *Black Fire* (1968), the most influential anthology of Black Arts writing.[37] Her writing assignments became political; after showing students a picture of three babies, two white and one black, she instructed: "Write a rhymeless poem. . . . If you feel it would be better for the world if all these cute little babies had white faces or black faces, say so in the context of your poem."[38] However, while Brooks's encounter with the Rangers changed her pedagogy, it did not fundamentally alter her underlying concept of literary form. In a 1969 workshop, she presented her students with the following statement, which she described as the "academy's attitude" toward art: "Literature and life are not the same." She juxtaposed this with a Black Arts claim drawn from Baraka and Neal's anthology: "The black man's art is . . . of a piece with his past, his present, his destiny." She concluded with her own credo, "Art is refining and evocative translation of the materials of the world."[39] Although Brooks presented this credo as a response to Black Arts theory, it was not altogether different from her early claim that poets must cook the raw dough of experience; Brooks continued to insist on art's mediating function, in contrast with Black Arts writers who demanded that art be one with the life of the community.

Brooks's late 1960s pedagogy outlined the pattern of her response to the Black Arts movement; she tests its central claims but tacitly rejects them in favor of a politically oriented version of her own late-modernist poetics. This pattern is evident throughout her poetry from the same period. In particular, Brooks stages a strategic response to Baraka's process art in *In the Mecca*'s "Two Dedications," a pair of poems about the relationship between art and audience: "The Chicago Picasso" and "The Wall." Mayor Daley commissioned the first poem for the unveiling of Picasso's monumental sculpture in downtown Chicago. The poem is the last work by Brooks addressed to a mostly white audience; it is also the last in a series of public poems that Brooks composed for the Democratic Party.[40] The poem highlights the separation between art and audience implicit in Picasso's work: "Does man love Art?" the poem asks, then quickly answers that "it is easier to stay at home, / the nice beer ready." The problem, the speaker suggests, is that art rarely penetrates the viewer's everyday experience, to the detriment of both. Echoing Brooks's earlier comments on cooked art, the poem juxtaposes a "raw" private sphere entirely given over to bodily functions, the "commonrooms" where people "belch, or sniff, or scratch," with "cooked" public art institutions that refuse intimacy; tourists at the Louvre, the speaker complains, "do not hug the Mona Lisa" (412).

"The Wall," in contrast, is immersed in the Chicago-area Black Arts movement and commemorates an artwork absorbed into the life of the community that created it. The poem describes the unveiling of the *Wall of Respect*, a now-demolished mural, conceived by Bill Walker and painted on the side of an abandoned tavern, which depicted African American artists and heroes, including Charlie Parker, Malcolm X, and Brooks herself. Brooks underscores the mural's identification between art and audience with one of her simplest rhyming couplets: "All / Worship the Wall" (414). She also disrupts the late-modernist convention of impersonality by making herself the poem's confessional speaker:

> I mount the rattling wood. Walter
> says, "She is good." Says, "She
> our Sister is." In front of me
> hundreds of faces, red-brown, brown, black, ivory,
> yield me hot trust, their yea and their Announcement (415)

You have to be an avid reader of Brooks to appreciate the startling novelty of this moment; it is the only instance in her first four volumes of poetry when she sets aside her usual dazzling array of personas to enter one of her own poems. The poem employs a paradoxical temporality to underscore the collapse between artist and audience that takes place when the crowd yields to Brooks. The poem is a "Dedication," which implies that like the Picasso poem, Brooks composed it for the Wall's public opening. However, she describes her approach to the speaker's platform in the present tense, which suggests that the moment of composition, critical appreciation, and audience response all take place at the same instant. In contrast to her early work, the poem seemingly presents itself as a raw, unmediated evocation of a public event, as an example of the process aesthetic championed by Baraka. Art becomes life as Brooks recites her poem to the crowd. The poem concludes with the line "And we sing" (415), evoking her immersion in that crowd.

The poem, however, complicates this immersion and undercuts its own illusion of rawness. Describing an earlier speaker, the black actress and stage director Val Ward, Brooks comments that Ward "leans back on mothercountry and is tract, / is treatise through her perfect and tight teeth" as she leads the crowd in a chant of "Black Power!" (414). In Ward's case, the collapse between speaker, message, and audience is perfect; she becomes the Black Power ideology that she speaks. In contrast, Brooks's response to the Wall is enigmatic:

> No child has defiled
> the Heroes of this Wall this serious Appointment
> this still Wing
> this Scald this Flute this heavy Light this Hinge.
>
> An emphasis is paroled.
> The old decapitations are revised,
> The dispossessions beakless. (415)

D. H. Melhem has unpacked the allusions to public art in these lines; "Scald," for instance, is a Scandinavian term, referring to one who recites Norse heroic poems.[41] However, the lines withdraw from the public rhetoric of the poem's opening ("A drumdrumdrum, / Humbly we come" [414]) into the dense imagery and archaic diction characteristic of earlier poems like "The Anniad." At the moment when Brooks is folded into a community of readers—through Walter Bradford's commendation of her and through her portrait on the Wall—she reasserts her idiosyncratic style. Moreover, her use of the agentless passive voice ("An emphasis is paroled") suggests that she reasserts the objectivity that she sets aside when she adopts a first-person confessional speaker.[42] Brooks does not abandon a cooked for a raw aesthetic. Instead, "The Wall," like "The Chicago Picasso," insists that "we must cook ourselves and style ourselves for art" (412). The illusion of rawness depends on the artist's subjection to a lifetime of poetic discipline.

Brooks also underscores her critical appropriation of process art in the poems about juvenile delinquents that she includes in *In the Mecca*. For Black Arts poets like Baraka and for Community Action Agencies like the Woodlawn Organization, black juvenile delinquents were a key urban constituency they hoped to address with their participatory professionalism. Before *In the Mecca*, Brooks had already laid claim to juvenile delinquency as a literary topic in "We Real Cool," the most famous poem ever written on the subject and one that Brooks later pointed to as the most perfect realization of her aspiration to create accessible black art. *In the Mecca* returns to this topic with two poems, "Boy Breaking Glass" and "The Blackstone Rangers." The first poem, in particular, uses the figure of the delinquent to reflect on the process aesthetic embraced by younger poets. The poem begins by equating delinquency and art in a manner similar to that of Baraka's "Black People," with its rallying cry of "up against the wall mother / fucker! this is a stickup."[43] The broken window from the poem's title is a "cry of art," and the boy's exclamation links black crime with the process artist's destruction of traditional forms: "I shall create! If not a note, a hole. / If not an overture, a desecration" (408). As Melhem notes, the poem's first fourteen lines hint at a "shattered sonnet,"[44] written in a loose iambic pentameter with occasional off rhyme. With the boy's first exclamation this form starts to break down; he opens a hole in what otherwise might be read as a quatrain. His second exclamation thoroughly disrupts the form; it spills over from the fourteenth to a long fifteenth line that can no longer be scanned as an approximation to iambic pentameter: "Nobody knew where I was and now I am no longer there" (409). The poem's remaining twelve lines gesture toward reestablishing its broken form; the poem's stanzas are roughly symmetrical, and the poem ends, at it begins, with a sestet. However, in contrast with the first half, the lines in the second half vary wildly, from one to five beats. Brooks, in other words, equates the boy's broken window with her own deconstruction of the sonnet that had served her so well as a younger poet. In Brooks's account of her Blackstone Ranger workshop, she singled out the sonnet as the form that provoked the most hostility from her students. In

"Boy Breaking Glass," the poet engages in her own act of vandalism, smashing the sonnet to reach the delinquent on the other side. Brooks thus enacts the gesture that defined both Baraka's process art and the War on Poverty's Community Action Program. Professional expertise must be broken down to better serve the expert's social purpose.

However, "Boy Breaking Glass" disrupts this identification between delinquency and artistic creativity, instead highlighting the ineradicable distance between the boy and speaker, as well as the potential authoritarianism implicit in any attempt to pretend that this distance does not exist. As the poem makes clear, the boy's utterances, although put in quotation marks, are not actual transcriptions of his words; the boy speaks using Brooks's characteristically dense, imagistic diction rather than any of the colloquial black idioms that she also captures in her work. Instead, these utterances are the speaker's self-consciously inadequate efforts to translate wordless physical violence into rhetorical violence. The poem's penultimate stanza registers the boy's rejection of this translation: "It was you," the boy complains, "it was you who threw away my name! / And this is everything I have for me" (409). The speaker imagines the boy's vandalism as a reaction against people and institutions that reduce him to the generic category of delinquent. The poem, however, reproduces this reduction, leaving the boy unnamed. At the same time, the poem betrays the temporality of the boy's violence. As underscored by the present participle of the poem's title, "Boy Breaking Glass," this violence is instantaneous, meaningful only during its duration. The poem's first line, however, transforms this present participle into a noun ("broken window"). While the boy's violence literalizes the ambitions of process artists, Brook's poem leaves behind a durable object, preserved (like Baraka's poems from the same period) in a socially sanctioned cultural container: a book of poetry published by a major press.

Throughout *In the Mecca*, Brooks's purpose in offering this critical commentary on process art is to fashion a model of the engaged black artist distinct from Baraka's conception of the poet as prophet shaman. This alternative model is most explicit in the volume's title poem, which takes up half the book and doubles as a quasi-sociological exploration of tenement housing and as a self-reflexive commentary on Brooks's evolving art. "In the Mecca" is a narrative poem set in Mecca Flats, a Chicago tenement built in 1892 as a luxury apartment building, opened to African American tenants in the 1910s, and demolished in 1952 to make way for S. R. Crown Hall at the Illinois Institute of Technology.[45] The poem's plot focuses on the plight of Mrs. Sallie Smith, a black single mother with nine children who searches the building for her murdered daughter, Pepita. Most of the poem, however, is dominated by a series of vignettes of other tenement dwellers. The most important of these tenants is Alfred, a poet and high school teacher whose internal monologue takes up more space than that of any of the poem's other voices. Through this figure, Brooks articulates an aesthetic of caring distance or "hot estrangement" between the artist and the black community. This aesthetic, the poem suggests, is necessary to understand socially abject figures like Mrs. Smith.

As most of the poem's critics have noted, Alfred is a self-portrait, poised somewhere between the early Brooks who explored Mecca Flats in the late 1940s and the later Brooks who wrote about it in the 1960s.[46] He begins the poem as an ineffectual would-be modernist like Baraka's Roi; he "reads Shakespeare in the evenings or reads Joyce / or James or Horace, Huxley, Hemingway" (379). By the poem's end, he is a black nationalist and Pan-Africanist who admires the Senegalese poet and politician Léopold Sédar Senghor (392). This shift entails a changed relationship to the building and community he inhabits. In the poem's opening, Alfred is closed in his room, chastising himself for his failures and engaged in private pursuits (sleeping with women and drinking). Near the poem's conclusion, he leaves his room to lean against one of Mecca's courtyard balconies. He reflects that although he "hates it," "something in Mecca continues to call!" (403). This description of Mecca's call seems to prefigure Alfred's transformation into a Black Arts poet insofar as it echoes tropes of calling that run throughout late 1960s African American poetry. Most obviously, the trope is central to Baraka's "SOS," which Brooks singled out as characteristic of what she hoped to accomplish with her own Black Arts poetry: "My aim, in my next future, is to write poems that will somehow successfully 'call' (see Imamu Baraka's 'SOS') all black people."[47] Over the course of the poem, Alfred increasingly resembles Haki Madhubuti, the Chicago-based Black Arts poet whom Brooks anachronistically includes among her portraits of Mecca Flats' residents.[48]

However, throughout the poem, Alfred articulates an aesthetic theory that does not resemble that of any of Brooks's Black Arts contemporaries. Alfred outlines this theory in his first monologue:

To create! To create! To bend with the tight intentness
over the neat detail, come to
a terrified standstill of the heart, then shiver,

then rush—successfully—

at that rebuking thing, that obstinate and

recalcitrant little beast, the phrase!

To have the joy of deciding—successfully—

how stuffs can be compounded or sifted out

and emphasized; what the importances are;

what coats in which to wrap things. (378–379)

Creation, for Alfred, is a two-stage process: first, observing details; and second, discovering the phrases best suited to communicating their significance. Although the first half of his explanation suggests that these processes are distinct, the second half suggests that they run concurrently; without the right linguistic coats, the "neat detail" is indistinguishable from "things" and "stuffs." In Saussurian terms, literary creation resembles how children learn language; the poet encounters a "vague, uncharted nebula," which she divides "into distinct parts to furnish the signifiers needed by thought."[49] The poem concludes with an example of this act of creation in the rhyming couplet that Mrs. Smith's daughter Pepita composes before her death: "I touch . . . petals of a rose. / A silky feeling through me goes!" (403). Although these lines draw on common poetic conceits, they name precisely a previously inchoate subjective state.

This process of poetic naming, Brooks insists, is a political act with ramifications for the residents of Mecca Flats. Brooks underscores these political consequences through her portrait of Alfred. Immediately after describing his aesthetic, the speaker comments that he is an "untalented" poet because he cannot make the kind of distinctions required by his theory. The world remains, for him, an indistinct blur. In the morning, his classroom is "a smear / which does not care what he may claim or doubt / or probe or clear or want"; he cannot distinguish between students, which means that he "'fails' no one." In his sex life, similarly, he indiscriminately beds women. In his drinking, finally, he reaches a state where "the Everything / is vaguely a part of One thing and the One thing / delightfully anonymous / and undiscoverable" (379). This failure is critical given the poem's tenement context; the problem faced by Mecca Flats's residents is that outsiders similarly see them as an anonymous, indistinguishable mass. When "the Law" comes to investigate Pepita's disappearance, they characterize her as a "Female of the Negro Race" (391). In viewing his students in generic terms rather than adjusting his pedagogy to their specific needs, Alfred institutionally perpetuates the same social categorization that keeps

Meccans and other slum dwellers living in substandard housing. Brooks's poem, with its multiplicity of characters, works against this tendency to render the Meccans anonymous. Where the Law sees "the Negro Race," the poem discovers a complex social microcosm, in which schoolteachers live side by side with housemaids and former slaves.

"In the Mecca" charts Alfred's gradual realization of this aesthetic of specificity, as he learns to perceive and name his environment. As he tries to remedy his failures as a poet, he first turns to a romanticized vision of Africa akin to that perpetuated by many black cultural nationalists. He asks,

> Where there were all those gods
> administering to panthers,
> jumping over mountains,
> and lighting stars and comets and a moon,
> what was their one Belief?
> what was their joining thing? (379–380)

As Sheila Hughes notes, Alfred's initial conception of Africa is monolithic; he perceives it as a place unified by a single belief system and reduces it to generic stereotypes about panthers and mountains.[50] He perceives the continent more distinctly when he begins to admire Léopold Senghor, whose poetics of negritude enabled him to escape from European abstractions about "fairy story gold, thrones, feasts, the three princesses" (392) and instead pay attention to the particularity of Senegal; after Senghor's break from European culture, he "listens / to the rich pound in and beneath the black feet of Africa" (393). Senghor's example facilitates Alfred's turn to the particularities of his own locale. At first, Alfred attempts to imagine the Southern United States as a homeland akin to Senghor's Senegal, and the speaker registers his faltering efforts to bring together words and concepts:

> To be a red bush!
> In the West Virginian autumn.
> To flame out red.
> "Crimson" is not word enough,
> although close to what I mean.
> How proud.
> How proud.
> (But the bush does not know it flames.) (394)

However, there are no red bushes in Mecca Flats, and Alfred is forced to de-construct the terms he uses to visualize them; neither of the adjectives ("red" or "crimson") nor the metaphor ("flaming") adequately particularizes the au-tumn bushes.

Finally, Alfred discovers his subject matter when he leaves his flat to look at his fellow residents from the balcony. The call that he hears "builds to a reportage and redemption. / A hot estrangement" (403). These lines sum up Brooks's approach to the poem: what Brooks later called "verse journalism."[51] This approach combines the disinterested fact finding of journalism with an interested desire to make audible previously unheard voices. This conception of poetry entails a specific relationship between poet and community that differs from the immediate identification sought by Black Arts writers like Baraka and Madhubuti. Brooks captures this relationship in her paradoxical phrase "hot es-trangement." Like the impersonality promoted by many strands of modernism, hot estrangement entails a deliberate attempt to distance oneself from one's community. For Brooks, however, this distancing is a passionate act, done out of a sense of political responsibility for the people one serves as a poet. This hot estrangement is essential to the aesthetic of naming that the poem promotes. Those who stand at a cold distance from the Meccans, like Alfred in front of his classroom or the police investigating Pepita's disappearance, see only a blur. However, the same problem besets those who seek to eradicate this distance en-tirely. For instance, the poem presents two vignettes of would-be black nation-alists who cultivate fantasies about retaliating against white America: Amos and Way-Out Morgan. Amos fantasizes about raping a personified white America to remind her "of how she was so long grand, / flogging her dark one with her own hand" (395). Way-Out Morgan collects guns and paints "Death-to-the-Hordes-of-the-White-Men!" (400) above his bed in memory of police beatings he suffered and his sister's gang rape in Mississippi. These fantasies blind both men to the particularities of the forces that oppress them and the communities they believe they serve. Way-Out Morgan quickly drifts away from the particu-lar memory of his sister's rape to an abstract "Blackness stern and blunt and beautiful, / organ-rich Blackness telling a terrible story." Similarly, he is inca-pable of seeing the "yellow woman in his bed" because he is intent on finding justice for massacred "black bodies" against an equally anonymous white horde (401). African Americans are as much a "smear" for Way-Out Morgan as they are for Alfred before his transformation into a perceptive poet.

As "In the Mecca" insists, Way-Out Morgan's inability to particularize the experience of race and class oppression is common to most of Mecca Flats's residents and is a key effect of this oppression. As Craig Hansen Werner remarks, the poem's character vignettes form a catalog of "defenses against confronting the harshness of ghetto reality."[52] Most of the Meccans are incapable of seeing their environment. This failure falls into two broad categories. First, many of the poem's characters are distracted by the promise of the consumer culture they inhabit. When Mrs. Smith looks at her squalid kitchen, she exclaims, "I want to decorate!" The speaker comments: "But what is that? A / pomade atop a sewage" (380). Mrs. Smith hopes to disguise her apartment's dysfunctionality with a commercial beauty product specifically marketed to African Americans. She shares this strategy for coping with disagreeable circumstances with her daughter Yvonne, who uses "doublemint as a protective device" (381) to disguise the casualness of her relationship with her boyfriend. Similarly, many of the Meccan women are disciples of a religious charlatan, the Prophet Williams, who sells powders that promise to ward off all of the ills of ghetto life: "Pay-check Fluid, Running around Elixir, / Policy Number Compeller, Voodoo Potion" (397). All of these characters, like Alfred, are trying to find "coats in which to wrap things," but the wrappings they choose are commodities designed to hide the fact that African Americans have been relegated to an abject status—to sewage. This inability to perceive one's own abject status is especially devastating in a poem about a building that had, by the late 1940s, literally been assigned to the category of a waste space designated for slum removal. However, the opposing strategy—refusing wrappings and designating everything as waste—is equally problematic. "In the Mecca" thus juxtaposes Mrs. Smith with her second-eldest daughter, Melodie Mary, who hates commercial goods but "likes roaches / and pities the gray rat" (382). This identification leads to her fatalistic acceptance of her family's eventual disposal: "Trapped in his privacy of pain / the worried rat expires, / and smashed in the grind of a rapid hell / last night's roaches lie." Perceiving tenement dwellers as waste can, at best, provoke pity. The speaker insists on the limits of this sentiment, which is indistinguishable from cruel indifference: "there is a central height in pity / past which man's hand and sympathy cannot go; / past which the little hurt dog / descends to mass" (383). Finding the right response to tenement experience instead means understanding oppression in its particularity. "In the Mecca" tries to achieve this particularity; its portraits never collapse all of Mecca Flats's residents into a single category of "black-ness" or "waste" but instead explore the various ways they are marked by yet resist their abject status.

This insistence on perceiving particularity informs Brooks's engagement with sociological abstractions throughout *In the Mecca*—in particular, her portraits of delinquents and single mothers. Brooks's triptych of poems about the Blackstone Rangers ("As Seen by Disciplines," "The Leaders," and "Gang Girls") offers the reader a guide for how to penetrate generalizations about youth gangs perpetuated by black nationalists and Great Society liberals in the late 1960s. As Werner notes, the three poems proceed dialectically; each poem revises the previous one. As the first poem's title suggests, it voices the point of view of those who would discipline the Rangers, especially the police; the poem articulates what Werner calls a "sociological-penal" perspective.[53] The speaker leaves the Rangers unnamed, referring to them as "thirty on the corner" (416) and imagines them as figures who have willfully embraced social pathology; they are "sores in the city / that do not want to heal" (416). The second poem departs from this disciplinary perspective by naming the gang's four leaders: "Jeff. Gene. Geronimo. And Bop" (417). The poem echoes the romanticization of black male delinquents typical of Black Arts writers like Baraka and liberals associated with the Woodlawn Organization, for whom the gangs were authen-tic political organizations irreducible to existing models of black leadership; the Rangers are "Hardly Belafonte, King, / Black Jesus, Stokely, Malcolm X or Rap" (417). This organization is at once autocratic and flexible; all of the gang's decisions come from its "bitter bureaus" of top leaders, yet its "bureaucracy is footloose" (418). The poem's speaker strives for a poetic form that evinces the same combination of structure and flexibility. The poem is "footloose" in its shifting play with meter, rhyme, alliteration, and amplification ("they can-cel, cancelled images" [417]; "bitter bureaus [bureaucracy is footloose]" [418]) in a fashion that evokes the improvisatory nature of urban signifying. Just as "Boy Breaking Glass" initially suggests that physical and rhetorical violence are one and the same, "The Leaders" equates the Rangers' style of decision making with the speaker's poetic invention. If "As Seen by Disciplines" insists on a total split between the speaker and her subject matter, "The Leaders" insists on total identification.

The third poem, "Gang Girls," however, stresses the poet's need to find an intermediate stance between objectification and identification where the gang members' particularity becomes visible. Brooks achieves this stance by focusing on a single young woman—Mary Ann, one of the leaders' girlfriends—and by continually shifting the poem's point of view. The speaker alternates between third-person similes that reduce Mary Ann to an erotic symbol ("Mary is / a rose in a whiskey glass" [419]) and second-person lines that collapse the distance between reader and Rangerette ("swallow, straight, the spirals of his flask / and assist him at your zipper / pet his lips / and help him clutch you" [420]). Through this alternation, the speaker depicts Mary Ann as both a victim of her situation and as an agentive figure capable of negotiating her victimhood. She enacts the combination of escapist fantasy and constricted aspiration that Brooks's poetry has taught its readers to see as the chief psychological symptom of racism in black women; Mary Ann "sighs for Cities of blue and jewel" (419) but settles for the stolen goods that her boyfriend brings her. Even as the gang offers its male leaders an escape from typical patterns of racial oppression, it perpetuates those same patterns among the young women whom gang leaders treat as sexual adjuncts. However, even as Mary Ann makes love to her boyfriend, "Gang Girls" insists that she is a deliberate performer, never lost in the moment, who strategically uses her lover for the goods he brings her; she "pants carefully, peers at / her laboring lover" (420). Like all of Brooks's characters, Mary Ann exhibits the unique combination of passivity and agency in the face of environmental forces that define her as a particular person. This combination is evident only when the poet passes through the simple identification with an imagined black urban audience characteristic of process art.

Brooks achieves a similar twin perspective on the Smith family in "In the Mecca." At its core, the poem is about the kind of black, female-headed family pathologized by Moynihan and other poverty theorists. Mrs. Smith shares her apartment with her nine children. The eldest daughter, Yvonne, is having sex with boys in the park, while the eldest son, Briggs, is running with a gang. The poem seemingly replicates the circular causality that Moynihan's *The Negro Family* attributes to black matriarchs and their children; single black mothers breed delinquent children who in turn reproduce new broken families. The entire poem, moreover, foregrounds the influence of the tenement building itself, whose closed courtyards and narrow corridors create the conditions that ultimately doom Pepita. These deterministic frameworks, however, fail to encompass the specificity of the Smiths' response to their constrained circumstances. Brooks evokes this specificity in Mrs. Smith's cooking; although her tenement kitchen is "sick," and although she can only afford to feed her children ham, she keeps a pot of "water of many seasonings" (380) boiling on her stove, which will flavor the meat in a fashion unique to her home. Similarly, although Yvonne appears to be following the pattern of other tenement girls, the speaker insists on the specificity of her desire for her boyfriend. Yvonne is just one of many "tough girl[s]" the boyfriend sleeps with, potentially exchangeable with "a rough / Ruthie or Sue." However, the physical pleasure he gives her is as unique as his signature; even when he is in other girls' rooms, Yvonne fantasizes that he is "slicing a cold cucumber, / or is buttoning his cuffs, / or is signing with a pen / and will plan / to touch you again" (381). This specificity in the way that the Meccans fit into conventional ghetto roles opens up the possibility, finally, of breaking free from them. This possibility is embodied in Pepita, whose name, as Melhem notes, means "seed" in Spanish.[54] Not yet having "learned that black is not beloved," Pepita believes that she is "royalty when poised, / sly, at the A and P's fly-open door" (403). Whereas other Meccans find their lives narrowly confined by the walls and doorways of their building, Pepita is convinced of her sovereign control over her material surroundings. She is murdered before this childish belief can be tempered by experience, and she faces the risk that she will end up exactly like her brothers and sisters. Nevertheless, while poverty theorists like Lewis and Moynihan believed that the culture of poverty was a system that inevitably captured children shortly after birth, Brooks imagines Pepita as marking a potential break with the circular causality that defines her mother and siblings' lives. This potential is renewed with each new child born to the tenement, with each new seed that the Meccans sow.

Brooks's insistence on the hot estrangement necessary to perceive oppression in its specificity put her at odds with most other artists involved in the Black Arts movement, as well as with many of the liberal professionals who sought to address the problems of the inner city during the War on Poverty. In particular, Brooks's poetry avoids the drama of anguished separation from and reunification with the poor that informs Baraka's art and politics. Implicit in Baraka's work is an anguished conception of himself as an outsider who must become an insider by stripping away artificial forms of expertise. Brooks insists on a different conception of the artist's class status. The autobiography that she published after her Black Arts conversion, *Report from Part One* (1972), depicts a working-class childhood infused with sophisticated forms of cultural capital. Home meant a janitor father who read poetry to his children and a

"Duty-Loving mother who played the piano . . . who helped her children with arithmetic homework, and who sang in a high soprano."[55] Literary expertise, for Brooks, is rarely a foreign intrusion into the ghetto; rather, it is a strategy whereby writers achieve critical self-reflexivity without departing from the communities that nourish their work.

3 Legal Services and the Cockroach Revolution

Early in Oscar Zeta Acosta's 1972 novel, *The Autobiography of a Brown Buffalo*,[1] his protagonist, Oscar Acosta, quits his job as a War on Poverty–funded Legal Services lawyer in East Oakland, California, dumping his law license in the wastepaper basket. His resignation precipitates his search for racial identity in *Autobiography* and eventual transformation into Buffalo Zeta Brown, the activist Chicano lawyer in Acosta's sequel, *The Revolt of the Cockroach People* (1973), the best-known novel about the Brown Power movement.[2] Oscar/Brown's transformation enacts a triple rejection. First, he rejects the liberalism that led him to take on "the enemy our president [Lyndon Johnson] so clearly described in his first State of the Union address" (*A*, 22). Instead, Oscar/Brown adopts a militant Chicano/Chicana cultural nationalism at odds with the politics of integrationist Mexican American leaders affiliated with the Democratic Party.[3] This political turn mirrors that of other Chicano/Chicana activists from the same period, many of whom began their political careers as members of the Viva Kennedy Clubs that helped elect John F. Kennedy or as paid organizers in Johnson-era Community Action Agencies.[4] Second, Oscar/Brown rejects the professional aspirations that led him to get his license to prove "that even a fat brown Chicano like me could do it" (*R*, 24). Living communally with his clients and helping them bomb the courthouse, Brown declares that he's "the only revolutionary lawyer this side of the Florida Gulf. . . . I'm the only one who actually hates the *law*" (*R*, 214). Third, Oscar/Brown rejects the white American counterculture, which turned him into "a faded beatnik / a flower vato" (*R*, 53). He abandons the hyperindividualist ethos of countercultural writers like his friend Hunter S. Thompson in order to identify with a collectivist political movement. Although Acosta wrote his two novels after his involvement with Brown Power, he inscribes this transition in their form. While *Autobiography* is a peripatetic Beat novel, loosely modeled after Jack Kerouac's *On the Road*,

Revolt incorporates elements of agitprop, reiterating the Brown Power slogan, "Viva la Raza!" (104).[5] The two novels mirror Amiri Baraka's 1960s shift toward a collectivist version of process art in which the artist becomes one with his or her racially specific audience.

In spite of these rejections, *Autobiography* and *Revolt* remain indelibly marked by Acosta's early identification with the War on Poverty. Specifically, Acosta's work is shaped by his beginnings as a poverty lawyer, associated with one of President Johnson's signature domestic programs. Incorporated into the Community Action Program in 1966, Legal Services marked the beginning of federally funded legal representation for the poor, connecting and expanding the hitherto fragmented and underfunded network of private Legal Aid offices across the United States. In the first eighteen months of the program's establishment, the OEO "created a system of law offices and lawyers about the size of the United States Department of Justice and all of its U.S. Attorneys' offices,"[6] encompassing more than eight hundred offices in poor neighborhoods, including the Oakland office where Oscar begins to practice law. Echoing African American critics, who tend to see a radical split between liberal politics and the Black Arts movement, Acosta's readers generally argue that a fundamental shift occurs between *Autobiography* and *Revolt*, as Acosta's protagonist learns to challenge liberal conceptions of justice and legality. In Ramón Saldívar's terms, in joining the Brown Power movement, Oscar/Brown embraces a view of justice as something that "cannot be achieved within present institutions."[7] Brown's activist turn in *Revolt*, however, is less a rejection than a realization of the principles that inspired the Legal Services program. Although Oscar/Brown rejects the routine concerns of welfare clients to focus on what he calls "political" cases (*R*, 256), he does so to embrace a model of radical lawyering that strikingly resembles that outlined by the program's early theorists. In line with participatory orientation of the Community Action Program, Legal Services lawyers were supposed to challenge local welfare bureaucracies to make them more responsive to their clients' needs, a challenge that Oscar evades throughout *Autobiography* but takes up in *Revolt*.

More broadly, Acosta's fiction longs for, even as it seeks to complicate, the ideal that motivated Legal Services and other Community Action initiatives: the creation of a new, multiracial, and cross-class coalition to replace the fragmenting electoral coalition that underlay the New Deal welfare state. Over the course of the 1960s, the Democratic Party began to envisage itself as a party that would bring together urban professional and minority (especially African American and Mexican American) voters. As *Revolt* highlights, many cultural nationalists materially benefited from this strategy, even as they embraced political rhetoric and tactics that put them at odds with the Democratic Party. Brown's first political trial is the result of a smear campaign coinciding with the 1968 Democratic Primary; local Republicans hope to highlight Eugene McCarthy and Robert Kennedy's associations with radical elements in the Mexican American community by charging key activists with conspiracy. The Ford Foundation, a philanthropic organization closely associated with the Democratic Party, funds Brown's law office, and his activist clients "earn most of their coins from the Poverty Program" (*R*, 80). Even after his radicalization, Brown is nostalgic for the liberal rhetoric that shaped 1960s Democratic Party policy on civil rights, which he associates with John F. Kennedy and his brother Robert.[8] President Kennedy is "the man who dreamed Cockroach dreams" (*R*, 47), a term that Brown uses to designate the multiracial coalition of the poor for which he agitates throughout *Revolt*. Robert Kennedy is "the last hope for the Chicano"; his assassination marks the death of "the whole white liberal bit" (*R*, 64). Throughout *Autobiography* and *Revolt*, the Kennedy brothers embody the lost promise of a more thorough integration of Mexican Americans and other minorities into the Democratic Party establishment—a promise betrayed by the late 1960s. Brown's rejection of the nonviolent tactics of his early idol, César Chavez, is a despairing response to the Kennedy assassinations and to the subsequent election of Richard Nixon; immediately after Robert's death, one of Brown's clients comments, "Shit, I feel like throwing a bomb or something" (*R*, 64).

However, even as Acosta chastises the Democratic Party for its failure to create a true cross-class and multiracial coalition, he also pushes to the breaking point tensions that were always latent in that ideal. In particular, *Autobiography* and *Revolt* highlight concerns about the class fragmentation and gender dynamics of minority communities that Acosta believes are exacerbated by Legal Services and other War on Poverty programs. As imagined by the federal administrators who helped craft the Great Society, the new Democratic coalition would suture the class divide between the professional managerial class and urban underclass. In actual practice, the War on Poverty replicated that schism within minority communities themselves. In theory, the Democratic coalition would be masculinist; echoing priorities established in the New Deal era, most War on Poverty programs targeted unemployed young men. In practice, the

War on Poverty indirectly benefited poor women; one of the Great Society's chief effects was to facilitate the addition of millions of previously excluded single mothers onto AFDC welfare rolls. Throughout *Autobiography* and *Revolt*, Oscar/Brown struggles with his class alienation from the constituencies he claims to represent, as well as with the gendered nature of welfare benefits. These class and gender anxieties pervade his professional identity as a lawyer and writer, generating the strange combination of self-parody and hypermasculinity that is the hallmark of Acosta's fiction. These anxieties are crucial to his version of process art, which brings to the fore many of the tensions that similarly plagued Amiri Baraka's transition from Beat artist to cultural nationalist. Although Acosta wants to fashion a Chicano/Chicana nation through his fiction, he remains wedded to a subjectivist aesthetic that highlights his solitary role as author.

Welfare Professionalism in
The Autobiography of a Brown Buffalo

Legal Services, Oscar's employer in *Autobiography*, was one of several War on Poverty programs that tried to bring into being the Great Society coalition of professionals and minorities. The program's origins date back to the earliest antipoverty pilot projects funded by the Kennedy administration; many of these projects included lawyers who offered pro bono services to needy clients. One of these lawyers was Jean Cahn, an African American Yale law graduate who participated in a short-lived Legal Aid program associated with Community Progress, Inc. (CPI), a 1963 pilot project in New Haven, Connecticut.[9] The program collapsed after she aroused controversy by defending a black man accused of raping a white woman; faced with negative publicity, CPI closed down the law office. On the basis of this experience, Jean Cahn and her husband, Edgar, wrote a widely read article for the 1964 *Yale Law Review* proposing a unified, federally funded system of neighborhood law offices.

In proposing this new system, the Cahns hoped to remedy two problems. First, they wanted to correct flaws inherent in the older, charity-based Legal Aid system that had catered to the poor since 1876. Because this system was privately funded, lawyers lacked autonomy and generally avoided controversial cases that might threaten their individual and corporate donors. As a result, no Legal Aid lawyer fought a case before the US Supreme Court until 1965.[10] Federal funding, the Cahns believed, would free poverty lawyers from local pressures such as the ones that closed the New Haven law office, enabling them to take on more challenging cases. Second, the Cahns wanted to remedy problems that they had observed in the New Haven pilot project, which they feared would be institutionalized in Community Action Agencies across the United States. One of the War on Poverty's goals was to encourage "maximum feasible participation" by the poor—a phrase incorporated into the 1964 Economic Opportunity Act as a requirement for all Community Action Agencies. The Cahns feared, however, that community action would perpetuate welfare paternalism as usual. The War on Poverty would be "fought by professionals on behalf of the citizenry through service programs," which would undercut local leadership and exacerbate welfare dependency. In spite of organizers' best intentions, Community Action Agencies would be deaf to "the civilian perspective"—the voice of dissent emerging from the people. For the Cahns, the solution was not to turn over more administrative control to community representatives. Welfare clients "lack the critical means necessary to implement the civilian perspective": education, skills, organization, and resources. Rather, the solution was to provide the poor with lawyers, who would give voice to their needs in a way that social workers and other welfare professionals could not. According to the Cahns, lawyers embody a unique form of professionalism. They are necessarily partisan; their function is to present "a grievance so that those aspects of the complaint which entitle a person to remedy can be communicated effectively and properly to a person with power to provide a remedy." Moreover, lawyers' specialized expertise does not distance them from their clients but brings them closer. The lawyer is not obliged "to be apologetic about his middle class background, because the justification for his presence is that he is a professional advocate and that he possesses skills and knowledge not otherwise available."[11] The poverty lawyer thus seamlessly embodies the War on Poverty's goal of creating a coalition between professionals and the urban poor.

As this summary suggests, Jean and Edgar Cahn's proposal replicated, rather than resolved, many of the class contradictions that they identified in the War on Poverty's professional orientation. They assumed that legal representation was an unproblematic way of translating clients' needs into a language that welfare institutions could understand. Indeed, they emphasized the need for poverty lawyers to maintain their professional autonomy even as they serve the poor. To avoid the case overload characteristic of previous Legal Aid organizations, lawyers should choose cases with "broad institutional implications and widespread ramifications," strategically turning down needy clients. At the same time, lawyers must not let impoverished communities dictate how they choose their clients or advocate on their behalf. Alluding to Jean Cahn's New Haven experience, the Cahns explained, "The desire and need of the law firm for acceptance from the community should not be equated with blind submission to the prejudices of that community."[12] The poverty lawyer carefully filters the civilian perspective. At the core of the Cahns' article and the Legal Services program it inspired, then, was a radical rethinking of the professional/client relationship that left that relationship strangely intact.

In its actual implementation, however, Legal Services sometimes challenged this relationship in ways that the Cahns did not imagine. Predictably, most Legal Services offices funded by the OEO replicated the faults and limitations of their pre–War on Poverty predecessors. In the program's early years, poverty lawyers were overwhelmed with routine cases—especially divorce cases—with the result that few could focus on the institutional provocation and law reform that the Cahns envisaged.[13] At the same time, Legal Services helped give rise to the most radical—and most frequently overlooked—legacy of the War on Poverty: the welfare rights movement. This movement, spearheaded by the National Welfare Rights Organization (NWRO), was dominated at the grassroots level by a multiracial coalition of AFDC recipients, or welfare mothers. This organization embodied the idea that the Cahns seemingly embraced but ultimately rejected in their article: the notion that welfare clients might take a leading role in their own advocacy. Although the movement included legal strategists such as Edward Sparer, many of its leaders were welfare recipients, such as Johnnie Tillmon, NWRO executive director from 1972 to 1975. The movement transformed AFDC clients into community activists; the NWRO encouraged its members to participate in sit-ins and other acts of civil disobedience.[14] The organization helped millions of poor mothers enter the welfare rolls by challenging restrictions on AFDC eligibility that had been in place since the New Deal. Its goal was to revolutionize the welfare state by establishing welfare as a legal right rather than a charity.[15] The NWRO thus realized many of the War on Poverty's aims but did so in a fashion that liberal administrators found troubling and politically hazardous. The figure of the militant welfare mother, demanding an unprecedented expansion of the welfare state as a fundamental human right, was one that few on the left, center, or right of the American political spectrum were willing to embrace in the late 1960s.

Oscar Zeta Acosta's two autobiographical novels highlight many of the contradictions in the Cahns' vision of Legal Services, even as he avoids the solution to those contradictions developed by the welfare rights movement. Indeed, the first of Acosta's novels, *The Autobiography of a Brown Buffalo*, begins with a misogynistic assault on welfare mothers. His protagonist, Oscar, is a poverty lawyer who specializes in divorce cases; most of his clients are poor white, Latina, and African American women seeking to escape their abusive husbands to receive AFDC benefits. Oscar initially characterizes the War on Poverty as a manifestation of feminine waste. His clients crowd into his office with "their tits still hanging and their grubby, happy kids sliding on the linoleum floors"—an image of lower-class, reproductive irresponsibility. When one of them asks for a TRO (temporary restraining order), Oscar thinks she is using "ghetto euphemism for a sanitary napkin" (*A*, 21). Oscar's comment, which disturbingly conflates domestic abuse with menstruation, suggests that the War on Poverty is a temporary check against the recurring bloodletting of lower-class women. Oscar extends this imagery to his secretary, Pauline, a fifty-seven-year-old woman with "female problems" (*A*, 22) who guides him through the legal system and shields him from his most demanding clients. Pauline's female problems are the result of the disease that kills her on the morning that Oscar quits; Acosta implies that she suffers from ovarian or cervical cancer, a tumorous contamination of the reproductive organs that inverts the deviant reproductive capacity of the office's clients.

This portrait of Oakland's welfare mothers exemplifies the grotesque satire that, as Michael Hames-García notes,[16] runs throughout Acosta's two novels, especially the carnivalesque courtroom scenes in *The Revolt of the Cockroach People*. However, Oscar's satire of Oakland Legal Aid is closer to the reactionary grotesque aesthetics that Peter Stallybrass and Allon White discover in bourgeois European representations of the working class than it is to Mikhail Bakhtin's liberating carnival.[17] By emphasizing the welfare mothers' excess physicality, Oscar underscores their incapacity for discipline and self-denial. In so doing, he draws on grotesque representations of lower-class women that have informed American welfare policy since the New Deal. From its inception in the 1935 Social Security Act, AFDC stigmatized its female recipients as morally suspect, thereby reinforcing a long-standing distinction in American culture between the deserving and undeserving poor. This conception of welfare recipients shaped most War on Poverty programs, which were explicitly masculinist in their focus on male employment. In particular, throughout the 1960s, theorists and politicians associated with the War on Poverty imagined welfare mothers, especially those who belonged to visible minorities, as pathological figures, incapable of regulating their sexual behavior in the manner of white middle-class subjects. During an NWRO sit-in, Senator Long referred to the protesting mothers as "brood mares."[18] Such conceptions of lower-class mothers were central to the work of Oscar Lewis and Daniel Moynihan, both of whom linked single mothers to juvenile delinquency.

Oscar's emphasis on his clients' reproductive excess reflects this conception of lower-class minority women as damaging matriarchs. Like Moynihan, he imagines that welfare facilitates the proliferation of matriarchal families and enfeebles lower-class men; Oscar's own work helps women of color separate from their husbands. Indeed, Acosta imagines his office as both an extension of matriarchal social policy and as a female-headed family. "We aren't lawyers," Oscar complains; "we are simply counselors of old women. We listen to their tales because we have a mandate from Congress" (*A*, 20–21). Oscar's own maternal figure in the office is his secretary, Pauline, whose excessive solicitude keeps him from taking on challenging cases. "Right from the start," he reflects, "she has coddled me, burped me, protected me and preserved me for the serious work—the heavy research, which I just haven't quite gotten around to doing yet" (*A*, 22). Sheltered by an overprotective mother, Oscar becomes a spoiled child, who complains that the battered clients are oblivious to his physical ailments—his ulcers and indigestion. Pauline's sudden death from cancer destroys the office's maternal environment, precipitating Oscar's flight and subsequent adventures with the hypermasculine King, a thinly veiled version of Acosta's friend, the gonzo journalist Hunter S. Thompson. This flight replicates Sal Paradise and Dean Moriarty's escape from domestic entrapment; *Autobiography* becomes a road novel modeled after *On the Road* once Oscar leaves behind the welfare mothers who constrain his process art.

This misogynistic streak in Acosta's writing, noted by many critics, seems to put him at odds with both the spirit and practice of Legal Services, as envisaged by Jean and Edgar Cahn and as developed by the lawyers who advocated on behalf of the welfare rights movement.[19] However, this streak also highlights anxieties about Oscar's professional status that echo the Cahns' critique of the War on Poverty. Part of the reason for Oscar's scathing satire of Oakland Legal Aid is that the agency in no way resembles the kind of neighborhood law office that the Cahns hoped to establish nationwide. Instead, it resembles the older model of charity-run Legal Aid that the Cahns criticize in their work; Oscar never pretends to be anything other than a professional serving an entirely passive clientele. Unlike the neighborhood lawyer envisaged by the Cahns, Oscar never challenges the welfare rules and regulations that entrap his clients; he takes on only uncontested cases that he can process on a mass basis without litigation and avoids running afoul of what he calls "social worker logic" (*A*, 20). Meanwhile, he avoids the research needed to prepare test cases that might challenge the welfare establishment. His caseload also forces him to erect bureaucratic barriers between himself and his clients that imitate those of the regular welfare system. "When we Legal Aid lawyers don't want a case," he explains, "when the problem is one that we aren't accustomed to dealing with, if it's something we'd actually have to study for and fight about, why, I'm sorry ma'am, but I don't make the rules, I just work here" (*A*, 21).

This barrier between Oscar and his clients poses a problem for him, insofar as he is a recently accredited minority professional, with a background that closely resembles those of the people he serves. As Oscar reveals in flashbacks throughout *Autobiography*, he grew up in an impoverished Mexican American family and experimented with various failed careers before earning a law degree. The War on Poverty, if it does not do much to help Oscar's clients, does selectively transform token minorities like himself into urban professionals, surrounded by the symbols of white-collar prestige. Oscar's clients are all intently aware that he is the true beneficiary of the War on Poverty; "the absolute worst of it all," he reflects, "is the sleepy yet knowledgeable look she [his client] gives to me when I'm on the phone, the way she *notices* my red $567 IBM typewriter on my mahogany desk" (*A*, 29). As a member of one of the minorities that makes up Oakland's ghetto, Oscar is supposed to function as a more effective advocate for the poor; as an attorney, he is "a man who speaks for others . . . a mature person who helps others in distress" (*A*, 24). However, the circumstances of his position prevent him from doing this. The War on Poverty, in short, creates and reinforces within the minority community the class division (between professional and underclass) that it is supposed to bridge. Moreover, it establishes and maintains this division without actually helping minority professionals fully assimilate into the professional managerial class. Although Oscar's framed degree and IBM typewriter separate him from his clients, his privileged position perversely mirrors theirs.

Most members of the California Bar regard Legal Services as an occupational ghetto, riddled with the same pathologies as its clients; poverty lawyers, Oscar reflects, are "socialist creeps, incompetents who know nothing about a hard-earned dollar" (*A*, 22).

Oscar's problem, in other words, is that unlike Lewis, Moynihan, and other social scientists who depict lower-class mothers as grotesque figures, Oscar cannot adequately separate himself from them. As Héctor Calderón observes, Oscar's satire throughout *Autobiography* is first and foremost "directed inwards."[20] The novel begins with Oscar looking into the mirror and observing "an enormous chest of two large hunks of brown tit" (*A*, 11). In reinventing himself as a minority professional, Oscar has not been able to discipline his unruly body and behavior, which resemble those of the lower-class women he serves. Anxious that he is morphing into a version of his large-breasted clients, he engages in compensatory masculinist fantasies, in which he imagines himself as a variety of Anglo celebrities such as Charles Atlas, Humphrey Bogart, and Ernest Hemingway. The vehemence of Oscar's satire of welfare mothers, in other words, is partially explained by his need to make them abject; Oscar needs to rigidly police the boundary between himself and his clients to avoid becoming too much like them. The events of his last day of work highlight for him that this boundary is all-too porous. Trying to escape from a group of women seeking TROs, Oscar retreats into the toilet to vomit blood, a bodily discharge that echoes his anxieties about his clients' perpetually bleeding bodies.

Vato Loco Advocacy in *The Revolt of the Cockroach People*

When Oscar quits Oakland Legal Aid, he flees a situation in which he is at once too close and not close enough to his welfare clients. In becoming a welfare professional, Oscar severs himself from his cultural origins as the child of migrant workers. At the same time, he imagines that professionalization has imperiled his masculinity, turning him into a grotesque, middle-class version of a lower-class woman. Oscar's solution in *Autobiography* is to take off on the road in imitation of hypermasculine white countercultural writers like Jack Kerouac and Hunter S. Thompson. However, when Oscar reinvents himself as Buffalo Zeta Brown and returns to legal practice in *Revolt*, he must suture his professional identity. He must bridge the gap between himself and his clients, becoming a true minority professional. At the same time, he must regender his legal practice, rejecting the abject welfare mothers whom he represents in *Autobiography* in favor of the equally abject, but decidedly male, Chicano street youth, *vatos locos*, whom he represents in *Revolt*.

Brown allegorizes this regendering near the beginning of *Revolt* in a scene that chronologically introduces his use of the term "cockroach people" to designate his new, multiracial political constituency. In a cheap motel shortly after arriving in L.A., Brown overhears an alcoholic beating his wife—the kind of woman who might have been Oscar's client in *Autobiography*. Reiterating Oscar's indifference toward battered women, Brown tunes out the domestic abuse and tries to go to sleep. At this moment, he undergoes a conversion experience that leads him to accept his abject status as one of the cockroach people:

> My light is off and I curl my arm under my head, figuring at last to get some sleep. All of a sudden I feel a tingle on my right thigh. I'd seen enough James Bond flicks to know better than to strike or jump. Tense and gritting my teeth, I shut my eyes hard watching for the beast to move again. It is about three inches from my balls, but either my sex doesn't appeal to him or he just isn't hungry. The next thing I know it has crawled over my bulging muscular ass and disappeared into the bed and the night. I laugh and sing to myself:
>
> > *La cucaracha, la cucaracha,*
> >
> > *ya no puede caminar.*
> >
> > *Porque le falta,*
> >
> > *porque le falta,*
> >
> > *marijuana pa' fumar.* (R, 23)

In this sequence, the distance between Brown and L.A.'s underclass collapses, and Brown responds with the same panic that Oscar expresses throughout *Autobiography*; he fears contamination and emasculation. At first, Brown turns to the compensatory fantasy by which Oscar defends his imperiled heterosexual masculinity in *Autobiography*. Just as, when gazing into the mirror, Oscar tries to imagine himself as Charles Atlas, Brown imagines himself as James Bond—a virile, white, first-world spy in a third-world nation. This fantasy is resolved when the insect loses interest in Brown's genitals and crawls over his ass, an event that precipitates Brown's memory of the Mexican folk song "La Cucaracha." At this moment, Brown accepts both his Mexican American upbringing and the fact that he belongs in a bug-infested hotel room with other cockroach people. Moreover, through the song about the marijuana-deprived insect, he conflates that racial and class identification with excessive substance abuse in a way that seems at odds with his professional status as an upwardly mobile lawyer.

This resolution, with its erotic emphasis on Brown's "bulging muscular ass," evokes the homosocial bonding that marks Brown's relationship with the Chicano militants throughout *Revolt*. As Gutiérrez-Jones argues, this bonding at once presupposes male violence toward Chicanas and is shadowed by the threat and possibility of homosexuality, a threat figured by Brown's repeated association between Chicano militancy and anal rape.[21] This combined hostility toward Chicanas and homosocial desire for Chicanos carries over to Brown's legal practice. Henceforth, women like the battered wife in his hotel will no longer seem like political clients; Brown perceives the violence directed toward them as merely internecine, unlike the more authentic violence that the *vatos locos* direct toward the police and other outsiders. This rejection of domestic violence as a valid political concern echoes the logic of many male activists in the Brown Power movement, who self-consciously embraced machismo as a defining feature of Chicano culture.[22] It also echoes the dominant focus of the War on Poverty, as expressed in documents like the Moynihan report, which similarly minimized the problems of impoverished mothers to focus on empowering poor young men.

Once Brown reimagines his potential clientele as empowered and masculine rather than victimized and feminine, he is able to return to lawyering, now reimagined as a virile, militant, distinctively Mexican American activity rather than a feminine submission to Anglo social policy. Indeed, in spite of Brown's repeated insistence that he hates the law, *Revolt* traces out his transformation into a better lawyer, one who fully commits to his profession's adversarial imperative and who gives voice to his clients' needs in a way that Oscar is incapable of doing in *Autobiography*. Brown depicts this reconciliation of his lawyerly vocation and Mexican American (later, militantly Chicano) identity as a gradual process. When Brown first arrives in L.A., he does not identify with the Chicano/Chicana militants; instead, he hopes to exploit their story to write his novel and cement his middle-class status. He wants to "find 'THE STORY' and write 'THE BOOK' so that [he] could split to the lands of peace and quiet where people played volleyball, sucked smoke and chased after cool blondes" (*R*, 22). The militants, in turn, hope to exploit Brown's professional abilities. Brown's law license, which Oscar must discard to escape his white-collar existence in *Autobiography*, becomes his entry ticket into the Brown Power movement; the militants warm to his participation only when they see his bar card. After witnessing his first Brown Power demonstration—the 1968 East L.A. Walkouts, in which hundreds of students walked out of the city's high schools to protest the poor education available to Mexican Americans—Brown becomes a convert and lends his professional abilities to the cause. No longer merely a lawyer who helps minority clients, he becomes "Buffalo Z. Brown, Chicano Lawyer" (*R*, 48), as his business card announces.

Brown comes to see lawyering in much the same way as the militants do: as a resource to be exploited. At no point in *Revolt* does Brown identify with his profession, in contrast to his early enthusiasm for the law when he passed his bar exam. As César Chavez explains, after Brown tells the hunger-striking civil rights leader that he doesn't want to be a lawyer, "Who in his right mind would *want* to be a lawyer?" (*R*, 46). Wanting to be a lawyer entails an attachment to the profession's perks and privileges—the typewriter and framed degree in *Autobiography* that separate Oscar from his clients, perpetually reminding them of his token status as a recipient of federal largesse. Brown gives up these privileges in *Revolt*, eventually working out of his apartment, where he lives with several of his clients. Brown's disidentification with legal advocacy leads him to parody his profession's outward proprieties. Violating most of the regulations laid out in the California Bar's Rules of Professional Conduct, he prepares for trial by dropping acid, recites a poem during one of his summations, and shows up in court wearing a disheveled suit and carrying a briefcase with a Mexican flag painted on it. This disregard for outward proprieties highlights Brown's willingness, in his new role as a Chicano lawyer, to do anything on behalf of his clients—even if his antics land him in jail for contempt of court. His in-court theatrics also underscore his liberation from the administrative control that hampered his actions in Oakland; he embraces a charismatic model of professionalism, of the kind that New Left activists promoted in the 1960s.[23]

This new form of advocacy prompts Brown to challenge institutions that are biased against his clients, in a way that Oscar shies from doing in Oakland. In particular, Brown uses his cases to expose and challenge the legal system itself. Throughout *Autobiography* and *Revolt*, Acosta engages in what Hames-García calls an "extramural" critique of the law; Acosta shows that "material relationships defined as beyond legal consideration are crucial to the functioning of the law."[24] In particular, he shows how clients and lawyers' race and class status influence the outcomes of court cases. For instance, in his defense of the

Tooner Flats Seven—a group of defendants arrested during the 1970 Chicano Moratorium riots—Brown tries to prove that California's Grand Jury is a racist institution.[25] He subpoenas and cross-examines all trial judges in the L.A. County Superior Court, highlighting the systemic bias that leads the judges to select white grand jurors. At the same time, Brown engages in extralegal political activism to attack the material inequalities that underlie the legal system—most notably in his campaign to become sheriff of L.A. County, promising to dismantle the office. As Hames-García explains, *Revolt* embodies a "conception of legal practice that calls for action outside the legal system to challenge the factors with which that system maintains its dominance (that is, the social relations on which the capitalist system is founded)."[26] Brown becomes a community activist, leading "pickets at the School Board, pickets at the police stations, pickets at City Hall, demonstrations at poverty program offices, marches to the welfare offices" (*R*, 71). He ultimately joins his clients in bombing Safeway supermarkets and the courthouse itself.

However, the extreme kinds of civil disobedience that Brown engages in throughout *Revolt* also highlight anxieties, fundamentally shaped by his impoverished childhood, that underlie his conception of professionalism. According to the Cahns, poverty lawyers are distinct from other welfare professionals in that they do not need to apologize for or pretend to erase their middle-class status. Brown, however, does feel this need. When he first meets the militants, he tries to prove that he fits into their narrow, cultural nationalist definition of what it means to be a Chicano. "How many peaches have you picked?" (*R*, 34), he asks their leader, highlighting his upbringing as a migrant worker. Wanting to fit in means that he must take increasingly desperate risks to prove that he too is a *vato loco*—a tough-minded, macho street youth like his clients. Increasingly, Brown imagines that his clients are remaking him in their image. When a prosecuting attorney suggests that Brown is the militants' leader, he reflects, "Those guys wouldn't do what I told them to do if their lives depended on it. They are *vatos locos!* Nobody tells crazy guys what to do. . . . It is *they* who have converted me and driven me to this brink of madness. It is they who are watching and wondering and complaining about me. *I* am the sheep. *I* am the one being used" (*R*, 248). Driven to the brink of madness, Brown allows his lawyering to be shaped by *vato loco* culture. He carries a gun in his courtroom briefcase and brings drugs into court that he hurriedly passes on to other militants when he is arrested for contempt. This approach both enables and threatens his professional persona—allowing him to bridge the gap between himself and his clients yet also raising the danger that he might be disbarred. The problem he faces is that none of these efforts can erase that his utility to the movement lies precisely in the fact that he is different from his clients and can mediate between them and the Anglo-dominated courts. The militants rely on the police's differential treatment of Brown: "Leave Brown alone!" a police sergeant tells his officers during a demonstration; "he's their lawyer" (*R*, 19). Similarly, the court guards vigilantly search the militants but ignore Brown's briefcase. Even as Brown's new, militant style of legal advocacy brings him closer to his clients, it also distances them from him.

Moreover, Brown adopts many of the same criteria for choosing cases that the Cahns laid out in their 1964 article; he too mediates his clients' "civilian perspective." As the Cahns advocated, he selects cases for their precedent-setting potential, refusing to defend a *vato loco* arrested in a gang fight because the case is "personal" rather than "political" (*R*, 256). As in the Cahns' description, he sometimes offends the Mexican American community he claims to represent, even receiving bomb threats from devout Chicanos/Chicanas when he defends clients who challenge L.A.'s Anglo-dominated Catholic hierarchy. Brown's awareness of his role in professionally shaping his clients' demands becomes especially obvious when the court of appeals upholds his first major case, the East L.A. Thirteen, a group of militants arrested during the L.A. Walkouts. "We have established a new precedent in the prosecution of conspiracies in a political case," he announces. "So long as the Republic stands, defense lawyers will be quoting our case and I am assured of my place in legal history" (*R*, 181). As Brown's shift from the plural to the singular pronoun suggests, the case accomplishes different things for the militants than it does for their lawyer. For the East L.A. Thirteen, Brown's defense protects them from the draconian forty-five-year sentences the district attorney's office tries to impose; for Brown himself, the defense secures his legacy in the legal profession.

Brown's account of the inquest of Robert Fernandez allegorizes his unease with his mediating function. Attempting to resolve whether Robert committed suicide, as prison officials claim, or whether he was murdered by a guard or fellow inmate, Brown orders an autopsy. But this desecrates the corpse, repeating the youth's original murder and making Brown a party to it. Imagining the autopsy as a form of cannibalism, he hallucinates the coroner asking him, "How about those ribs? You want some bar-b-que ribs, mister?" (*R*, 103).

In the service of producing a legally meaningful narrative, the autopsy digests Robert's body, excreting it as professional discourse. In so doing, it disfigures the embodied narratives legible to those immersed in Chicano/Chicana street culture; at the autopsy's conclusion, Brown sees "the tattoo on his right arm . . . God almighty! A red heart with blue arrows of love and the word 'Mother.' And I see the little black cross between the thumb and the trigger finger. A regular *vato loco*. A real *pachuco, ese*" (*R*, 104). For the purpose of the inquest, the tattoo is meaningless in contrast with other bodily marks—such as bruises and old needle marks—that speak to Robert's police beating and criminal lifestyle. Indeed, the sheriff hires a psychologist to carry out a "psychological autopsy" (*R*, 115), which dismembers the complicating narratives surrounding Robert's life and replaces them with stock social-psychological arguments about Mexican American communities. "Fernandez was a Chicano," the psychologist concludes. "A poor boy. He had a history of drug abuse. He'd been in jail an average of three months of every year since he was twelve" (*R*, 116). All of Brown's efforts to speak to the courts, he realizes, mistranslate the barrio's stories or else become overwhelmed by the narratives of the Anglo-American establishment.

Moreover, even as Brown assimilates the militants' machismo into his legal practice, he reproduces the abject categories through which lower-class Chicanos are generally viewed; in his efforts to affirm the *vato loco* lifestyle, Brown develops a version of the culture of poverty thesis that Oscar Lewis similarly applied to lower-class Mexicans and Puerto Ricans. Chicano street youth, Brown reflects, are present oriented: "Tooner Flats is the area of gangs who spend their last dime on short dogs of T-Bird wine, where the average kid has eight years of school. Everybody there gets some kind of welfare. . . . There is no school for the *vato loco*. There is no job in sight. His only hope is for a quick score" (*R*, 90). Unlike most liberal theorists, Brown does not believe this present-oriented, lumpenproletariat culture generates political passivity: "the *vato loco*," he reflects, "has been fighting with the pig since the Anglos stole his land in the last century" (*R*, 91). This animus against the police, however, is anarchic, reducible to no political ideology, including the militants' own Chicano nationalism. When Brown and his clients contemplate bombing a target in retaliation against the Fernandez inquest ruling, Brown struggles to make them choose an appropriately symbolic target; the militants either want to hold up a convenience store or shoot the first white man they see. Brown's legal advocacy can do nothing to channel or change this anarchic energy; indeed, the courtroom tends to dissipate the *vatos locos'* militancy, which is one reason why Brown and his cohorts attempt to bomb it.

Processing the Revolution

Brown's attempt to suture his professional identity by turning himself into a *vato loco* lawyer also shapes what he imagines to be his true vocation—writing novels. In line with the participatory aesthetic championed by Black Arts writers like Baraka, Acosta presents *Revolt* as a collectivist work of art, one that speaks on behalf of the Brown Power movement in Los Angeles, telling its history and articulating its aims. *Autobiography* begins by allegorizing the solipsism of Acosta's first-person confessional voice: "I stand naked before the mirror. Every morning of my life I have seen that brown belly from every angle" (*A*, 11). *Revolt*, in contrast, opens with Brown immersed in a Christmas Eve protest outside St. Basil's Roman Catholic Church, confident in his ability to speak for the crowd: "It is a dark moonless night and ice-cold wind meets us at the doorstep. We carry little white candles as weapons" (*R*, 11). Acosta's collectivist aspirations are captured in a scene in which the Mexican American actor Anthony Quinn addresses a rally during Brown's mayoral campaign. Leading the rally in a chant of "VIVA LA RAZA," Quinn inspires "an orgy of nationalism," in which "the crowd melts into one consciousness" (*R*, 175). Brown's problem, however, is that his fellow activists perceive novel writing as a private activity, one that cannot generate the collective consciousness that Brown experiences at the rally. Near the novel's conclusion, the militants become increasingly distrustful of Brown as he returns to his original plan to transform the militants' struggle into "THE BOOK" (*R*, 22) that will launch his literary career. His book contract comes about through literary connections inaccessible to his clients—most notably, his friendship with the journalist Stonewall, another thinly disguised version of Hunter S. Thompson. "The book offer," Brown explains, "has made me enemies. That I would think to make money off the struggle for freedom of the Cockroaches has made some people whisper traitor, *vendido*, *tio taco*, uncle tom, and a capitalist pig to boot" (*R*, 230). The novel ends with Brown abruptly leaving, taking off on the road in a repetition of Oscar's earlier abandonment of his welfare clients in *Autobiography*. At this moment, Brown's narrative voice fragments; as he flees Los Angeles, he alternates between the past and present tense, and between the third person, first-personal singular, and first-person plural. Rather than create a collective through his process art, Acosta insists on the schizophrenic self-division of his authorial persona.

Brown's transformation into a writer embodies the same anxieties about professional-client relationships provoked by his work as a lawyer throughout *Revolt*. The crux of these anxieties is the dilemma that the Cahns and other Legal Services lawyers encountered in response to the OEO's demand for maximum feasible participation: How can professionals subordinate themselves to their clients' needs without abandoning their professional autonomy? This same problem troubled Baraka, Brooks, and other Black Arts writers who sought to create a process art that would allow writers to speak directly to lower-class African Americans. How can writers address an inner-city audience without sacrificing literary complexity or authorial independence? Brown's contradictory response to this anxiety is captured in his parting reflections: "Somebody still has to answer for Robert Fernandez and Roland Zanzibar. Somebody still has to answer for all the smothered lives of all the fighters who have been forced to carry on, chained to a war for Freedom just like a slave chained to his master" (*R*, 258). Brown's narrative is driven by his need to keep alive the cases of his two dead clients—Robert the *vato loco* and Roland the Chicano journalist, both martyred for the Chicano/Chicana cause.[27] At the same time, it is driven by his need to liberate himself from that same cause. The recurrence of the Fernandez case here is especially telling, given that Brown has already inculpated himself as partly responsible for the young man's second death in the autopsy room. His problem is that, in trying to find justice for Robert through his fiction, he ends up repeating the same discursive cannibalism he diagnoses in the legal system. Rather than create a process art that dissolves the boundary between himself and his client, he processes Robert's body into a professional product. Acosta used the chapter describing the autopsy to promote *Revolt*; in 1973, he published a slightly condensed version in *La Gente de Aztlán* (*The People of Aztlán*).[28] In both versions, Acosta highlights the violence implicit in literary representation, which inevitably creates dead art products rather than living processes. "The week after McIntyre got the ax," the chapter begins, "I first encountered death as a world of art" (*R*, 89), and later in it Brown reflects that the autopsy "reminds me of the title of my first book: *My Cart for My Casket*" (*R*, 99), a reference to Acosta's first, unpublished novel. His dilemma is further exacerbated by the fact that *La Gente de Aztlán* was a UCLA student newspaper associated with the Chicano/Chicana movement: he is selling Robert's narrative to upwardly mobile students anxious about their own class status and eager to purchase easily consumable narratives of lower-class Chicano/Chicana authenticity.

Indeed, *Revolt* as a whole processes the barrio's cause in ways that parallel Brown's courtroom mediation of his clients. One of the paradoxes that the historical Acosta confronted was that to litigate on behalf of impoverished Chicanos/Chicanas, he often needed to represent clients who were not, strictly speaking, poor at all. In public documents written on behalf of the Brown Power movement, Acosta claimed that militants spoke for "their poverty-ridden, black-eyed *camaradas*."[29] However, most of the militants whom Acosta defended in court were upwardly mobile university students, some of them working on graduate degrees. Acosta's narrative, which speaks on behalf of the cockroach people, repeats this sleight of hand. As Louis Gerard Mendoza comments, in comparison to most other accounts of the Chicano/Chicana movement, students are "conspicuously decentered in Acosta's account as the source of energy and the primary actors."[30] *Revolt* elides internal class differences within the Brown Power movement to portray Brown's clients' organization, the "Chicano Militants," as lumpenproletarian. Of the novel's East L.A. Thirteen, only one is a student, and the remaining militants have little use for what they call "college sellouts" (*R*, 55).[31] The Chicano Militants themselves are a fictional creation synthesizing two distinct (and sometimes antagonistic) organizations whose members Acosta defended in the late 1960s / early 1970s: the student-dominated United Mexican American Students (UMAS) and the *vatos locos*–dominated Brown Berets. The differences between these groups fleetingly manifest themselves in minor inconsistencies in the militants' characterization. When Brown first meets the Chicano Militants, they are young intellectuals; Gilbert Rodriguez, editor of their newspaper, is a painter and "the poet laureate of East LA" (*R*, 16). By the end of the novel, the same characters are anti-intellectual *vatos locos*; Gilbert and the Chicano Militants, Brown reflects, are all "politicized lowriders," examples of the lower-class street youth who "knows from birth he is a lowdown cockroach" (*R*, 67). Brown's sutured representation of himself as a *vato loco* professional, in short, depends on a similarly sutured representation of his clients.

Ultimately, the historical Acosta's efforts to mediate the various contradictions that he outlines in *Autobiography* and *Revolt* alienated him from the Brown Power movement. As he commented in a 1971 letter to Hunter S. Thompson, after returning to L.A. to face drug charges, "How is it that a folk hero such as I was in East L.A. this past year is suddenly without a single fucking sup-porter?"[32] Such isolation reflects his efforts to bridge the class divide between the *vatos locos* and the Chicano/Chicana students—the divide that he writes out of existence in *Revolt*. For the Brown Berets, Acosta was too middle class due to his connections to white intellectuals like Thompson; after he helped Thompson research a *Rolling Stone* article on the movement, he received death threats from fellow militants. For the Chicano/Chicana law students associ-ated with MALDEF (Mexican American Legal Defense and Educational Fund), he was too much of a *vato loco* after his drug bust. Acosta intended this dual alienation to be the subject of his third novel, *The Rise and Fall of General Zeta*, outlined in a letter to his agent shortly before his mysterious disappearance in Mexico. In this plot summary, the novel's newly renamed General Zeta strug-gles to find followers willing to help him carry out various schemes against the US government—including plans to assassinate President Nixon. Harassed by the FBI and betrayed on all sides by Chicano militants, civil rights lawyers, and the publishing industry, General Zeta is debarred and, Acosta speculates, "Perhaps he dies of an overdose?"[33] In thematizing his own divided loyalties, Acosta reveals that in spite of his hatred of Johnson-era liberalism and the legal movement it inspired, he inherited the War on Poverty's irresolvable tensions. In his person, his texts, and his legal practice, Acosta tried and failed to con-struct his own version of the Great Society coalition between professionals and impoverished minorities.

4 Writing Urban Crisis after Moynihan

Joyce Carol Oates's National Book Award–winning novel, *them* (1970),[1] concludes with an apocalyptic account of the 1967 Detroit riot that indicts the Community Action Program's participatory professionalism. The riot, Oates suggests, is a planned event, partially orchestrated by a group of New Left radicals who run an antipoverty agency called United Action Against Poverty. The organization's spokesman, a sociologist named Mort Piercy, confides to an associate, "The riot is set for this weekend, we're almost certain, Saturday night. Unless it rains or something" (421). He uses government funds to purchase guns and plans on "blowing up the bridge and the tunnel and the expressway intersection" (447). His goal, he explains in a television panel after the riot, is to clear the way for white and black radicals to build a new world: "Our society must be leveled before a new, beautiful, peaceful society can be erected. This means the end of the world as we have known it, we middle-class whites" (472). As the novel heavy-handedly underscores, Mort cannot really see the ghetto that he claims to represent. After the riot, his glasses are broken when he tries to interview a group of black youth (477).

Oates's account has little basis in the actual etiology of the Detroit riot, which began when police raided an unlicensed drinking club during a party celebrating two black GIs returning from the Vietnam War.[2] Instead, it echoes many of the War on Poverty's late 1960s critics, who similarly linked Johnson's domestic policies with inner-city violence. According to these critics, the riots were collaborations between two increasingly vilified social groups: white middle-class liberals and the urban underclass. Daniel Moynihan became the most articulate spokesman for this point of view. In *Maximum Feasible Misunderstanding*, he offered a postmortem of the Community Action Program, based on his insider's knowledge of the deliberations leading to its implementation in the Johnson administration.[3] The book provided a liberal imprimatur for the Nixon administration's partial dismantling of the War on Poverty, which Moynihan helped oversee in his role as one of Nixon's domestic advisers. According to Moynihan, there was no grassroots pressure for a national antipoverty program in the early 1960s: "The American poor, black and white, were surpassingly inert." The pressure to institute the program came from professional reformers: social scientists studying juvenile delinquency, who came up with the idea that the War on Poverty should encourage the poor to challenge local welfare institutions. Once up and running, the Community Action Agencies were staffed with radical intellectuals like Oates's Mort Piercy: "young idealists suffused with what Norman Mailer terms the 'middle-class lust for apocalypse.'"[4] These idealists aroused unreasonable expectations among the poor and stirred up hitherto dormant racial tensions, provoking the confrontations that exploded into riot.

For Moynihan, the solution to late 1960s urban unrest was to replace participatory professionalism with a much more limited model of social scientific intervention in the ghetto. Social science, he believed, should serve a strictly critical role, assessing the effectiveness of government programs and chastening reformers' expectations.[5] By the late 1960s, most liberal social scientists agreed, although for different reasons than the ones Moynihan articulated in his book. For these social scientists, the problem did not lie with poverty warriors' middle-class radicalism. Rather, it lay with their class and racial disconnection from the ghetto. After the controversy that surrounded Moynihan's use of the culture of poverty thesis in *The Negro Family*, liberal poverty theorists questioned "their own use of the cultural framework, believing that it had been hopelessly corrupted in what had degenerated into a debate over the 'undeserving poor.'"[6] This framework was so entrenched as to endanger any ethnographic representation of the poor, leading social scientists to abandon the richly detailed studies that proliferated in the United States during and immediately after the War on Poverty: books like Kenneth Clark's *Dark Ghetto* (1965), Elliot Liebow's *Tally's Corner* (1967), and Lee Rainwater's *Behind Ghetto Walls* (1970).[7] Instead, poverty researchers turned to policy analysis: quantitative studies evaluating the successes and failures of government programs aimed at helping the poor.[8] According to Herbert Gans, an early proponent of the culture of poverty thesis who renounced it after the Moynihan controversy, "if the prime purpose of research is the elimination of poverty, studies of the poor are not the first order of business at all."[9]

Social science, Gans concluded, should retreat from direct engagement with the ghetto into the less contentious ground of political economy.

As I argue in this chapter, this crisis in participatory professionalism afflicted late 1960s literary representations of the ghetto, especially those that directly responded to the Community Action Program. I focus on two influential texts from this period: Oates's *them* and Tom Wolfe's New Journalistic *Radical Chic and Mau-Mauing the Flak Catchers* (1970).[10] Each book draws on a tradition of urban writing that resists the process imperative to break down barriers between author, audience, and urban subject matter. Oates's working-class chronicle draws on the naturalist tradition—a tradition that insists on the novelist's empirical detachment from her subject matter. Wolfe's book, which brings together two essays about the War on Poverty, similarly insists on its journalistic objectivity: Wolfe's capacity to remain clinically removed from the people and situations he observes. This formal insistence on the writer's removal from the inner city reflects the shared concern that animates Moynihan and Gans's respective critiques of social scientific activism during the War on Poverty. Oates and Wolfe distrust white liberals' claims to identify with and speak for the ghetto. At the same time, both writers complicate their literary objectivity by incorporating aspects of the very participatory professionalism that they seek to delimit. At strategic moments in *them*, Oates includes metafictional interludes that draw attention to her own experiences teaching first-generation students at the University of Detroit. These interludes at once enable and disrupt the naturalist objectivity that she tries to establish throughout the novel. Wolfe's New Journalism, meanwhile, is rooted in his own version of process art, stylistically and thematically influenced by Kerouac and other Beat writers from the 1950s.

As the novels' diverging politics highlight, this twin exclusion/incorporation of participatory professionalism ranged across the political spectrum during the Nixon era. Oates's book heralded her emergence as the foremost writer in a new generation of feminist realists concerned with inequality in post-1960s America. Wolfe's book marked his transformation into America's most prominent conservative satirist. Indeed, the two novels demarcate liberals' and conservatives' respective responses to white writing about the underclass from the 1970s onward. After the Moynihan report, liberal social scientists like Gans abandoned their epistemological certainty that they could speak for the ghetto, viewing their own knowledge of it as inevitably compromised. Echoing this uncertainty, Oates's book undermines its representational conditions of possibility, ultimately calling into question any white writer's capacity to describe Detroit's underclass. Her novel articulates a version of literary identity politics, whereby no writer can be certain of her authority to write about any experience different from her own. In contrast, in the 1970s and 1980s, conservative writers gained confidence that they could displace liberals as authoritative experts on the inner city. While Wolfe distrusts liberal efforts to speak for the ghetto, he similarly attempts to ground his journalistic project in his process-based, intuitive knowledge of it.

Naturalism and the Detroit Riot

Two-thirds of the way through *them*, Oates interrupts her narrative with a pair of letters from one of her white working-class characters, a troubled young woman named Maureen Wendall. The novel's metafictional conceit, established in its prefatory "Author's Note," is that Maureen was one of Oates's students at the University of Detroit, where Oates taught between 1962 and 1967. The letters became the genesis for *them*; after reading Maureen's story, Oates subjected it to "careful research," correcting it whenever its "context was confused" (6). The result, Oates claims, is a "work of history in fictional form" (5), rooted in a "naturalistic" (6) strand of empirical storytelling. On a formal level, the novel fits into the naturalist tradition stretching back to Émile Zola, foregrounding the accumulated realist detail and sensationalistic violence typical of the genre. Oates's metafictional framework, however, at once enables and frustrates any effort to read *them* as a naturalist novel. The literary naturalism of the late nineteenth and early twentieth centuries typically depended on the author's distance from his or her materials. For Zola, this distance was ensured by the author's application of the experimental method: "We should operate on the characters, the passions, on the human and social data, in the same way that the chemist and the physicist operate on inanimate beings, and as the physiologist operates on living beings."[11] Few of Zola's American imitators went so far in insisting on their work's scientific accuracy. However, in trying to understand the turbulent changes wrought by the American Industrial Revolution, they too established and then mediated a carefully calibrated distance between themselves, their readers, and their (usually) lower-class subject matter. In Jude Davies's terms, American naturalists set out "to interpolate readers as fellow members of the middle-class and offer them access to the public, domestic, and laboring spaces of those who work manually or who are unemployed."[12] According to Oates, however, *them* never achieves this distance. Rather, the novel originates in her uncontrolled absorption in her materials. As Oates writes the Wendalls' story, their "lives pressed upon mine eerily, so that I began to dream about them instead of about myself, dreaming and redreaming their lives. Because their world was so remote from me it entered me with tremendous power, and in a sense the novel wrote itself"(6).

This account of Oates's absorption in her lower-class characters' lives gestures toward the process aesthetic that, I have been arguing, characterized an important strand of postwar literature. That aesthetic sought to bridge the gap between middle-class writers and the poor by calling into question the formalism characteristic of post–World War II academic poetry and fiction. Oates's account of her writing process sometimes resembles that of writers like Kerouac and Baraka. In interviews shortly after *them* made her a literary celebrity, Oates admitted that she "doesn't do much rewriting" and that she writes her books quickly.[13] However, Oates's inability to achieve authorial distance from her characters in *them* has little to do with process art's participatory impetus. Both Kerouac and Baraka viewed the poor as bearers of an antiformalist aesthetic that they tried to channel through their improvisatory art. Oates, in contrast, conceives of poverty as a formal threat to art. That threat is exemplified by Maureen's childhood as a sensitive, bookish child subjected to the brutal violence of a dysfunctional working-class family. When Maureen is a teenager, she is attracted to Jane Austen, whose novels seem more "real" (166) to her than her own family. However, after being pushed into prostitution by her mother and savagely beaten by her stepfather, she learns that reality cannot be found in books. "*This is not important*," she reflects as Oates reads *Madame Bovary* to the class, "*none of this is real*" (312). Maureen brings to Oates's classroom the same challenge that process artists brought to postwar academic art. When Oates explains that "literature gives form to life," Maureen asks, "What is form? Why is it better than the way life happens, by itself?" (318). Maureen's problem, however, is that having discovered that life resists literary form, she is left with no resources for making sense of it. While Oates knows "so much that never happened, in a perfect form," Maureen has "lived a lifetime already and turned myself out and got nothing out of it" (320).

Literary form, for Oates, is a protective barrier against the antiformalist suffering that prevents Maureen from gaining knowledge from experience. This barrier, however, is dangerously thin; Maureen's suffering continually threatens to break through Oates's art. "Everybody," Maureen insists, "is flawed with it, a crack running through them. In you it is filled for a while. You feel no pain" (317). Oates's representational problem is that Maureen's young adulthood is both like and utterly unlike her own. In Freudian terms, Maureen is uncanny, or *Unheimlich*, in the etymological sense that she reminds Oates, who grew up in a working-class home, of the class origins that she tried to leave behind. As Maureen puts it, "I am writing to you because I could see, past your talking and your control and the way you took notes carefully in your books while you taught, writing down your own words as you said them, something that is like myself" (309). Literature, for Oates, is the means that she uses to impose form on her life; she achieves the class mobility that allows her to avoid Maureen's fate by reading and writing books. When Oates gives Maureen a failing grade for her course, she offers only the following comment: "lack of coherence and development" (315). Maureen is an incoherent, undeveloped version of Oates— someone who lacks the luck, talent, and willpower to force her way out of the working class. The novel thus stages what McGurl calls Oates's "class shame," her feeling that "class identity (who you feel yourself to be) lags behind class positionality (where you currently stand)."[14] For McGurl, the primary site of this class shame is the literature classroom, the place where Oates, as a student at the University of Syracuse in the 1950s, began her literary career. In *them*, the literature classroom actively engenders shame, thereby enforcing class distinctions between teachers and students. When Oates fails Maureen, she becomes an agent of the middle-class institutions that have kept Maureen poor.

Oates's metafictional frame underscores her major concern in *them*, which encompasses both her attempt to create a new kind of naturalist novel and her critique of the War on Poverty. Oates's encounter with Maureen sets up the novel's recurring interclass dynamic, whereby middle-class characters confront lower-class characters who embody the kind of pathologies that 1960s social scientists similarly attributed to the poor. These pathologies, however, closely mirror ones barely (and sometimes not at all) kept in check by the middle class themselves. Moreover, any attempt to make sense of or help alleviate those pathologies through literature or welfare activism risks amplifying them for both classes. Oates's chronicle of the Wendall family addresses one of the central problems of postwar poverty discourse: how to explain the persistence of poverty (especially white poverty) in an affluent society. As Maureen's mother,

Loretta, puts it, the postwar "world was pulling into two parts, those who were hopeless bastards and weren't worth spitting on and those who were going to get somewhere" (12). For most of the novel, the Wendalls belong in the first category; they exemplify the "case" poverty that John Kenneth Galbraith claimed resisted postwar affluence: poverty "related to some characteristic of the individuals so afflicted," such as "mental deficiency, bad health, inability to adapt to the discipline of industrial life, uncontrollable procreation, alcohol, . . . or perhaps a combination of several of these handicaps."[15] These dysfunctions, 1960s sociologists argued, are passed down from generation to generation. In Oscar Lewis's *La Vida*, the Ríos family has a history of female prostitution; in the Moynihan report, single mothers pass on their own deficient impulse control to their delinquent sons and promiscuous daughters. The Wendalls, similarly, are afflicted by a recurring propensity for male violence and masochistic, female submission to that violence. The boys become delinquents while the girls become prostitutes or battered wives. This cyclical pattern prevents the family from taking advantage of the postwar economy and welfare state. During the 1930s, Americans "began getting jobs again, back from government projects and optimistic from government checks that became as regular and permanent as the cycle of the seasons itself" (18). Loretta's father, however, loses his job in construction, never recovers from the Great Depression, and never works again. The entire family seems trapped in that era; Maureen's brother, Jules, "has the look of being permanently out of the sunlight, a depression baby" (424).

Oates thus draws on 1960s sociological accounts of intergenerational poverty to provide the deterministic framework typical of naturalist fiction, replacing the hereditary and environmental determinism characteristic of Progressive-era naturalism with a psychological determinism adapted to postwar conceptions of urban poverty.[16] This deterministic framework provides the form that allows Oates to make sense of the Wendalls' lives. Each generation of Wendalls seems doomed to repeat the catastrophes of the previous one, in a pattern that resembles the cycles of poverty described by Lewis, Moynihan, and others.[17] This cyclical repetition especially afflicts the Wendall women: Maureen and her mother, Loretta. The novel opens in 1938 with Loretta's traumatic entry into womanhood at the age of sixteen; she is startled awake by a gunshot and finds herself lying next to the corpse of her teenage lover, Bernie. The murderer is her brother, Brock, whose motivations for killing Bernie are opaque; nobody in the family really cares about Loretta's chastity. The act thrusts Loretta into a hitherto unseen world of male violence. Looking around her family's cramped apartment, she becomes aware for the first time of "all the unconscious living that had gone on in it!—all of those years, unconscious" (33). This unconscious life frustrates Loretta's attempts to improve her circumstances. When Loretta takes a police officer—her future husband, Howard—into her home to help her deal with Bernie's corpse, he succumbs to a lawless passion similar to the one that drove Brock to kill the boy; he rapes Loretta in her kitchen. The scene establishes the pattern for Maureen's adolescence. Attempting to escape from her dysfunctional family, she turns to public, educational institutions—the library and the school—as mechanisms of upward mobility. Both institutions, however, fail to counter the familial dysfunctions that similarly doomed her mother. Loretta stigmatizes Maureen's attraction to the library and school, insinuating that her good behavior is a front for shoplifting and sex with boys.[18] This assumption drives Maureen to realize Loretta's perverse reading of her behavior; she prostitutes herself to older men while wearing her school uniform, then hides the money she earns in a library book. Through this prostitution, Maureen regresses to her mother's occupational horizons; Loretta also tries to earn money as a prostitute when her first husband, Howard, is away in World War II. When Loretta loses her virginity to Bernie, she is working in a laundry; when Maureen loses hers to her first client, she compares him to "a machine, one of those machines at the Laundromat where she dragged the laundry" (194). In a traumatic repetition of her mother's coming of age, this promiscuity invites masculine violence; when Maureen's father-in-law discovers her prostitution, he beats her into unconsciousness. This cyclical repetition, the novel suggests, continues to haunt Maureen even after she establishes a toehold in the middle class at the novel's end. As Jules warns her when he visits her suburban house, "Don't forget that this place here can burn down too. Men can come back in your life, Maureen, they can beat you up again and force your knees apart, why not?" (478).

However, even as Oates depicts the cycle of poverty that traps the Wendalls, she also undercuts one of the central assumptions shared by 1960s poverty theorists and the naturalist tradition within which she locates the novel. In addressing itself to a middle-class audience, naturalist fiction invited that audience to see itself as fundamentally different from the mostly lower-class characters it portrayed. In Davies's terms, "The naturalist text differentiated its readers from its typical subjects precisely by virtue of their implied capacity for self-determination, in contrast to the Maggies, McTeagues, Carries, Hurst-woods, and others, whose narratives are determined by social and biological forces."[19] Poverty theory in the 1960s, similarly, drew a distinction between the present-oriented poor and future-oriented social scientists and their readers. In contrast, *them* refuses its readers this assurance that they are immune to the problems that afflict the novel's characters. While sitting in the library, writing her letter to Oates, Maureen realizes that all of the people around her, silently reading books, are barely restraining the same violent and masochistic impulses that culminated in her hospitalization and madness: "Those people would like to throw the books out of the windows, break the lamps and chairs, hit one another over the head with anything they could grab" (310). The novel is filled with wealthy characters who cannot maintain this restraint. When Maureen's brother Jules, who drops out of school and becomes a delinquent, tries to abduct an upper-class teenager named Nadine, he discovers that her family history is just as dysfunctional as his own. Her uncle deserts his wife to become a gangster and ends up dead in a downtown rooming house. Nadine herself helps Jules steal her parents' car, abandons him when he falls sick, and eventually tries to murder him. As Oates similarly emphasizes in her society satire, *Expensive People* (1968), the major difference between the suburbs and the slums is that the wealthy are better at hiding their dysfunctions and much better at covering the costs. Oates herself, Maureen warns, has a crack in her life that is only "filled in for a while" (317). This crack risks opening once more as Oates writes the novel. Her claim that the Wendalls' world "entered me with tremendous power" (6) echoes Jules's insistence on the fragility of Maureen's suburban home, which men can enter at any time.

This insistence on universal pathology seems like it might enable a version of process art's attempted eradication of the distance between author, reader, and lower-class subject matter. In *them*, however, it achieves precisely the opposite result. As Adolph Reed Jr., points out, one of the most enduring characteristics of poverty discourse is its creation of social categories like the underclass that "exist only in the third person."[20] These categories are terms of abjection used to demarcate groups whose lives supposedly do not match the behavioral norms of middle-class America. Ultimately, they undermine public support for the welfare state, turning underprivileged groups against each other. With its lower-case, third-person title, *them* exemplifies this process of abjection, which it insists derives from psychological and cultural similarities between insider and outcast groups. These similarities alternately give rise to feelings of disgust and fetishistic desire for people who belong to a different class or race. As Loretta, for instance, collects AFDC after the birth of her fourth child, she complains about black welfare mothers: "Them niggers have a birth rate twice as much as white people, or ten times, I forget which, and they're all on ADC and play poker with the checks" (117). The obvious irony is that the behaviors she attributes to black single mothers (prostitution, cheating the system, drinking welfare money) are ones that she also exhibits. Nadine, meanwhile, worries that Jules has been contaminated by his proximity to inner-city blacks: "I've always been afraid that you might have some kind of disease. . . . I was thinking of where you lived, the way things are in the city, and Negro women, girls" (352). However, this very proximity makes Jules an object of fetishistic desire. Echoing 1950s Beat mythology, Nadine imagines Jules as a white Negro, a rootless drifter who lives closer to his skin than suburbanites like herself. All her life, she explains, she has seen poor men hitchhiking on the highways: "They seem very wise, very nasty. They put their thumbs out and wave for a ride, watching everything, mocking. They're very dangerous, I think" (368).

Instead of enabling cross-class and cross-racial identifications, universal pathology leads to an atomized aesthetic, one in which any attempt to write about members of another class or race risks making them abject. Oates is intensely aware of this risk in *them*, and she takes steps to limit it. In her preface, Oates insists that *them* "is truly about a specific 'them' and not just a literary technique of pointing to us all" (5). This specific "them" is that section of the white working class unable to take advantage of the postwar affluent economy. This focus on the white working class complicates the novel's claim to be a "history in fictional form." Critics generally praise *them* for its attempt to understand the tensions that led to the Detroit riot; the novel conveys "an exhaustive—if necessarily partial—view of the urban experience that culminates in the social unrest of 1967."[21] The riot marks the moment when, in Lukácsian fashion, personal destiny intersects with broader historical events.[22] During the riot, Jules shoots and kills a police officer, enacting symbolic revenge on his abusive father, who worked for the police, and on an officer who beat him as a teenager. On a broader scale, the riot manifests many such grievances; in concluding with the riot, Oates implies that her family chronicle will help readers understand mass violence as a culmination of tensions building in the ghetto since the Great Depression. This apparent etiology, however, is undermined by the fact that Jules is white; the Detroit riot was a race riot, provoked by specifically African American concerns about employment discrimination, segregated housing, and police brutality. The novel allegorizes its own distorted etiology in the television panel that follows the riot. After interviewing Mort, the moderator asks one of his coworkers to provide the ghetto's perspective: "The camera moved to show a young Negro dressed in a suit, but this must have been a mistake—the Negro shook his head, frightened to indicate that he wasn't one of the co-workers" (473). The camera then moves to Jules, who becomes the voice of Detroit's inner-city poor. The scene reflects a broader pattern in the novel; the only nonwhite character who speaks more than a few words is a pimp who lets Jules know that the girl he has been prostituting needs bail money. Indeed, the entire novel originated in an act of racial substitution. According to Greg Johnson's biography, Oates came up with the idea for *them* after a series of conversations with novelist Daniel Curzon, who told her about a black student who visited his office at Wayne State. The student, who had "been raped by somebody and had gone into a decline, a semi-coma for a year or more,"[23] became the basis for Maureen.

However, even as *them* whitens its cast of characters, it also foregrounds the problem of race; while there are few black voices in the novel, race is omnipresent. As McGurl comments, the novel problematizes the category of whiteness itself; *them* deprives "the privilege of whiteness the further privilege of presenting itself as an unmarked universality."[24] The Wendalls, in particular, are intensely aware of their racial privilege. When Jules and his mother, Loretta, visit his uncle Brock in the hospital ward, she comments, "Aren't you glad you're not a nigger, at least? . . . Jesus, how'd you like to be a nigger and sick on top of it?" (322–323). Throughout the novel, Loretta and other white working-class characters insist on their difference from African Americans, generally at moments when they are most in danger of being lumped in with them. This difference is, in fact, one of the Wendalls' only assets. In spite of the repeated disasters that befall them, the Wendalls achieve some degree of middle-class respectability by the novel's end. Maureen seduces and marries her college English teacher, Jules is heading to California to work with Mort, and Loretta is poised to marry her third husband—a postal worker she meets in an emergency shelter after her home is bombed in the riot. All three characters exemplify a pattern repeated throughout Oates's fiction; the story that she returns to again and again is that of a white-working class protagonist escaping, often irreparably damaged, from his or her class origins. This basic story, however, is usually set against a background of black working-class characters who do not achieve similar success.[25]

Oates, in short, pointedly avoids the kind of cross-racial literary representation that characterizes the work of white process writers like Kerouac and Mailer. Throughout her massive oeuvre, she predominantly focuses on characters who come from a background similar to her own; she is the premier novelist of the American white working and lower middle class. Oates wrote *them* at a time when American writers were becoming increasingly sensitive to the problem of white appropriation of black voices. American novelists went through their own version of the Moynihan controversy after the publication of William Styron's *The Confessions of Nat Turner* (1967), a novel that ventriloquized the nineteenth-century slave revolt leader. Black reviewers criticized the novel for many of the same reasons that black social scientists attacked the Moynihan report. The novel, Lerone Bennett Jr. complained, pathologizes Turner in terms inspired by Moynihan, imagining him as the "impotent" son of a fatherless, "ADC slave family."[26] More broadly, an emerging generation of African American intellectuals claimed authoritative knowledge about black literature, culture, and history, rejecting white interpreters who had hitherto dominated these fields. As Oates's metafictional frame highlights, this same problem of appropriating another's voice informs Oates's effort to depict the pathologies that afflict the class from which she arose; Oates renders the Wendalls abject by writing their story. As McGurl points out, Oates's work returns again and again to figurations of whiteness as an atomized identity. "I am only a *writer*," Oates lamented in a 1993 letter after hearing that Toni Morrison won the Nobel Prize in Literature; "I have no socio/historical definition; no 'constituency'; I represent no one & nothing—not even (I suppose) myself."[27] The phrase underscores the reductio ad absurdum logic implicit in Oates's radical rejection of process art. That rejection finally dissolves the authorial self, an entity that inevitably crosses class and cultural boundaries over the course of its history.

The pattern of shared pathology giving rise to abjection in *them* finally informs Oates's distrust of Community Action as a solution to the urban tensions that she traces throughout her novel. As Oates's parody of United Action Against Poverty makes clear, members of the professional class who try to intervene in the inner city end up playing out their own pathologies. Through Mort, for instance, Jules seduces Vera, a middle-class girl who reads Frantz Fanon in Mort's introduction to sociology course and relocates to the ghetto to work for his agency. Vera is tormented by her anxiety that she does not really fit into the middle class that she belongs to by way of her family and education: "I failed English composition," she confesses, "I couldn't organize my thoughts" (436). Under Jules's tutelage, she lives out this anxiety, becoming his prostitute and letting him beat her with a coat hanger when she fails to bring in enough money. Indeed, the novel suggests that any attempt to improve conditions in the inner city is doomed because of the pathologies that afflict both reformers and the people they would like to help. In the post-riot television panel, Mort and an Anglican priest offer the typical range of late 1960s left-liberal explanations for Detroit's urban unrest. For Mort, the riot dramatizes the need for a complete reordering of society. For the priest, the riot reinforces his belief in piecemeal, liberal reform: "My total commitment is for education, enormously enlarged funds for education and the cleaning up of slums, in order to bring about a new America for all our children" (474). Both panelists interpret the riot instrumentally, as an irrational outpouring of violence by the urban poor that they can direct or chasten. Mort and his fellow academics hope to use the riot to help foment a revolution, imagining themselves as "generals, guiding everything" (447). The priest hopes to use it to create an expanded welfare state. Jules, in contrast, rejects his copanelists' instrumental interpretations:

> I would like to explain to everyone how necessary the fires are, and people in the streets, not, as Mort says here—Dr. Piercy—so that things can be built up again, black and white living together, no, or black living by itself, by themselves—no, that has no importance, that is something for the newspapers or the insurance companies. It is only necessary to understand that fire burns and does its duty, perpetually, and the fires will never be put out. . . . Violence can't be singled out from an ordinary day! . . . The rapist and his victim rise up from the rubble, eventually, at dawn, and brush themselves off and go down the street to a diner. Believe me, passion can't endure! It will come back again and again but it can't endure! (473–474)

The riot, for Jules, is an expression of human passions—the same passions that drive Brock to kill Bernie, Howard to rape Loretta, and Pat to brutalize Maureen. No one can channel or control these passions; they appear and disappear in a mercurial fashion.

Jules's speech highlights the strangely apolitical nature of Oates's novelistic response to urban politics in the late 1960s. Her novel insistently gestures toward political themes—like the racial tensions that gave rise to the Detroit riot—only to fold them back into her characters' dysfunctional family dynamics. When Jules insists that "fire burns and does its duty," for instance, he alludes to a childhood experience when he discovers his own capacity for unruly violence by accidentally burning down his in-laws' barn. He also alludes to Vinoba Bhave, Mahatma Gandhi's most famous disciple. Jules discovers the quote in the mid-1950s, when he takes his grandmother to a welfare clinic and picks up a recent issue of *Time* magazine. The first article he reads is about "the Negroes of America—'A Decade of Prosperity'—the achievement of equality, of justice, affluence in Harlem" (95). The second is a profile of Bhave. The two articles present an idealized picture of an early moment in the civil rights movement, which mainstream news outlets like *Time* interpreted as a peaceful movement toward black integration, led by a responsible middle class. However, Bhave's pacific aphorisms haunt Jules as he tries to make sense of his own poverty and Detroit's racial divisions: "We are all members of a single human family. . . . My object is to transform the whole of society. Fire merely burns . . . Fire burns and does its duty. It is for others to do theirs" (95). In proclaiming universal membership in a common family, Bhave affirms the politics of sympathy that subtends both the civil rights movement and the welfare state that provides at least a limited degree of care for Jules's grandmother. That politics encourages observers to imaginatively inhabit the lives of another race or class. In the novel's context, however, belonging to a family does not guarantee sympathy; instead, it lays you bare to the destructive unconscious life that runs through all families and that erupts in the fires that burn in 1967 Detroit. The aphorism captures the reason why Oates connects the Wendall family chronicle to the Detroit riot and why Jules imagines that the post-riot rapist and his victim will "brush themselves off and go down the street to a diner" (474). All of the riot's participants—white and black, wealthy and poor—belong to the same human family, and Oates envisages the riot as a species of domestic abuse.

Even as Oates's insistence on universal pathology dismantles the categories that conservatives would use to render the poor abject from the late 1960s onward, it lends itself to deeply pessimistic conclusions about the middle class's responsibility toward the ghetto. Jules's final claim that Maureen's suburban house "can burn down too" (478) leaves the reader with three options. First, the reader can welcome the inevitable destruction of the social order, becoming a rioter and murderer like Jules. Second, the reader can cling to that order at all costs, becoming a law-and-order conservative, which is what Maureen morphs into by the novel's end. Pressed on her opinion about anti-Vietnam protests, Maureen responds, "People like this shouldn't make trouble. Marching around like that, it makes things confused" (412). Last, the reader can therapeutically attend to his or her own pathologies. The last option seems to be the one tacitly recommended by *them*. It is an option that cedes the ghetto as a space of political engagement, which is the course pursued by many white liberals after the crisis that befell participatory professionalism in the late 1960s.

Limousine Liberals and Ghetto Pimps

Even more so than *them*, Tom Wolfe's *Radical Chic & Mau-Mauing the Flak Catchers* consolidated many Americans' distrust of the kind of cross-racial identifications that characterized late 1960s liberalism; it popularized the term "radical chic" and became a favorite text for conservative intellectuals.[28] The book combines two essays. The first describes a 1970 fund-raising party that the conductor Leonard Bernstein held for the Black Panthers in his thirteen-room Park Avenue penthouse. The second collects a series of vignettes about confrontations between ghetto residents and OEO bureaucrats in San Francisco's poverty program. Both essays reinforce the conservative narrative about racial liberalism first articulated in Moynihan's *Maximum Feasible Misunderstanding*: that it furthers the interests of "limousine liberals" (9) and black radicals without doing much to improve conditions in the ghetto. At Bernstein's party, wealthy liberals indulge in "nostalgie de la boue" (27), romanticizing revolutionaries like the Black Panthers to reinforce their own class standing. The Black Panthers and other militant groups, meanwhile, play into this romanticization to get the funds they need to establish their street cred and compete with other black organizations. In "Mau-Mauing," a militant leader coaches his followers before heading to the poverty office: "When you go downtown, y'all wear *your ghetto rags*. . . . You wear your *combat* fatigues and your leather *pieces* and your shades" (85). According to Wolfe, liberals and black militants never actually communicate with each other at the level of ideology; as a Panther representative explains the party's ten-point program, one of Bernstein's guests interrupts: "I won't be able to stay for everything you have to say . . . but who do you call to give a party?" (24). Instead, the two groups communicate at the level of style. Bernstein organizes his party to differentiate himself from the middle class; by inviting the Panthers, he conveys "the arrogant self-confidence of the aristocrat as opposed to the middle-class striver's obsession with propriety and keeping up appearances" (27–28). The Panthers, meanwhile, stylistically differentiate themselves from middle-class organizations like the NAACP (National Association for the Advancement of Colored People) and the Urban League. *"These are no civil-rights* Negroes *wearing gray suits three sizes too big"* (5), Bernstein's guests enthuse as they observe the Panthers' unkempt Afros.

This perception, that Bernstein and the Black Panthers are playing different games, intersecting only at the level of style, derives from Wolfe's social theory, which conceives of American society as a series of distinct but interlocking strategies for acquiring in-group status. Surveying US culture at the beginning of his journalistic career in the early 1960s, Wolfe observed that America underwent a fundamental transformation after World War II. The war "made massive infusions of money into every level of society. Suddenly, classes of people whose styles had been practically invisible had the money to build monuments to their own styles."[29] Whereas status games used to be restricted to wealthy elites, they now became universally available to Americans of all classes. The result was a proliferation of lower- and middle-class subcultures, which Wolfe set out to document in his early journalism, writing about phenomena such as stock car racing, surfing, teenage disk jockeys, and California hippies. Each subculture developed an idiosyncratic style, and each embodied an alternative status structure, or "statussphere." This explosion of pop styles ultimately reshaped the upper class itself, as the rich drew on those styles in their own efforts to establish status within fashionable society. Wolfe thus articulated an exceptionalist vision of postwar American affluence, in which class conflict gives way to stylistic play enabled by mass consumerism; the United States, he insisted, had become the worker's paradise envisaged by nineteenth-century utopian thinkers.[30]

This vision relied on a series of obvious omissions. Beginning with Galbraith's *The Affluent Society*, most accounts of America's postwar wealth acknowledged the persistence and indeed retrenchment of severe forms of poverty. For Wolfe, however, even the poorest Americans are remarkably privileged compared to their counterparts in Europe and the third world; they experience only "relative poverty."[31] Even more obviously, before *Radical Chic*, Wolfe's exceptionalist vision ignored race; all of the subcultures that Wolfe wrote about were white.[32] Wolfe parenthetically addressed this gap, acknowledging that America's "happiness explosion" was racially specific: "World War II and the prosperity that followed pumped incredible amounts of money into the population, the white population at least, at every class level."[33] However, this erasure of race skewed Wolfe's thesis about subcultural styles and statusspheres, insofar as most of the subcultural art forms and styles reshaping American mass culture in the 1960s were originally black. Unlike Las Vegas and demolition derbies, these styles were not the products of mass affluence wedded to proletarian and lower-middle-class tastes; rather, they were innovative efforts to make do with limited resources.

Radical Chic is Wolfe's attempt to rectify this erasure; for the first time, he traces stylistic play in the ghetto. While the Black Panthers dress in militant garb to differentiate themselves from middle-class civil rights leaders, most inner-city youth affect what Wolfe calls the "pimp style": "The pimp is the dude who wears the $150 Sly Stone-style vest and pants outfit from the haberdasheries on Polk and the $35 Lester Chambers-style four-inch-brim black beaver fedora and the thin nylon socks with the vertical stripes and drives the customized sun-roof Eldorado with the Jaguar radiator cap" (113). As Wolfe makes clear with his priced catalog, the pimp style is not a manifestation of material lack. Rather, it is the product of African Americans' ability to benefit from an affluent society overflowing with consumer goods, even when that society denies them gainful employment. In the ghetto, "it seemed like nobody was going to make it *by* working, so the king was the man who made out best by *not* working, by *not* sitting all day under the Man's bitch box" (113). African Americans are not an exception to Wolfe's theory that American society is fragmenting into a series of alternative statusspheres; rather, they are the ultimate proof of that theory. Denied access to the normal status system, they develop an alternative one, which consists of conspicuous displays of consumer goods acquired through illegal hustling. Indeed, urban blacks more perfectly realize the proletarianization of aristocratic style than any other social group. In the 1960s and 1970s, while white college students were dressing "like the working class of 1934," unemployed black youth had "become the Brummels and Gentlemen of Leisure, the true fashion plates."[34]

Radical Chic thus arrives at much the same perception that governs Oates's critique of racial liberalism in *them*, albeit from a completely different direction; for both writers, poverty warriors' cross-class and cross-racial identifications disguise more basic affinities between them and their clients. Like Oates, Wolfe undercuts the culture of poverty thesis that dominated most liberal and conservative accounts of the urban underclass. However, whereas Oates universalizes that thesis, attributing its pathologies to everyone, Wolfe discards its basic terms. The opposition between present and future orientation is null in a society in which everyone, regardless of his or her class or race, is struggling to define his or her place in one or more status hierarchies by drawing on the endless resources of a leisure society. This nullification is especially evident in Wolfe's depiction of delinquent teenage subcultures, like the surfer gangs that he writes about in "The Pump House Gang" (1968). For most postwar sociologists, delinquent violence was a response to limited occupational opportunities; deprived of a middle-class career by virtue of their class or racial origins, delinquents seek criminal shortcuts. Wolfe's delinquents, in contrast, are post-career and post-class. Buoyed by the West Coast's "magic economy,"[35] they form juvenile communities defined by their in-group argot and dedication to aristocratic leisure. In *Radical Chic*, Wolfe underscores the similar conditions that shape limousine liberals and the underclass by bookending the collection with two scenes of gluttony. In "Radical Chic," the partygoers enthuse over the Bernsteins' appetizers: "Mmmmmmmmmmmmmmmm. These are nice. Little Roquefort cheese morsels rolled in crushed nuts. Very tasty" (2). "Mau-Mauing" ends with an OEO applicant bringing an army of ghetto children to the mayor's office, armed with "the greatest grandest sweetest creamiest runniest and most luscious mess of All-American pop drinks, sweets, and fried food ever brought together in one place" (125). Both Park Avenue and the ghetto are awash in consumer goods and the status competitions they enable.

Indeed, as the mayor's terror in the face of the junk food riot that threatens to engulf San Francisco's City Hall demonstrates, the problem with liberalism is its failure to understand the nature of consumer culture. The War on Poverty, Wolfe suggests, is the product of American politicians and intellectuals' inability to come to terms with a society that makes the means to pursue status available to all. Faced with a culture dedicated to unlimited "ego extension," they retreat to "the old restraints, the old limits, of the ancient ego-crusher: *Calamity.* . . . I was impressed by the profound relief with which intellectuals and politicians discovered poverty in America in 1963, courtesy of Michael Harrington's book *The Other America.*"[36] Liberals are concerned about poverty because it seems like a real issue that transcends the play of style that marks 1960s culture. Their attraction to African American causes comes from the same impulse; Bernstein's guests fetishize the Black Panthers because they seem more real to them than other civil rights activists: "The very idea of them, these real revolutionaries, who actually put their lives on the line, runs through Lenny's duplex like a rogue hormone" (4). This belief in the reality of poverty and black militants derives from liberals' attempt to impose an old-fashioned model of status on the ghetto. Liberals, Wolfe suggests, imagine that all ghetto residents want the straight jobs that whites themselves find inadequate vehicles for expressing status in a leisure society; the War on Poverty's emphasis on job training, however, will never help the ghetto, since there are "so many kids who—rather than have job training so they could get some job paying $75 or $80 in an office, at a low level, some routine repetitive work—would rather live the street life."[37] Liberals also imagine that the ghetto's status hierarchy is a singular system, with identifiable leaders and followers. Faced with the need to cool down the summer riots, War on Poverty officials seek out "the 'real leaders,' the 'natural leaders,' the 'charismatic figures' in the ghetto jungle" (105), whom the officials imagine belong to gangs. This conception overlooks the atomization of the ghetto, which mirrors the atomization of society at large. Although the ghetto produces militant organizations like the Black Panthers, the majority of ghetto residents are "individualists" (112), more interested in the pursuit of status than in political causes. In spite of liberals' misconceptions about the ghetto, the War on Poverty cannot escape the play of style. Instead, by feeding more money into the ghetto, the poverty program accelerates urban minorities' hunt for subcultural status in a style-driven, affluent society. The War on Poverty will never help ghetto children get jobs, but it might lend a degree of official respectability to the street life itself for those cunning enough to get OEO funding: "As a job counselor or neighborhood organizer you stood to make six or seven hundred dollars a month, and you were still your own man. . . . You were still on the street, and you got paid for it" (120).

However, even as Wolfe's critique of the War on Poverty, like Oates's, draws on his perception that white liberals and the urban underclass are psychologically identical, he draws opposing conclusions about that perception's implications for his own writing. For Oates, universal pathology threatens to disable literary representation. Wolfe, however, encounters no explicit representational crisis when writing about people who belong to a different race or class; indeed, his signature accomplishment as a New Journalist is his ability to enter into his subjects' heads by using third-person-omniscient techniques more commonly found in fiction. Wolfe opens "Radical Chic" with a dramatic example of this technique, narrating Bernstein's late-night vision of one of his concerts being interrupted by an unnamed black man who exposes the flimsiness of

Bernstein's liberal pieties. Elsewhere, Wolfe addresses the reader in the second person, so he or she becomes, first, a guest at Bernstein's party and, second, an applicant for poverty funding: "Wonder what the Black Panthers eat here on the hors d'oeuvre trail? . . . Deny it if you wish, but such as the *pensées métaphysiques* that rush through one's head on these Radical Chic evenings" (2–3); OEO bureaucrats "sat back and waited for you to come rolling in with your certified angry militants, your guaranteed frustrated ghetto youth, looking like a bunch of wild men" (83). As James Stull points out, this capacity for narrative omniscience derives from Wolfe's careful manipulation of his status theory. Everyone is engaged in the pursuit of status, and Wolfe's authority derives from his construction of himself as "the only player—the omniscient narrator—who has full knowledge of the social game."[38] This conception of himself as an outsider informed his reportorial technique; he established a calibrated distance from his subjects symbolized by his tailored white suits, which he wore regardless of his assignment. This distance, Wolfe claimed, ensured his journalistic objectivity; the New Journalism's advantage over fiction lies in "the simple fact that the reader knows *all of this actually happened.*"[39] Wolfe, in other words, achieves the clinical distance between author and subject that eludes Oates's naturalist narrator in *them.*

At the same time, Wolfe's narrative omniscience draws on the resources of process art in ways that strategically eradicate this distance. Like many experimental writers of the 1960s, Wolfe was influenced by the antiformalist prose style popularized by Kerouac in the 1950s. Although he insisted that he was "an outline man," for whom "spontaneous writing is a waste of time,"[40] his idiosyncratic journalistic style originated in an act of automatic writing akin to Kerouac's liberation from New Critical formalism when he wrote *On the Road.* His first New Journalist article, "There Goes (Varoom! Varoom!) the Kandy-Kolored Tangerine-Flake Streamline Baby," began with a case of writer's block, as he tried to fit his material into the formal requirements of feature writing. In a marathon overnight session, Wolfe wrote out his impressions of American hot rod culture, which *Esquire* published with almost no edits. In this article and other early pieces, Wolfe fashioned an oral style, one that threw aside the stodgy conventions of news writing and aimed at immediate communication with the reader.[41] At the same time, Wolfe developed a process conception of his relationship with his subjects. Reflecting on his technique for writing *The Electric Kool-Aid Acid Test,*[42] his in-depth account of Ken Kesey's Merry Pranksters, Wolfe described how he would "review my notes for a certain chapter, then I would close my eyes and try to imagine myself, as a Method actor would, into the scene . . . going crazy, for example . . . how it feels and what it's going to sound like if you translate it into words—which was real writing by radar."[43] This confidence in his ability to replicate his subjects' consciousness differentiated Wolfe from contemporaneous New Journalists like Joan Didion and Hunter S. Thompson, who were intensely aware of the potential distortions implicit in the journalist's narrative voice.

Wolfe counterposed this reportorial practice against the formalist aesthetic that he believed dominated postwar fiction. He associated this aesthetic with the academy, an institution that he left behind in 1957 after completing his doctorate in American studies. Conflating all postwar fiction with the 1940s and 1950s "new fiction" that Malcolm Cowley criticized in *The Literary Situation*, Wolfe insisted, "Almost all 'serious' American novelists today come out of the universities," and they create "a puzzling sort of fiction . . . in which the characters have no background, no personal history, are identified with no social class, ethnic group or even nationality, and act out their fates in a locale that has no place name." According to Wolfe, these novelists abandoned social realism due to their perception that "bourgeois society was breaking up, fragmenting."[44] This left fertile territory for the feature writers who invented New Journalism in the 1960s, who took for granted the disappearance of bourgeois society and explored the subcultural fragments that it left behind. Wolfe's account of the New Journalism's genesis parallels the career trajectory of process writers like Kerouac and Baraka, who similarly fled institutional confinement in the academy to cultivate a new kind of literary expertise outside it. For Wolfe, the New Journalist was uniquely poised as an expert interpreter of popular culture, capable of articulating its logic in a way that its unconscious practitioners could not; in spite of its sophistication, the hot rod culture he described in "Kandy-Kolored" is inaccessible to most outsiders, since its teenage enthusiasts "are not from the levels of society that produce children who write sensitive analytical prose at age seventeen."[45] At the same time, the New Journalist's anti-academic expertise threatened the literary establishment, shattering the status system that had governed it since the nineteenth century and exposing it to its outside. In that system, novelists and poets were the aristocrats, critics were the middle class, journalists the proletariat, and feature writers the "lumpenproles." With the rise of the New Journalism, the lumpenproles challenged novelists at their own game, dismantling "class lines that have been almost a century in the making." His bid to revolutionize the literary field was announced with his editorship of *The New Journalism* (1973), literary journalism's first anthology. Commenting on the institutionalization that usually goes hand in hand with anthologies, Wolfe hoped that New Journalism's revolution would be permanent: "With any luck at all the new genre will never be sanctified, never be exalted, never given a theology."[46]

In "Mau-Mauing," Wolfe extends this reportorial revolution to the ghetto, usually regarded as a privileged site of the real in American journalism and fiction. According to Wolfe, the problem with the bureaucrats who run the OEO is similar to the one that plagues postwar writers. Embedded in the self-perpetuating institutions of the federal government, they have no conception of an outside world. The poverty program is the federal government's attempt to force some sort of contact with this outside, creating opportunities for confrontation with ghetto leaders who will tell the government what to do. The program, however, perpetuates the very autotelic system that it tries to disrupt. Cunning game players, ghetto leaders reinforce bureaucrats' stereotypes about racial minorities, enacting their "deep dark Tarzan mumbo jungle voodoo fear of the black man's masculinity" (103). The result is the practice of "mau-mauing," whereby minorities ritualistically play the savage to intimidate government officials. Wolfe's literary example of mau-mauing is Eldridge Cleaver's *Soul on Ice*. In one of the essay's set pieces, a white female teacher ritualistically reads Cleaver's memoir to her English students at San Francisco State, closing the book "very softly under her chin, the way a preacher closes the Bible." Wolfe's point, articulated by the classroom's sole black student, is that the memoir does nothing to disrupt the classroom's circulation of educational capital. The book is "written for the white middle class. They published it and they read it" (110).

The War on Poverty's participatory professionalism, in other words, does not close the gap between government and the ghetto. Indeed, Wolfe insists that the War on Poverty's confrontations are carefully managed to have as little impact on government operations as possible. Wolfe's account of San Francisco's poverty program leaves out the young idealists drawn to many Community Action Agencies. In their place, Wolfe constructs a new caricature, distinct from both the radical chic liberal and the minority pimp: the flak catcher. In "Mau-Mauing"'s first fully realized scene, a multiethnic group of militants descends on the office of a flak catcher: an OEO bureaucrat whom they hope to intimidate into giving them more Community Action Program funding. The flak catcher, in Wolfe's scenario, has no social work expertise and offers no pretense of wanting to encourage lower-class participation in the poverty program. The only trace of the Community Action Program's participatory imperative is the bureaucrat's stance as he listens to the militants: he sits "backwards, straddling the seat and hooking his arms and his chin over the back of the chair. . . . It's like saying, 'We don't stand on ceremony around here'" (93–94). His sole function is to gauge the frustration of the War on Poverty's clientele, acting as an intermediary between the politicians and intellectuals who create the poverty program and the underclass who benefit from it. This flak-catching function, Wolfe suggests, pervades the entire bureaucratic corps of the US government. Flak catchers are not unique to the poverty program; they staff all offices where the government interfaces with the public: "Poverty, Japanese imports, valley fever, tomato-crop parity, partial disability, home loans, second-probate accounting . . . whatever you're angry about, it doesn't matter" (95).

The flak catcher is an ironic counterpoint to Wolfe, who similarly presents himself as an intermediary with the ghetto. Like Wolfe, the flak catcher stands outside the status games that the ghetto residents play. Unlike the radical chic liberals who support the poverty program, he has no personal stake in those games. His purpose is to sacrifice personal status to protect the government he serves; he absorbs assaults on his "dignity" and "manhood" (96) to allow the militants to feel like they have successfully challenged the system. This lack of status is reflected in his absence of style, which stands out in a society entirely dominated by it. His clothes are "stone civil service," permitting no deviation: "wheatcolor Hush Puppies" that "cost about $4.99" and a "wash'n'dry semi-tab-collar shortsleeved white shirt" (93). His bureaucratic speech is similarly bland:

> At this point I see no reason why our project allocation should be any less, if all we're looking at is the urban-factor numbers for this area, because that should remain the same. Of course, if there's been any substantial pre-funding, in Washington, for the fixed-asset part of our program, like Head Start or the community health centers, that could alter the picture. (95–96)

This abandonment of style and status allows the flak catcher to channel information to his readers; by absorbing assaults to his dignity, he communicates the relative militancy of different ghetto groups to the government without endangering any elected officials or the liberals who vote for them. Wolfe underscores this juxtaposition between the flak catcher and the reporter through a bravura display of New Journalistic style, as he describes the bureaucrat's shirt: "Sticking out of the pockets and running across his chest he has a lineup of ball-point pens, felt nib, lead pencils, wax markers, such as you wouldn't believe, Paper mates, Pentels, Scriptos, Eberhard Faber Mongol 482's, Dri-Marks, Bic PM-29's, everything. They are lined up across his chest like campaign ribbons" (93). This catalog contrasts with the flak-catcher's dry bureaucratic speech, dramatizing the journalist's superior command of language. At the same time, the pens and pencils underscore the fact that the flak catcher is a kind of writer, charged with transforming the ghetto into written reports for the benefit of white readers. He is, however, a petty, restricted version of the New Journalist—as evidenced by the difference between his mass-produced white shirt and Wolfe's custom-made white suits.

This juxtaposition buttresses Wolfe's authority to write about the ghetto, but it also betrays anxiety about his success in this endeavor, suggesting that like the flak catcher, he acts more like an information buffer than an in-depth reporter. Although Wolfe presents himself as a confident expert on the inner city, "Mau-Mauing" does not, in fact, get inside the heads of its minority subjects; the story is surprisingly devoid of details about status conflicts as experienced by the minorities themselves. Indeed, only one of the story's set pieces is actually set in the ghetto; the remaining scenes take place in downtown offices where would-be ghetto leaders meet the bureaucrats. Even when the story does venture into the ghetto, Wolfe's reportorial eye remains safely shielded within the autotelic enclosure created by the OEO. The story's singular ghetto scene is a meeting between gang leaders and OEO bureaucrats at the gang's clubhouse. The bureaucrats wait anxiously in the building listening to the muffled thuds as gang members beat a wino in the alley outside. "Mau-Mauing" prefigures a problem that beset Wolfe when he wrote his first novel, *The Bonfire of the Vanities* (1987).[47] As Joshua Masters observes, Wolfe describes the bonds between tradesmen and lawyers in this novel "by way of their class standing and status symbols," especially their clothing. In contrast, when describing minority characters, he relies on a "semiotics of the body which translates physical differences into moral and intellectual signifiers."[48] Similarly, in "Mau-Mauing," Wolfe constructs a ghetto bestiary, in which different races become caricatures based on their physical differences from whites. Samoans are "Polynesian monsters" (99), each with a "skull the size of a watermelon" (92). The black gang members sit at their clubhouse meeting "like a bunch of secretary birds" (114). When Wolfe uses these metaphors, he abandons the second-person point of view, instead presenting them as stereotypes invented by white observers unfamiliar with the ghetto. Wolfe describes the Samoans from the flak catcher's perspective; he describes the birdlike pimps from the point of view of the bureaucrats at the clubhouse. At one point, Wolfe itemizes the fears that different races evoke in the white psyche: "The white man pictured the Chinese as small, quiet, restrained little fellows. He had a certain deep-down voodoo fear of their power of evil in the Dark" (91). By characterizing ghetto residents in this way— as figures who embody white fears—Wolfe performs the same function for his readers that the flak catcher performs for the OEO. Rather than channel the consciousness of ghetto dwellers, he registers the degree of terror they instill in the white mind.

Wolfe's tactic—claiming an intuitive knowledge of the ghetto while recycling primitivist tropes—is not especially new. The same tactic is central to Jacob Riis's 1890 journalistic book, *How the Other Half Lives*, which provides a taxonomy of the different races and ethnicities that inhabit New York's tenement districts. Similarly, the journalists who wrote in-depth exposés on the underclass in the 1980s, such as Ken Auletta in *The Underclass* (1982), drew on a primitivist terminology extending back to the nineteenth century. The underclass, Auletta argues, "usually operates outside the generally accepted boundaries of society. They are often set apart by their 'deviant' or antisocial behavior, by their bad habits."[49] Wolfe's use of primitivist metaphors, however, stands out because it jars with his ostensibly universalistic theory of human nature. Jacob Riis's taxonomy, which ranks New York's races hierarchically from the Chinese at the bottom to the Germans at the top, is rooted in his implicit reliance on a late nineteenth-century social evolutionist paradigm. Auletta's work draws on the equally deterministic, conservative version of the culture of poverty theory outlined by Edward Banfield. Both of these paradigms assume that the poor are essentially different from the white middle class. Wolfe, in contrast, assumes that the poor are tactical game players just like other Americans; their crimes are merely further convolutions of the universal search for status. Unable to observe those games, Wolfe nevertheless presents himself as an omniscient guide to the ghetto.

The apparent confidence with which he does so registers conservatives' increasing dominance of poverty discourse after the War on Poverty. Devoid of

Oates's anxiety about appropriating others' voices, Wolfe uses a revised process aesthetic to construct himself as an inner-city expert. This confidence underlies a project that similarly insists that the ghetto be left to its own devices. For Wolfe in *Radical Chic*, the Community Action Program does nothing to create lasting wealth in the inner city or alleviate its violence. It merely goads the underclass to invent con games that play on white liberal anxieties and sympathies.

5 Civil Rights and the Southern Folk Aesthetic

When a new generation of black women writers began to publish in the 1970s, the War on Poverty was effectively over. Although the OEO survived until 1981, most of its programs were gutted by the Nixon administration. Even as objects of derision, War on Poverty programs seemed irrelevant to writers in the post-Johnson era, as did the urban-oriented racial liberalism that gave rise to those programs. Drawing on the historical model of Zora Neale Hurston's anthropology and fiction, black womanist novelists instead explored the folkways of rural black communities, many of them situated in the Jim Crow South. These communities were shaped by racial oppression yet operated according to a completely different cultural logic than that of the white communities that surrounded them. In particular, novels like *Sula* (1973), *Song of Solomon* (1977), and *The Color Purple* (1982) offered nostalgic visions of a cohesive black people bound together by root magic and other spiritual practices. These fictions helped spur an organic conception of black folk community that would influence literary intellectuals from the 1980s onward. In Cornel West's terms, Jim Crow–era communities had fashioned "powerful buffers to ward off the nihilistic threat, to equip black folk with cultural armor to beat back the demons of hopelessness."[1] For West and other post-1980 black intellectuals, the destruction of these communities was one of the worst disasters to befall African Americans, and neither the Black Arts movement nor the War on Poverty helped reconstitute them in the inner city.

Yet the War on Poverty left an indelible stamp on black women writers in the 1970s. Two cases in point are Alice Walker and Toni Cade Bambara. Both began their professional lives as social workers, employed by the New York Department of Social Services in the 1960s. At the time, social work was one of the few occupations open to college-educated black women; it was also a job that attracted young women interested in social justice issues. "We were all radical movement people who wanted to save the world," Walker commented; "we believed that working for the welfare department would give us a chance to help people."[2] Both women were disabused of this belief when they encountered the department's heavy caseloads, and this dissatisfaction drove them to Great Society projects that challenged social work's status quo. Walker moved to Mississippi to work for Head Start, where she taught older women who would, in turn, become teachers for black rural youth. Bambara taught in City College's Search for Education, Elevation and Knowledge (SEEK) program, which helped low-income minority youth prepare for university. These experiences galvanized both writers' literary careers: Walker's work in Mississippi inspired her first novel, *The Life of Grand Copeland* (1970), while Bambara made the contacts at City College that allowed her to publish *The Black Woman* (1970), the anthology that sparked the black womanist movement. The experiences also provided the template for the two women's subsequent activism; both writers, in their fiction and community work, believed that they were carrying out social work by other means. In so doing, they extended many of the process assumptions of the Black Arts movement, conceiving of their fiction as a vehicle for transmitting useful knowledge to lower-class black communities.

Perhaps unsurprisingly, the organic communities these writers imagined in their fiction replicated the promises and problems of Great Society–era Community Action Agencies. As Madhu Dubey argues, the Southern folk aesthetic offered a solution to a crisis of representation that troubled black writers from the 1960s onward. In the face of the class fragmentation brought about by the Great Migration, this aesthetic sought "to establish an exact identification between the writer and the 'black folk'—in other words, to authenticate the writer's claims to addressing and speaking for a clearly recognizable black community."[3] During the Black Arts era, black writers worried that literature was a product of the white culture of expertise that separated the black educated elite from the urban underclass. Turning to the South allowed those writers to imagine literature as an outgrowth of the same Southern folkways that shaped black urban culture; Henry Louis Gates Jr. offered the most influential version of this argument in *The Signifying Monkey* (1988), which conceptualized the entire history of black writing in America in terms of Southern storytelling practices. This notion of a lost folk community, however, often reinforced the very divisions it sought to eradicate. As Kenneth Warren argues, by the 1980s and 1990s, appeals to Southern organicism had become a routine component of underclass discourse. Surveying the work of Cornel West, Houston Baker Jr., and others, Warren concludes that the Southern folk aesthetic helped perpetuate an account of the black underclass as victims of cultural disorientation brought about by the Great Migration. This account, Warren argues, allowed black intellectuals to present themselves as guardians of lost cultural traditions and possible saviors of the race: "We find ourselves in a world where the presumed pathologies and behavioral shortcomings of the lower orders are taken to be symptomatic of a failure on the part of natural, organic authorities to impose order upon and exact obedience from the nation's impoverished citizens."[4]

Walker and Bambara's use of a folk aesthetic to suture divisions between black professionals and the underclass is especially evident in two novels that directly address the legacy of community action and the Black Arts movement: *Meridian* (1976) and *The Salt Eaters* (1980).[5] Both novels explore the possibility of reviving black organic communities in the post–civil rights present. *Meridian* locates this possibility in the Student Nonviolent Coordinating Committee (SNCC), for which Walker was an activist in the early 1960s. The novel engages with SNCC's specific brand of community action, which evolved at the same time as early, Kennedy-era experiments like Harlem Youth Opportunities Unlimited and Mobilization for Youth. The SNCC's efforts to bring together black professionals and the rural working class are central to the novel's account of a poet and former SNCC activist who returns to the South in the late 1960s, trying to reconnect with the black folk that she left behind when she became a college student. The effectiveness of this effort, however, remains ambiguous at the novel's end. In particular, the novel struggles to reconcile the critical expertise embodied in Meridian's postsecondary education and activist training with the folk knowledge that originates in the South. This struggle also marks the novel's form, which simultaneously affirms its continuity with and autonomous separation from folk art. This interest in community action and black literature's capacity to suture the black community recurs in Toni Cade Bambara's *The Salt Eaters*, a novel about a civil rights activist who undergoes a faith healing at an Afrocentric health center. More directly than Walker, Bambara embraces a Southern folk version of process art, envisaging her novel as a folk ritual that will heal divisions between black professionals and the underclass. At the same time, the novel highlights the material underpinnings of community action:

white liberal patronage, which reinforces the class divisions that the novel tries to overcome. Formally and thematically, both novels gesture toward community action–inspired organic communities that they can never realize.

Alice Walker's Other College

Speaking in 1970 to the Black Students' Association at her alma mater, Sarah Lawrence College, Alice Walker offered one of the earliest versions of the Southern folk aesthetic. Echoing Baraka and other Black Arts writers, she insisted, "The artist then is the voice of the people, but she is also The People." Whereas Baraka found his people in the urban slums of Harlem and Newark, Walker found hers in the South—in Georgia, where she grew up, and in Mississippi, where she relocated in 1967 after completing her college degree: "When I write about the people there, in the strangest way it is as if I am not writing about them at all, but about myself." This capacity to write about the people was both enabled and disabled by her college studies. At Sarah Lawrence—an elite liberal arts college where Walker was one of only six black students—she found the "freedom to come and go, to read leisurely" denied to her in rural Alabama. At the same time, because Sarah Lawrence did not teach black authors, she had to unlearn much of her formal literary education after graduation. She left Sarah Lawrence to enroll in "another college," taught by "the oldest old black men and women I could find" and "students and dropouts who articulate in various bold and shy ways that they believe themselves to be without a valuable history." This other college was the Head Start program in rural Mississippi, where Walker worked as a consultant in black history for Friends of the Children of Mississippi. Walker's return to the South thus followed the same trajectory as other 1960s process artists. Through community action sponsored by the War on Poverty, Walker learned to dismantle artificial forms of expertise acquired in the university. The project ended quickly; Walker's salary came "from the OEO, which apparently frowns on black studies for Headstart teachers."[6] From this experience, however, she acquired much of the impetus for her early fiction.

Walker's transition from college to community action reflects a tension that runs throughout her work. Even as she claimed that Southern folkways were the entire content of her art, she also insisted that she could learn to write about those folkways only by separating herself from them for a time. Moreover, she brought to the South an autonomous conception of the artist and intellectual that she cultivated at Sarah Lawrence, a place where she "felt no teacher or administrator breathing down my neck." Teaching black history to the rural women who ran Head Start classrooms, she discovered that they were "educationally crippled" with little conception of history; many believed in the curse of Ham. Immersion in a folk tradition that labeled black women "the mule of the world" reinforced their historical amnesia and double oppression. A few years later, in the essay that most succinctly captured the Southern folk aesthetic, "In Search of Our Mothers' Gardens" (1974), Walker evoked the same tension. Tracing a forgotten lineage of black female creativity through her mother and grandmother's generations, Walker found its expression in folk arts such as quilting, gardening, and storytelling. These arts, however, were products of a cultural tradition that sharply restricted black women's expressive range. Even as Walker insisted on her debt to her foremothers, she suggested that their work was chiefly valuable because it prepared the way for her own, more self-conscious writing. Alluding to the South's systematic neglect of black literacy, Walker claimed that her foremothers passed on "a sealed letter they could not plainly read."[7] Walker articulated a central paradox of the Southern folk aesthetic: folk art, the product of lived immersion in a materially constrained culture, can be perceived as aesthetic only once one achieves a critical distance from it. This distance, for Walker, meant removing oneself from the folk community by becoming a professional.

The novel in which Walker most explicitly allegorizes this process of professionalization is *Meridian*, her most autobiographical work of fiction. Both thematically and formally, the novel dramatizes the "return South" that Walker claimed was central to the Southern folk aesthetic. The novel tells the story of Meridian Hill, an activist and poet who grows up in small-town Georgia, where she becomes involved in the civil rights movement. After attending college, she comes home to recommence her civil rights work, long after the movement itself has ended. This return is embodied in the novel's form. Walker described *Meridian* as a "crazy quilt,"[8] in contrast with the realism of her first novel, *The Third Life of Grange Copeland* (1970); the nonlinear novel is divided into short, discontinuous chapters, some of them only tangentially related to the novel's overarching narrative. However, even as *Meridian* thematically enacts Meridian's return to "the people" and formally exemplifies Walker's aspirations to create a literary version of folk art, the novel insists that these two returns will never be complete. Meridian's college education continues to separate her from the rural people she serves, and the novel underscores the foreignness of

Walker's brand of literary art within the black rural communities she describes. Even as the novel gestures toward a participatory professional eradication of the differences between welfare experts and their clients, artists and their audiences, it insists that this eradication remains incomplete.

Meridian filters this account of participatory professionalism through the specific experiences of civil rights organizing. Although the novel never names the civil rights organization that Meridian joins, Walker provides enough details for readers to identify it as the SNCC.[9] In particular, the novel draws on the SNCC's experiments in community action, which preceded and influenced many War on Poverty–era Community Action Agencies. When the SNCC first came into being, shortly after the Greensboro and Nashville sit-ins, it focused on direct action aimed at desegregating lunch counters and public facilities. Beginning in 1961, the organization turned to voter registration, which entailed a different kind of engagement with local communities. SNCC activists could no longer come into a community from the outside for brief actions that challenged unconstitutional state and municipal laws; they needed to work with the people they hoped to register, living among them and helping cultivate local leaders. As SNCC activists soon learned, any attempt to tell sharecroppers what to do usually backfired, leading to the perception that the SNCC were outsiders who would abandon locals as soon as white retaliation became too fierce. As a result, SNCC members tried to blend into rural communities, adopting a rural drawl and farmers' clothing: work shirts and blue jeans or overalls.[10] The SNCC also created alternative, community-controlled institutions, which coincided with Kennedy administration and Ford Foundation pilot projects such as Mobilization for Youth. In the summer of 1964, the SNCC established community projects across Mississippi, which enabled residents to challenge local governments for better services, including health care, education, and agricultural subsidies.[11] The SNCC's freedom schools, in particular, pioneered new modes of pedagogy that emphasized "student participation and the Socratic method."[12] Many of the federally funded Community Action Agencies that emerged throughout the South after 1964 simply enveloped these SNCC initiatives; the Head Start program where Walker taught was originally a freedom school. The SNCC, then, was an experimental laboratory that helped create the participatory model of expertise that reshaped the practice and ethos of professionalism in the 1960s. Along with Students for a Democratic Society, the SNCC took seriously the imperative to dissolve boundaries between experts and nonexperts.

As in the case of other participatory professional organizations, this imperative went hand in hand with a romantic conception of the poor's ontological difference from the middle-class students who populated the movement. Especially during the 1964 Freedom Summer, which drew a mass influx of white students to the organization, many activists embraced a mystique of poverty. James Stembridge, the SNCC's first executive secretary, claimed that rural blacks enjoyed "a closeness with the earth . . . a closeness with each other in the sense of community developed out of dependence . . . the strength of being poor." This mystique led some activists to doubt the utility of the skills they brought into the field; according to one Freedom School director, many workers "withdrew into shells of guilt and meek deference to those who were poorer and less educated, apologizing for Harvard and Smith and Berkeley. Apologizing for knowing how to spell." The SNCC ultimately fragmented because of tensions between some activists' insistence on the need for professional competency and others' idealization of the poor. After the Freedom Summer, the organization split into two factions. On the one side, hard-liners like James Forman and Cleveland Sellers called for greater centralization and bureaucratization to make the SNCC more effective. On the other, frontline activists worried that the organization had already become too professionalized. Organizers, literary project director Maria Varela argued, had to abandon "the habits that come from a system of values almost all of us have had—that is that educated, better-off people naturally dominate under-educated, less well-off people." Field secretary Charles Sherrod insisted that activists should instead embrace "the wisdom of the pinched toe and the empty belly."[13]

In *Meridian*, Walker's title character embodies the SNCC's participatory professionalism in a more complex fashion, since she comes from the urban folk whose wisdom movement activists extolled. In Meridian's case, civil rights activism becomes a vehicle for upward mobility into a cross-racial professional class represented by the novel's three other activist characters: Truman Held, Anne-Marion Coles, and Lynne Rabinowitz. Meridian grows up in small-town Georgia, the victim of a transgenerational pattern of stalled upward mobility. Her mother escapes from an abusive home to become a schoolteacher but must abandon her career to marry and have children. Meridian is an intelligent young woman with an IQ of 140 but drops out of high school when she too becomes pregnant. The movement puts Meridian back on her mother's interrupted trajectory, singling her out as a special beneficiary of its policy of eradicating differences between students and nonstudents. Through a movement donor, she gets a scholarship to attend Saxon College, a historically black all-girls' institution in Atlanta. At Saxon College, Meridian is groomed to become a member of the black bourgeoisie. However, the college is mired in an older regime of black education fashioned in the Jim Crow era; Saxon girls are trained to "become something—ladies—that was already obsolete" (95). Like Naxos College in Nella Larsen's *Quicksand*, Saxon exemplifies the disciplinary regime that Roderick Ferguson identifies as typical of historically black colleges in Jim Crow America. It establishes rigidly heteronormative expectations of female sexuality, which it codes as white, then actively undermines any attempt by black women to live up to those expectations.[14] By the 1960s, this disciplining of black female sexuality was becoming an impediment, rather than a prerequisite, for membership in the professional class.

Meridian finds a clearer path toward the new black elite within the movement itself, which invites its activists to be political and sexual risk takers; male and female members dress in the same uniform (overalls with clodhoppers), get arrested in the same protests, and openly engage in sexual liaisons. In Alvin Gouldner's terms, the movement is suffused with a "culture of critical discourse,"[15] which challenges and disrupts the traditional beliefs that constrain rural black women like Meridian. As Walker underscores through her portrait of male activists like Truman, this culture has not yet revolutionized gender roles; as Lauren Cardon notes, the movement "carves out a space for women as narrow as the working-class domesticity that confined Meridian's mother."[16] Nevertheless, the movement provides Meridian a critical consciousness about gender absent in her Jim Crow community. Before her involvement in the movement, Meridian's understanding of gender roles is circumscribed by her mother's cryptic warnings about being "fast" (88) and by the "fantasy" (75) lives of white women she reads about in magazines. She acquiesces silently and without pleasure to sex and then marriage with her high school boyfriend. The movement disrupts her state of complacency, making her "aware of the past and present of the larger world" (73) and enabling her decision to put her infant child up for adoption and go to college. With this decision, Meridian breaks her community's central expectation of black mothers—that they put their children's well-being before their own. As Walker recounted in nonfiction essays about her own involvement with the SNCC, this sudden awareness of the mutability of previously unquestioned cultural taboos was typical of the movement's impact on rural blacks: "If knowledge of my condition is all the freedom I get from a 'freedom movement,' it is better than unawareness, for-gottenness, and hopelessness, the existence that is like the existence of a beast." Walker described her participation in the movement as the means she used to escape from a state of unconsciousness that kept her trapped, like Meridian, in a pattern of stalled upward mobility. Before the movement, Walker's hopes and aspirations were those of a "typical high-school senior." The movement helped her expand those aspirations. "Knowing," she concluded, "has pushed me out into the world, into college, into places, into people."[17]

However, by facilitating the individuation of young activists like Meridian, the movement risks betraying its own participatory ethos. Meridian's upward mobility, predicated on a radical reevaluation of all of the customs and in-herited notions that determine racial and gender identification, is a solitary process, one that does not lend itself to SNCC-style political organizing. When asked if she thinks she can change the cultural climate of the South, Meridian explains, "I can change . . . I hope I will" (152). Civil rights activism in *Meridian* is not so much oriented toward changing society as refashioning the self; when Meridian is beaten unconscious by racist police during a sit-in, she welcomes the violence for the "inner gaiety" and "sense of freedom" (97) it provides her. The movement ostensibly extends the possibility of personal transformation to everyone affected by it. However, for most rural blacks, the material benefits of this transformation are fleeting or nonexistent. When Meridian and Truman try to register a poor black couple who have been reduced to collecting dis-carded newspapers to roll and sell as firewood logs, the husband complains, "What good is the vote if we don't own nothing?" Although voting seems like an obvious mechanism for improving social conditions, its immediate results are negligible; the vote will not get the couple "free medicines" or "a job no one can take away." Meridian explains that voting can "be the beginning of the use of your own voice. You have to get used to using your voice, you know. You start on simple things and move on" (204–205). However, whereas Meridian's discovery of her voice provides her, at least for a time, with material rewards, this same discovery probably will not change the couple's condition.

Even more problematically from the perspective of the Southern folk aes-thetic, when it makes rural women like Meridian aware of a "larger world" (73) outside the Jim Crow South, the movement threatens the customs and myths that allowed segregated communities to survive centuries of racial oppression.

The student activists at Saxon realize this threat when they cut down the college's ancient Sojourner tree. The tree embodies a tradition of black women's storytelling; its roots are nourished by the severed tongue of Louvinie, a first-generation slave punished for telling a story that stopped the heart of one of her master's children. The tree also embodies the college's mixed history of female oppression and resistance; once a year, students commemorate the death of Fast Mary, a student who committed suicide in the 1920s after becoming pregnant and killing her newborn child. Last, the tree's name alludes to the abolitionist Sojourner Truth, pointing to a history of black female activism dating back before the Civil War. Rather than engage with these various histories, the students eradicate them altogether. Confronted with a political movement dedicated to cultural amnesia, Meridian struggles with a dilemma that also beset Walker's attempt to fashion a womanist philosophy distinct from the feminism of the white women's liberation movement. In Keith Byerman's terms, Walker tried "to integrate feminism with folk values so that each enhances the other." This integration would "link ideology to a concrete history" while also giving "direction and force to an often fatalistic folk wisdom."[18]

In *Meridian*, Walker achieves a dialectical resolution of this conflict between folk tradition and the culture of critical discourse by reimagining the black church. For much of the novel, Meridian experiences the black church as a confining institution; as a child, she refuses to convert, rejecting her mother's unthinking belief in the church's authority.[19] When Meridian returns South, however, she returns to a church transformed by the civil rights movement. Entering a church during a ceremony commemorating a civil rights martyr, she realizes that between the early and late 1960s, black religion has changed. The music has become "martial" (195), the preacher forbids the young men in his congregation from participating in the Vietnam War, and the church's stained-glass window portrays B. B. King wielding a guitar and bloody sword. For the first time, Meridian feels that all African Americans are organically connected; her life "extended beyond herself to those around her because, in fact, the years in America had created them One Life" (200). This organic connection is effected by the rituals and traditions that the community passes on from one generation to the next; Meridian describes the church hymn as the "song of the people" (201). This song, however, is not static; it changes as it incorporates the experiences of each generation, including the new radical generation that questions the basic tenets of that tradition. The congregation's martial song assimilates the death of the civil rights martyr; Meridian imagines the singers addressing the martyr's grieving father: "If you will let us weave your story and your son's life and death into what we already know—into the songs, the sermons, the 'brother and sister'—we will soon be so angry we cannot help but move" (199).

Meridian's self-transformation through movement activism thus gestures toward a collective transformation of the black community, achieved through a gradual evolution of the community's songs and prayers as it absorbs her experiences. Near the beginning of her movement activism, Meridian confronts an old woman who refuses to register to vote, insisting instead on the efficacy of prayer. Whereas Lynne, freshly arrived in the South from her all-white college, wants to continue to persuade the woman, Meridian insists that she is "beyond the boundaries of politics" (102). By the end of the novel, Meridian achieves a new vision of civil rights politics perpetually confronting this boundary. In spite of the novel's interest in moving beyond the civil rights era, this political vision is solidly rooted in the era's debates about the limits and possibilities of social change. From the end of World War II to the Freedom Summer of 1964, the debate over racial segregation was dominated by two positions. Beginning with Gunnar Myrdal's *An American Dilemma* (1945), racial liberals argued that the solution to American racism was largely educational. Liberals must appeal to the egalitarian "American Creed" against the nation's racist prejudices.[20] Southern traditionalists, in contrast, drew on Charles Graham Sumner's concept of "folkways" to insist on the intractability of racist customs. "Folkways," Sumner argued, "are not creations of human purpose and wit. They are like products of natural forces which men unconsciously set in operation, or they are like the instinctive ways of animals."[21] At stake in this debate was a conflict over the nature of folk culture. For Myrdal, folk culture was a tissue of beliefs susceptible to rational persuasion; for segregationists, it was thickly embodied in static rituals passed down from generation to generation. Echoing previous black intellectuals from the civil rights era such as Ralph Ellison, Walker tries to synthesize these two theories.[22] The old woman Meridian encounters cannot be swayed by the activists' reasoned arguments; her belief in prayer is too deep-seated. However, the prayers themselves will gradually evolve in response to the activists' suffering.

This dialectical relationship between critical consciousness and tradition, however, does not suture the rift opened up within Meridian herself when she becomes an activist. Unlike Truman and Anne-Marion, Meridian refuses to use movement activism as the basis for a professional career. Instead, she remains attached to the SNCC model of community action, long after the movement itself abandons this tactic. When she leaves New York to return South, she resolves to "go back to the people, live among them, like Civil Rights workers used to do" (31). She sloughs off the advantages of her college degree, sliding back into the working-class jobs for which she was destined as a high school dropout: "From being a teacher who published small broadsides of poems, she had hired herself out as a gardener, as a waitress at middle-class black parties, and had occasionally worked as a dishwasher and cook" (32). This downward mobility, however, never leads her back to the people; she remains an outsider in rural Georgia, marked as different by her nontraditional behavior and beliefs, and unintegrated into local kin networks. Her in-between status—no longer one of the folk but not quite a professional—is highlighted by the sole decorations she attaches to the walls of her ramshackle houses: letters from her mother and Anne-Marion. The letters from her mother contain Bible verses that underscore Meridian's departure from traditional mores; the letters from Anne-Marion castigate her for failing to understand Marxist theory (23). This in-between status is a precondition for Meridian's work; her value to the community consists in the fact that she does, in fact, have access to knowledge that they do not and can connect them to services they need. The "wisdom of the pinched toe and empty belly,"[23] extolled by SNCC workers, is strikingly limited in *Meridian*. For instance, in one of the novel's concluding vignettes, Truman accompanies Meridian on a voter registration visit to a sixty-nine-year-old woman who is convinced that she is pregnant after losing her virginity to a house painter. Her certitude is based on her traditional belief that retribution follows sin. Meridian disrupts this certitude by encouraging her to go to the doctor's office for a consultation. In this instance, folk belief cannot be changed through the gradual evolution of ritual; it must be doused in the cold truth of professional expertise.

This awareness of the potentially ineradicable tension between tradition and expertise puts into question the possibility of the kind of process art that Walker wanted to create when writing *Meridian*. Throughout the novel, Walker depicts art as a predominantly middle-class endeavor, rooted in the professional cultures of Saxon College and the movement. Both Anne-Marion and Truman use the movement to jump-start their careers as artists, and these careers take them away from the people they once served as activists. Anne-Marion abandons the Black Power movement to become "a well-known poet whose poems were about her two children, and the quality of light that fell across a lake she owned" (201). In the 1960s, Truman embraces a Black Arts aesthetic, painting portraits of voluptuous black women with "breasts like melons and hair like a crown of thorns" (168). By the 1970s, however, this aesthetic has been fully absorbed into the American art establishment; he makes "a statue of Crispus Attucks for the bicentennial" (189). When Meridian joins the movement and attends college, she similarly discovers her aesthetic sensibilities; she slips "off the heavily guarded campus at five in the morning to photograph a strange tree as the light hit it just the right way" (39) and writes and publishes poems. However, when she returns South, she does not seek to create art that might speak to the rural folk. She abandons or burns her poems as further signs of her middle-class status that she must shed to become one of the people (145). While college turns Meridian into an aesthete, civil rights organizing turns her into an ascetic who eschews beauty and pleasure.

This identification of art with middle-class privilege also characterizes the novel's "crazy-quilt" form. Although this form gestures toward folk art, it registers Walker's uncertainty about the possibility of translating that art into a work of fiction. In the same interview where she described *Meridian* as a quilt, Walker also compared it to Romare Bearden's collages. The latter comparison better captures the novel's tension between folk sensibility and modernist ambition.[24] The novel's chapters are focalized through the free indirect discourse of the novel's four activists. As Madhu Dubey notes, this narrative choice establishes a clear boundary between organizers and organized: "The standard English of Meridian and the narrator sets them apart from 'the people,' who usually speak a form of Southern black dialect." The novel, in other words, involves the reader within a fractured collective of civil rights experts, one that pointedly excludes the rural communities they try to help. For Dubey, this "inability to assume the untroubled collective voice of black oral forms" demarcates Walker and other black women writers' distance from the Black Arts aesthetic championed by figures like Baraka. In particular, Dubey draws attention to one of the few moments in the text where the narrative attempts to encompass the first-person voice of the organized: Meridian and Truman's visit to an unnamed teenage girl in prison who murders her baby. Switching between first and third person, the passage "strains awkwardly toward a fusion of the narrator's and character's voices, betraying the narrator's inability to represent 'the voice of the people,'"[25] and it ends abruptly when the girl tells Meridian and Truman to "go the fuck away" (212). The girl, a black teenage single mother, is in a position analogous to Meridian's when she joins the movement; Meridian also fantasizes about killing her child before giving him away. The girl represents the kind of woman Meridian might have become had she not found the movement in time. The girl's murder of her child, however, places her beyond the reach of participatory politics and art. Immediately after Meridian and Truman leave the prison, the text abruptly returns to its habitual narrative voice, focalized through Meridian and Truman. The novel allegorizes this failure to encompass the girl through Meridian's subsequent return to writing poetry. When she goes back to her home, she writes "with such intensity and passion the pen dug holes in the paper" (213), underscoring her desire to penetrate the barrier between life and art by speaking directly to the girl in a way that she could not in the prison. The poem she writes, however, is a first-person lyric, the most intimate and insular of literary forms. She attaches the poem to her wall and never reads it again, underscoring its disconnection from any audience.

In interviews after she published *Meridian*, Walker insisted that in spite of the novel's autobiographical content, she was not much like her title character: "My life has been, since I became an adult, much more middle class than Meridian's." While Walker, like Meridian, returned to the South after college, she never renounced her desire to be a professional writer or gave up the privileges of a middle-class life. However, when she articulated what it meant to be a writer, Walker often came back to the same conflicts that shape Meridian's poetry and civil rights work. While Walker claimed that the black writer should be "the people," she also insisted on her absolute autonomy as an author: "I try, first of all, to know what I feel about what I think and then to write about that. And if there's an audience, well, fine, but if not, I don't worry about it." Throughout her career, Walker refused to speak for a singular black community, a claim usually made by Black Arts–affiliated writers whose patriarchal vision of that community excluded independent female intellectuals like herself. Indeed, Walker's notion of "the voice of the people" narrowed with each book that she published in the 1970s, even as her audience grew. After the publication of *The Color Purple*, which Ishmael Reed and other male authors criticized for its depiction of black men, this conception of her audience became autotelic—an imagined community located only in the pages of her work. As she wrote *The Color Purple*, she reflected, "I thought about the people I was writing it for. The people I was writing it for are the people who are in the book. That's who I was writing it for."[26]

Community Action's Magic

Unlike Alice Walker, Toni Cade Bambara never cultivated any doubts about her work's political function. She viewed her fiction as a seamless extension of her activism, describing herself as "a teacher who writes, a social worker who writes, a youth worker who writes, a mother who writes." Fiction, for her, was a practical activity that should be of use to a specific community. At a local level, Bambara imagined herself as a worker with skills she could barter. "I was the neighborhood writer," she claimed about the years she lived in Atlanta. "You want to sell your Ford wrecker? Fine, and I would write the contract. Give me a piece of paper and a pencil. That's what a writer does: a writer writes." Also unlike Walker, Bambara believed that her work was shaped by her audience, with whom she enjoyed a face-to-face relationship: "The audience that gives me the most feedback tends to be folks I run across in the wash house or on a bus or on the train or just sort of traveling around."[27] This insistence on practical art oriented toward a specific community meant that Bambara envisaged her work as a critical reworking of the process aesthetic conceptualized by Black Arts theorists in the 1960s. Indeed, Bambara arguably went further than any other black woman writer of the 1970s in adapting that aesthetic to fiction, especially in *The Salt Eaters*.

This process aesthetic informs the novel's experimental form, in ways that sharply differentiate it from *Meridian*. The two novels share obvious thematic links. Set in the late 1970s in the fictional Southern town of Claybourne, *The Salt Eaters* focuses on a civil rights activist named Velma Henry. Almost two decades of activism have destroyed Velma's marriage and estranged her from her adopted son. Meanwhile, the Claybourne activist community she belongs to is falling apart, splintering into the various factions that characterized black radical politics after the civil rights movement. Physically weak and psychologically drained, Velma attempts suicide, and the novel traces the efforts of a faith healer, Minnie Ransom, to rescue her from catatonic despair. Like *Meridian*, then, *The Salt Eaters* is a therapeutic novel focused on healing its protagonist, whose body registers the traumas of movement activism. However, whereas Walker's novel insists that this healing process is a solitary effort, with only a tangential connection to the work that must be done to bring together a divided black community, *The Salt Eaters* erases this division between the individual and the collective.[28] The novel's free indirect discourse jumps midchapter from Velma and Minnie to a series of other characters who have gathered outside the infirmary to participate in the town's annual carnival. Through this shifting point of view, the novel suggests that the private ritual that takes place inside the infirmary is connected to the public ritual that takes place outside in the streets. At the culmination of the healing, this separation disappears entirely; Velma's spirit, hitherto confined to exploring events in her personal history, escapes the infirmary walls and participates in the carnival celebration. Pragmatically, Velma's healing will help suture her community since she is the only one capable of speaking to its various factions. At a more mystical level, Minnie's healing radiates outward to encompass Claybourne and eventually, a nationwide network of activists. According to Bambara's conception of the novel, this ritual also encompasses the reader. Speaking about her ambitions, Bambara explained, "The very shape of the book itself is a ceremony, a series of steps, a process that the author is taking the protagonist through but also asking the reader to go through."[29] *The Salt Eaters* thus enacts the experience of becoming "One Life" that eludes Meridian throughout most of Walker's novel; the boundaries separating her characters' consciousnesses become permeable, as does the boundary separating author and reader.

This enactment of community draws on the theory of intersubjectivity implicit in process art since the 1950s. Echoing Charles Olson's account of poetry as energy transfer from poet to reader, Bambara described literature as "a spirit informer—an energizer. A lot of energy is exchanged in the reading and writing of books."[30] In *The Salt Eaters*, Bambara literalizes this energy transfer at the culmination of Velma's healing. As the ritual draws to a close and Velma's spirit roams the streets, a storm breaks out, and supernaturally loud thunder shakes the town. As most of the novel's critics have pointed out, even as this energy release traverses all of the characters, it does not eradicate the conflicts that divide them. Bambara "does not show the moment of achieved unity" promised by Velma's healing.[31] Instead, the healing restores the townsfolk's capacity to make decisions that might create this unity in the future. When the storm breaks out, Claybourne's militants and police force are bent on a confrontation that threatens to destroy the town; the militants have hidden stolen guns in one of the carnival floats, and the town's police are planning a show of force of their own. At the moment the thunder shakes the town, the deterministic logic that pits these forces against each other is interrupted; outside the infirmary window, "choices were being tossed into the street like dice, like shells, like kola nuts, like jackstones" (294). Depending on the choices made by those caught up in the storm, the thunder might sound the death "knell of the authoritarian age, the thunderous beginning of the new humanism, the new spiritism" (248). Alternatively, it might prefigure an age of social chaos and environmental disaster when "the suffix '-curies' would radically alter all assumptions on which 'security' had once been built" (245–246). The reader, the novel suggests, must make similar choices. These choices begin with the reading itself; the events of the last two chapters are ambiguous, forcing the reader to actively participate in the text.[32]

As I have been arguing, this theory of art as energy exchanged between artist and audience was part of a broader experiment in the practice of professionalism that flourished in the 1960s and was promoted by the federal government through the Community Action Program. Process art, as a way of connecting with inner-city youth, appealed to both black nationalists and liberal poverty program administrators, with the result that the federal government and Ford Foundation funded process art projects seemingly at odds with those organizations' ideological imperatives. Most of the work Bambara published in her lifetime emerged from similar institutional convergences between liberal poverty programs and the Black Arts. Her edited collection, *The Black Woman* (1970), which virtually defined discussions of black feminism in the 1970s, originated in her work for SEEK in the late 1960s. When Bambara wrote *The Sea Birds Are Alive* (1977) and *The Salt Eaters*, she was associated with the Neighborhood Arts Center (NAC), a federally funded institution established in 1975 by the city's first black mayor, Maynard Jackson, with a mission to bring arts programs to Atlanta's black working class. Her fiction was an extension of her work for these organizations. More explicitly than any other US writer, Bambara imagined her fiction as a literary Community Action Agency, one that would bring together local, national, and international communities of oppressed people and organize them to confront specific political problems. *The Salt Eaters*, in particular, attempts to dissolve the boundary between expert writer and inexpert reader and to elicit that reader's maximum feasible participation.

Indeed, Bambara's fiction insistently returns to community action as a vehicle for fashioning coherent communities and provoking them to cultivate a political consciousness. One of the paradoxes of Bambara's work is that as 1960s-style community action played an increasingly smaller role in African American political life, it played a greater role in her fiction. In her first collection of short fiction, *Gorilla, My Love* (1972), two of the stories, "Playin with Punjab" (1967) and "The Lesson" (1972), feature community organizers who try to work with ghetto neighborhoods. In her second collection, *The Sea Birds Are Still Alive,* five stories are set in community centers that are holdovers from the War on Poverty/Black Arts era. In *The Salt Eaters,* similar community centers form the institutional medium through which Minnie's magic affects the town, the nation, and ultimately the world. The activist community in Claybourne revolves around two such institutions: the Southwest Community Infirmary and the Academy of the 7 Arts. The infirmary, where Minnie heals Velma, is a public health center that synthesizes traditional African American healing methods and modern medicine. The academy, run by her husband, Obie, is an alternative school, arts, and political center modeled after Baraka's BARTS and Spirit House. These two institutions are home to both the forces that threaten to fracture the community and those that promise to bind it together. The division between the infirmary and the academy itself embodies a split between "medicine people" and "warriors,"[33] which Bambara believed to be fundamental to the post–civil rights era. Severed from each other, these two factions become impotent; healers like Minnie Ransom retreat into ever more esoteric forms of spiritualism, while warriors like Obie carry out desperate acts unmoored from the community's traditions and customs. At the same time, both institutions reach out to Claybourne's poorest residents, offering them free services and organizing them to challenge the town's government and industries. Meanwhile, a third organization, a traveling, feminist multimedia troupe called the Seven Sisters, represents the possibility of coalition-based community action politics branching out from Claybourne to communities of color across the nation and the world. Each of the seven women in the troupe comes from and stands for a different US racial minority, and they travel to prisons, towns, and universities enacting political dramas. Their organization originates in the War on Poverty; at least one of the sisters began her activist career working for Mobilization for Youth (238), one of the chief community action pilot projects of the Kennedy era.

When Minnie heals Velma, the outpouring of energy activates the central promise of community action: to bring together professionals and the underclass. Since both of these groups in *The Salt Eaters* are black, this encounter promises to suture the class divisions torn open during the civil rights era. Bambara dramatizes this suturing through the figure of Dr. Meadows, a visiting medical intern who dismisses Minnie's healing as nonsense and wanders out of the infirmary to explore the town. When he blunders into Claybourne's working-class neighborhood, he steps on the foot of a black youth lounging on a stoop, surrounded by his friends. The youth evokes Dr. Meadows's stereotypical fears about black juvenile delinquents. Dr. Meadows identifies him as a "welfare man," one of the "small-change half-men who lived off of mothers and children on welfare" (182). These men, for Meadows, are at once effeminate "boymen" (183) because of their secondhand dependence on AFDC and threatening hypermasculine figures because of their propensity for violence. When the men threaten Meadows, it appears that they will become the stereotype he fears. However, Claybourne's institutions have already influenced the town's black youth; when they learn that Meadows is associated with the infirmary, they invite him to drink with them and discuss their grievances against Transchemical, the factory that employs many of the townsfolk. At the moment the thunder strikes, Meadows in turn abandons his insular professionalism. He vows "to give the Hippocratic oath some political meaning in his life" (281) and becomes an activist doctor.

In constructing this vision of community action as collective healing, however, Bambara confronts a problem that troubles all of her fiction and that shaped her activism. The Academy of the 7 Arts is an idealized version of the NAC, which hired Bambara as its first writer-in-residence. Although Bambara promoted the NAC throughout the years she lived in Atlanta, she quit her official position in 1976 after becoming dissatisfied by signs that the institution was too willing to make compromises to satisfy its liberal funders.[34] The problem that Bambara faced in the NAC was one that recurred throughout the history of the Black Arts movement: how to pursue a radical agenda in an institution funded by the government? In trying to work out the possibilities of community action, Bambara's fiction distinguishes between community action that organically arises within a neighborhood and community action shaped by outside organizations. This distinction, for instance, is central to "Playin with Punjab," a story from her first collection that focuses on a mid-1960s Community Action Agency in Brooklyn.[35] The program is run by a white social worker named Miss Ruby, who "came all the way out here to Brooklyn to straighten us folks out and get the rats taken care of and get us jobs and stuff like that" (*G*, 69–70). At first, Miss Ruby successfully organizes the neighborhood. Her greatest achievement is winning over Punjab, a pimp and loan shark who murders those who don't pay him back. Miss Ruby's efforts, however, unravel when she holds an election to pick community leaders to represent the neighborhood on the poverty council. With federal money flooding into Brooklyn, the community assumes that Punjab is "going to get his cut, him being the only kind of leader we could even think of." However, almost nobody votes, and the election goes to a local preacher and "Ann Silver's grandmother" (*G*, 73). After Punjab retaliates by destroying Miss Ruby's office, she abandons the project, and he resumes his usual loan business in the local poolroom.

The story hinges on Miss Ruby's failed attempt to impose a new model of political leadership on the residents of Brooklyn. For the residents, Punjab's leadership is a product of his central position in the community's criminal economy and the ruthless justice he embodies. They perceive this authority as an inevitable outgrowth of ghetto conditions; Violet, Miss Ruby's assistant, imbibes a respect for men like Punjab "along with the vitamins and the dextrose and all them other nutrients that comes tubing in when you're huddled up there in the dark waiting to be born" (*G*, 71). The War on Poverty, the community believes, exists to reinforce Punjab's power; "a whole lotta bread" is coming into the area, and "anybody in a position to be calling themselves doing good is always doing well" (*G*, 73). In understanding the War on Poverty in this way—as a payoff to criminals capable of managing the locals—the residents see the program as an extension of the Democratic Party's traditional mechanism for incorporating ethnic communities into its electoral coalition: the boss system that dominated urban politics until the 1940s. Indeed, the War on Poverty sometimes functioned in exactly this way; Community Action Agencies sought out heads of gangs like the Blackstone Rangers as de facto ghetto leaders. Miss Ruby, in contrast, is trying to bring a democratic model of authority to the community, in which every resident gets one vote and every neighborhood gets two seats on the poverty council. This model challenges Punjab's authority by threatening to dissolve its unspoken, charismatic basis. Punjab does not earn the community's respect by making electoral promises; he gets it by violently retaliating against anyone who crosses him.

For Bambara, the problem with Miss Ruby's challenge to Punjab is not that she promises to bring democracy to ghetto residents unused to exercising their political voice. When the residents complain about the election results, Miss Ruby retorts by invoking recent civil rights victories for African Americans: "If you didn't exercise your right as a voter, shut the hell up" (*G*, 74). Rather, Miss Ruby is doomed because of her contradictory role as a federally funded community organizer. Miss Ruby's purpose is to galvanize the people of Brooklyn to challenge both the city welfare establishment and local criminal underworld. Both of these forces use violence to discipline Brooklyn's residents; welfare workers have "an open line to the cops" (*G*, 71), while Punjab controls a network of thugs.[36] To negotiate the welfare system and underworld, Miss Ruby needs an in-depth understanding of the community's customs; however, as she admits to Violet, she does not "speak negro too good" (*G*, 71). In particular, she is unaware of the extent to which her own office survives only as long as it does because of criminal protection; Punjab stomps those who stare "too hard at Miss Ruby's hips" (*G*, 73), while others keep "the little kids off her car and bricks off her head and panes in her windows" (*G*, 70). Meanwhile, the federal government is powerless to back up Miss Ruby's efforts; hence, the story ends with a nameless federal bureaucrat, armed only with a clipboard, inspecting the ruins of her office. The story underscores the impotence of federal efforts to challenge local power hierarchies by merely importing well-meaning, activist social workers into the ghetto. Any effort to organize the ghetto must originate from within, must be guided by an understanding of local mores, and must be independent of outside funding.

In *The Salt Eaters*, Bambara imagines both the infirmary and the academy as local institutions, deeply rooted in Claybourne's history and Southern folk wisdom. The infirmary dates back to 1871, when it was established by the "Free Coloreds of Claybourne." Even its architecture is a product of traditional custom rather than bureaucratic decision making. The builders ignore "surveyors and other standing-about-with-pipes experts" when choosing a site for the building, instead relying on "wise ones" who "spat a juicy brown glob into a can, shaded their eyes and took a reading of the sun and then pointed—that spot and no other" (120). Other residents plant a sacred tree behind the infirmary, haunted by a loa that protects the building. For over a hundred years, the institution resists successive efforts to assimilate it into the medical establishment; it holds fast "against the so-called setting of standards, the licensure laws, the qualifying exams, the charges of quackery or charlatanism or backwardness" (107). The academy, a product of the Black Arts movement, is of more recent provenance. However, it too is rooted in the community's history. Its building, directly facing the infirmary, was once the "Mason's Lodge" that housed the infirmary's builders before becoming "the Fellowship Hall where the elders of the district arbitrated affairs" (120) and then the academy. Because of this historical provenance, the administrators of the infirmary and academy do not suffer the same problem as Miss Ruby in "Playin with Punjab." The residents recognize them as their own, as natural charismatic leaders akin to Punjab. When Dr. Meadows wanders into Claybourne's working-class neighborhood, he discovers that its residents are on a first-name basis with both Obie and Doc Serge, the man who runs the infirmary.

At the same time, *The Salt Eaters* cannot evade the material underpinnings of community action that plague Miss Ruby's social work in "Playin with Punjab." In constructing Claybourne, Bambara resists the utopian impulse that motivated other black women writers' attempts to imagine Southern folk communities in the 1970s and 1980s. As Dubey points out, both Toni Morrison's *Song of Solomon* (1977) and Gloria Naylor's *Mama Day* (1988) invent Afrocentric communities that are literally no places. In *Song of Solomon*, the town of Shalimar, Virginia, which the novel's protagonist, Milkman Dead, visits in search of his ancestral roots, does not exist on Texaco's road map. In *Mama Day*, Naylor locates her black folk community on an island, Willow Springs, which is not under American jurisdiction and is connected to mainland Virginia only by a fragile bridge. Both communities are entirely self-sufficient, with no government, no social services, and no industry. According to Dubey, by insisting on the impossibility and isolation of Shalimar and Willow Springs, Morrison and Naylor evade an obvious problem raised by black women writers' attraction to organic communities that flourished under Jim Crow: "to acknowledge the real horrors of the segregated South (and thus to support its destruction) but also to rescue from it a paradigm of community." Their version of the Southern folk aesthetic "is viable and sustaining only for literary culture,"[37] which explains why they project it into utopian spaces untouched by the material constraints that shape actual black communities. *The Salt Eaters*, as part of its process-based insistence on dissolving boundaries between art and life, refuses this evasion. Bambara locates Claybourne in a modern-day, urbanized South and insists on the town's imbrication in its region's economy. In particular, Claybourne is both dependent on and threatened by Transchemical and the nuclear plant, the town's principal employers and polluters.

This insistence on identifying the economic underpinnings of community action, however, poses a problem for Bambara. Both the infirmary and academy offer free services to ghetto residents, which means that they can never be economically self-sustaining. Instead, they are dependent on suspect figures capable of attracting outside funding. In the case of the infirmary, this figure is Doc Serge, the hospital administrator. Doc Serge disguises the means he uses to keep the infirmary solvent, portraying himself as a magician who has mastered the power of money. When a student asks him about his administrative prowess, he takes out a dollar bill and explains its arcane symbols. Pressed further, Doc Serge appeals to his own understanding of the natural laws that govern the universe: "Take money. If you want it, getting it is the easiest thing in the world. One need understand just a few simple principles that govern supply and demand. . . . Simple laws is all. Laws as inexorable as gravity" (126–127). In a novel about faith healing, in which characters practice clairvoyance, the greatest magic lies in the ability to conjure money. In particular, money's central mystery lies in its ability to yoke together capitalism and black nationalism. Explaining the dollar's symbolism, Doc Serge draws attention to its Latin inscription, *Novus Ordo Seclorum* (new order of the ages). When the founding fathers invented this slogan, they were thinking of America's manifest destiny, imagining that "the new age and the new order began with [their] arrival on these shores." They neglected the nation's "latent destiny," which is "a Neptunian thing, a Black thing, an us thing" (134). Evoking Freudian hermeneutics, Doc Serge imagines black nationalist institutions like the infirmary and academy as a return of the American repressed; the black labor force that the American economic system exploited for centuries is finally becoming visible and laying claim to its own communities.

However, Bambara offers a decidedly nonmagical interpretation of Doc Serge's administration of the hospital, one that reintroduces the class divisions supposedly overcome by community action. Before running the infirmary, Doc Serge was a pimp and gangster who ran a gambling house. Successful pimping, he explains, depends on the same mastery of natural law as successful administration. If you're going to be a "prime player" rather than a "mere pussy peddler" (134), "you've got to study the principles that govern the game. . . . Principles such as the law of reciprocity, the principle of attraction and repulsion, good ole supply and demand" (133). The latent content of American capitalism is not black nationalism but rather the exchange of bodies for money that characterizes pimping, slave ownership, and wage labor. Administering the infirmary, Doc Serge suggests, is not so much a break from this practice as an extension of it; Doc Serge pimps out his institution to white liberals in exchange for the funds he needs to run it. At various points, Doc Serge reflects that his management of the healers who staff the infirmary is identical to his former relationship with his prostitutes. Observing Velma in the final stages of her recovery, aware that after the ordeal she will become a powerful healer like Minnie, Doc Serge reflects that Velma is "like the women in his stable years ago . . . women who studied themselves for some tangible measure of their allure, their specialness, but never quite knowing what it was. Money was the tangible evidence he offered of their attractiveness and his, their power and his, till they would do anything to keep his attention and his answers" (268). For Doc Serge, money is intimately linked to sexual attraction and faith healing. It is the pimp/administrator's way of providing evidence of the prostitute/healer's power. At the same time, it allows the pimp/administrator to appropriate that power, to keep his women in thrall to him as he sells their abilities to others.

The divisive consequences of outside funding are even more apparent in the case of the academy, which relies on grants provided by a black liberal politician named Jay Patterson, whom the academy supports for public office in an effort to bring more black faces to local and state government. In one of the novel's flashback sequences, Velma and a group of female activists working for the academy highlight the gender inequities that result from this association. The academy's women do most of the organizational work to ensure Patterson's election: drawing up mailing lists, catering, booking halls, printing flyers. In return, the academy's men amass the symbolic and material rewards of Patterson's patronage. "Everybody gets paid off but us," Velma complains. "Do any of you have a grant for one of us? Any government contracts? Any no-work-all-pay posts at a college, those of you on boards?" (36–37). Like the infirmary, the academy depends on a kind of pimping. The institution's men sell female labor to enjoy upper-class luxuries available to them only through outside connections; women tolerate their exploitation out of a sense of loyalty to the cause. This practice has roots in the civil rights movement; Velma remembers a demonstration in the 1960s, which was supposed to culminate in a speech by a prominent civil rights leader. The demonstration is rained out, leaving the activists, who are mostly women, stranded in a muddy field with little food and inadequate medicine or shelter. Going to a nearby hotel for help, she discovers the speaker, his cronies, and a group of high-class prostitutes they have hired, "hair glistening fresh under stocking caps and fro cloths, the men carrying silver ice buckets and laughing with the women" (39). Civil rights leaders, Velma suggests, established themselves as a new elite through exploitation of the rank and file. The demonstration's speaker, in particular, represents what Velma perceives as the professionalization of civil rights leadership, as he elevates the style of protest leadership over its substance: "He looked a bit like King, had a delivery similar to Malcolm's, dressed like Stokely, had glasses like Rap, but she'd never heard him say anything useful or offensive" (35). This professionalization, enabled by liberal funding, reintroduces splits between leaders, activists, and community members that Bambara, unlike Walker, imagined could be sutured through community action.

The Salt Eaters also points to another danger, one that finally threatens to unravel the participatory professionalism that subtends both Walker and Bambara's process aesthetic. Both *Meridian* and *The Salt Eaters* envisage a new breed of civil rights workers whose activism is equally informed by professional disciplines like medicine and social work and by folk practices dating back to African Americans' first arrival on the continent. This vision informs their respective notions of the Southern folk aesthetic; black woman authors will similarly synthesize folk wisdom and the literary arts. Figures like Meridian Hill and Velma Henry embody this new synthesis; Meridian resolves to keep alive "the song of the people" (201) through her future activism, while Velma, after her healing, is "ready for training" (293) in Minnie Ransom's lore. *The Salt Eaters*, however, highlights the shape this synthesis was taking in the 1970s and 1980s: folk wisdom was itself becoming professionalized, turning into a specialized knowledge cultivated by experts trained in the arts of new age medicine. Velma's healing, which takes place in an infirmary observed by "visiting interns, nurses and technicians" (9), exemplifies this routinized root magic. The healing is part of a tightly scheduled itinerary meant to reinforce the infirmary's reputation in "radical medical circles" (10). The Seven Sisters, the multiracial, feminist troupe who travel the United States giving multimedia performances informed by their respective cultures, embody a similar professionalization of new age knowledge. The women, Courtney Thorsson comments, draw on the same syncretism as Bambara's novel; "they make use of tools as diverse as tarot cards and computers."[38] As they sit on the bus to Claybourne, "fumbling with cameras, tape recorders, weird machines, clipboards, note pads, babbling about corn and rice and plutonium bombs and South Africa and Brer Rabbit and palm oil and the CIA and woodcuts" (67), they are overheard by the black bus driver, Fred Holt, who reflects that their discourse is "baffling" (68) to working-class people like himself. Reading this scene, critics tend to moralize about Fred's obtuseness; Fred's "oppressive working conditions" are "inseparable from the labor concerns the women wish to address," and "whether or not he knows it, he is connected to labor issues worldwide, especially in communities of color."[39] However, Fred's bafflement in the face of the Seven Sisters' activism points to a problem that besets Bambara's entire novel, which she claimed she was writing for an audience very much like Fred—an audience of men and women whom she met on the bus or in the wash house.[40] *The Salt Eaters* makes extraordinary demands of that audience. Not only must they enjoy a work that puts into play a range of high-modernist literary techniques; they must also accept the validity of tarot, astrology, faith healing, communication with the dead, and other new age beliefs and practices. When Bambara published her novel, those practices were chiefly marketed to middle-class consumers as a simulacrum of the very folk wisdom that Bambara wanted to preserve in her book. Reading Bambara's process art, in other words, depends on the very expertise that the novel tries to dissolve. Ultimately, neither Walker's appeal to the dialectic of civil rights activism, nor Bambara's appeal to magic, can heal the class divisions they identify in their fiction. Both novels attempt to enact a process aesthetic, formally dissolving the boundaries between literary expertise and folk tradition. However, the novels reinscribe those same boundaries, turning folk tradition into a retrospective creation of literary experts.

6   Who Belongs in the University?

One of the central conceits of Philip Roth's *The Human Stain* (2000) is that the protagonist's plight mirrors that of President Bill Clinton.[1] The novel traces the downfall of Coleman Silk, a former dean of Athena College who becomes a pariah after his innocent classroom query about two absent students, "Does anybody know these people? Do they exist or are they spooks?" (*HS*, 6). The two students are black, and they accuse him of racism, an accusation picked up and amplified by the college's politically correct faculty. During the summer of 1998, in the midst of the Monica Lewinsky scandal, Coleman's notoriety deepens when he dates a college janitor, a domestic abuse survivor less than half his age. Both Coleman and Clinton are victims of what Roth's narrator, Nathan Zuckerman, calls "an enormous piety binge, a purity binge" (*HS*, 2). Nathan's goal is to understand Coleman's all-too-human failings and cast him as an authentic American type. By extension, he will do the same for Clinton; while William F. Buckley calls for Clinton's castration, Nathan dreams of a banner draped across the White House, reading "A HUMAN BEING LIVES HERE" (*HS*, 3).

This parallel between Coleman and Clinton is not completely surprising in the context of Roth's work. As is the case with the writers that Michael Szalay discusses in *Hip Figures* (Norman Mailer, John Updike, Ralph Ellison, and Joan Didion, among others), the Democratic Party has always been central to Roth's oeuvre. When Roth imagines a dystopian alternative reality in *The Plot against America* (2004), it is one in which the Democrats lose the 1940 election and the victorious Republicans launch an anti-Semitic pogrom.[2] For Roth, the Democrats are inextricably linked to the Jewish American ethnic identity that he explores throughout his work; to be a Newark Jew in the 1940s is to vote for the party of Franklin Delano Roosevelt. Indeed, *The Human Stain*'s analogy between Coleman and Clinton is central to the novel's political allegory: Coleman's college faces the same challenges as the liberal coalition embodied by the Democratic Party. Both of these entities are threatened by outsiders, and the novel institutes a series of strategies for defending the academy and coalition. At Athena College, these outsiders take the form of Coleman's student accusers. As Coleman comments in the disciplinary hearing that follows the charges, the two students do not "belong in school" (*HS*, 18). The college's problem, Coleman suggests, is that it has become too open to those who do not belong, and this openness imperils the institution. Similarly, as Roth shows throughout his American trilogy (*American Pastoral* [1997],[3] *I Married a Communist* [1998], and *The Human Stain*), the Democratic Party's liberal coalition has been strained by trying to encompass groups (especially lower-class African Americans) whose political demands exceed what the party can accomplish. Academic political correctness is merely the most recent instantiation of this impulse to include the excluded.

As I have shown throughout the previous chapters, including the excluded was central to the participatory professionalism that flourished in the 1960s during the War on Poverty. This inclusion took the form of a partial dismantling of expertise in an effort to dissolve boundaries between experts and the poor. This supposed inclusion, however, came at a cost: the insistence that participatory professionals had to cross an ontological divide generated by the poor's cultural difference. During the Clinton era, this conception of the poor's cultural difference culminated in the Democratic Party's strategic embrace of the underclass discourse that the American right had propagated since the 1970s. This strategy was part of the Democratic Leadership Council's (DLC) attempt to appeal to white working- and middle-class voters who had defected to the Republicans in the 1980s. Calling for a return to "the promise of equal opportunity for all to get ahead and special privilege for none,"[4] the DLC promised the "end to welfare as we know it." This policy culminated in Clinton's support for two signature pieces of legislation that defined his administration's impact on minority communities: the Violent Crime Control and Law Enforcement Act (1994), which accelerated the mass incarceration of black and Latino/Latina men; and the Personal Responsibility and Work Opportunity Act (1996), which terminated AFDC, the primary New Deal program that helped low-income mothers. Under the Clinton administration, the War on Poverty gave way to the War on Welfare, and the Democratic Party largely abandoned the participatory professionalism it promoted in the 1960s in favor of neoliberal policies that pushed low-income Americans into low-wage, temporary work.

In the American trilogy, Roth traces the racial tensions that helped spur the rise of the DLC and, at times, seems to affirm the necessity of the Democratic Party's 1990s conservative turn. *The Human Stain* satirizes liberal academics who extend "special privileges" to minority students who expect equal results without demonstrating equal capability; the trilogy as a whole traces this attitude to the 1960s, when liberals were sympathetic to the demands of the Black Power Movement and New Left. Instead, Roth affirms an alternative vision of the welfare state creating meritocratic institutions that reward anyone with the right combination of intelligence and work ethic, regardless of his or her class or race. This vision informs Nathan's hagiographic portrait of Coleman, an African American secretly passing as a Jewish American classics professor. While Coleman's black accusers do not belong in the university, Coleman does by virtue of his capacity for humanistic learning, which allows him to transcend his black working-class origins. This conception of the academy, I argue, is rooted in Roth's career-long rejection of midcentury process aesthetics. Roth became a novelist in the process era, and early reviewers alternately hailed and derided his most popular fiction, *Portnoy's Complaint* (1969),[5] as an example of that era's antiformalist literary art. However, Roth consistently rejected the idea that literary texts can or should seek to dissolve boundaries between authors and readers. Instead, he insisted that literary works create transclass and transracial communities of autonomous readers who submit to the discipline required by the text. In *The Human Stain*, Roth conceives of the academy in similar terms, as an antiprocess institution that rewards students who approach it on its own terms.

At the same time, the novel deploys a sociological understanding of the conditions that allow class and racial outsiders to take advantage of educational institutions, an understanding largely absent from mid-1990s DLC policy and rhetoric. Coleman's trajectory from his working-class origins in East Orange, New Jersey, to his deanship at Athena College parallels that of the 1940s generation of Jewish Americans whose identity he appropriates; by becoming Jewish, Coleman joins the vanguard of the expanding postwar professional class. However, as the American trilogy underscores, this trajectory is dependent on specific historical conditions: a combination of post–World War II affluence, Keynesian economic policies, and the mass expansion of postsecondary education. These conditions erode with urban deindustrialization in the 1950s and 1960s, making it more difficult for future generations of working-class men and women to follow the same path. Even more problematically, Coleman's

upward mobility depends on a specific kind of humanistic cultural capital that
was devalued with the rise of the postwar professional class. In his role as dean,
Coleman facilitates this devaluation; attempting to implement meritocratic
standards for faculty and students, he modernizes postsecondary education at
Athena in ways that render his own expertise obsolete. The novel thus highlights the fragility of humanistic learning and the transracial, meritocratic elite
that it supposedly enables. Ultimately, Coleman falls victim to the currents of
creative destruction that he helps unleash within the academy; as his calumny
following the spooks scandal demonstrates, he too no longer belongs at Athena.
His presidential double, Bill Clinton, fell prey to a similar dynamic. During
the Monika Lewinsky affair, he became stained with the same abjection that
he militated against black welfare mothers and criminal men in his attempt
to modernize the American workforce. Ultimately, *The Human Stain* suggests,
while the distinction between the deserving and undeserving undergirds the
New Deal social order that Roth nostalgically evokes throughout his trilogy, it
also sows the seeds of that order's destruction. In so doing, that distinction also
imperils Roth's own sense of the value and possibility of a literary vocation.

Against Promiscuous Institutions

When Roth published *Portnoy's Complaint*, reviewers struggled to reconcile the
novel with his earlier fiction. While early books like *Goodbye, Columbus* (1959)
and *Letting Go* (1962) established him as the "literary heir of Henry James,"[6]
Portnoy revealed Roth to be a looser, more transgressive writer, in tune with
countercultural currents reshaping the literary field.[7] Roth himself confirmed
this alignment of his novel with antiformalist trends in contemporary literature. The atmosphere of the 1960s inspired him "to try out a new voice, a fourth
voice, a less page-bound voice than the voice of *Goodbye, Columbus*." However,
Roth stopped short of identifying his work with process art. In particular, he rejected reviewers' tendency to read *Portnoy* as a confessional work that collapsed
the distinction between art and life. The voice he developed in *Portnoy* was a
stage act, a "comic impersonation" that still adhered to the modernist principle
of authorial impersonality. More specifically, in terms that echo William Wimsatt Jr. and Monroe Beardsley's affective and intentional fallacies, Roth insisted
that his fiction's meaning is independent of reader response and authorial intent. Asked about his intended audience, he claimed that he had no audience in
mind when he wrote: "what I want is for the work to communicate itself as fully

as it can, in accordance with its own intentions. Precisely so that it can be read, *but on its own terms.*" These textual intentions were distinct from his own ideas as an author; he often used fiction to test ideas that he distrusted, and these ideas were opaque to him until they had been run "through the blades of the fiction-making machine, to be ground into something else."[8] This New Critical insistence on his work's objectlike independence culminated in the ever-more elaborate games that he built into his fictions after *Portnoy*.[9] Especially in his novels featuring his three authorial stand-ins, David Kapesh, Nathan Zucker-man, and Philip Roth, he enacted the readerly temptation to interpret his books as process fictions. However, he repeatedly undercut that temptation, insisting on his work's independence from his own or his readers' lived experience.

Not coincidentally, *Portnoy*, the novel in which he first enfolded process fiction within his product-oriented modernist art, is also the text in which he most directly addressed the War on Poverty and the participatory professionalism it engendered. Roth's protagonist, Alexander Portnoy, is an archetypal poverty warrior; in his role as "Assistant Commissioner for The City of New York Commission on Human Opportunity" (*PC*, 107), he investigates instances of discrimination against minorities, helping them vent their grievances against hospitals, landlords, trade unions, and other institutions. He is the kind of lawyer whom Jean and Edgar Cahn, the chief theorists behind Legal Services, imagined would be central to the War on Poverty: someone who channels the "civilian perspective" to challenge the bureaucratic institutions of the welfare state.[10] This profession, however, is only one side of Alexander's life; he is also a sexual pervert, involved in a sadistic affair with The Monkey, a semi-illiterate lingerie model whom he picks up on the streets of Manhattan. Both Alexander and his psychoanalyst, Spielvogel, believe that his liberalism and sexual perversion contradict each other; Portnoy's Complaint is "a disorder in which strongly felt ethical and altruistic impulses are perpetually warring with extreme sexual longings, often of a perverse nature" (*PC*, 1). However, the novel suggests that these two sides of Alexander are one and the same. The Monkey is the kind of white Appalachian whom President Kennedy imagined would be the face of antipoverty efforts in the 1960s; she is born in rural West Virginia, a "woman who could neither read nor write nor count all that high, and to top things off, hadn't a single molar in her head" (*PC*, 154). Their affair unfolds as a perverse allegory for the Community Action Program. Alexander educates her, attempting to turn her into a self-conscious, proletarian-born member of the professional class. He does so through a literary curriculum that, he thinks, speaks directly to her class origins. His reading list, which he titles "Humiliated Minorities: An Introduction," reveals "the entire history of brutality and terror practiced by and upon the American laboring class, from which she was descended" (*PC*, 208), with texts drawn from Popular Front culture of the 1930s and 1940s. The problem with this pedagogical effort is that, in attempting to elicit The Monkey's participatory response, it reinforces her cultural difference, interpellating her as representative white trash. Indeed, Alexander's educational program is undermined by the fact that he both abhors and fetishizes that difference; The Monkey is the archetypal, lower-class promiscuous shiksa of Alexander's masturbatory fantasies.

Alexander's education of The Monkey highlights the aesthetic and political practices that Roth eschews in his fiction. Roth assails literary texts and political gestures that pretend to incorporate readers and disempowered persons in the cocreation of literary meaning and political power. In contrast, he affirms texts and politics that facilitate readers' transformation into autonomous cultural and political agents. Hence, Alexander's sole success in educating The Monkey occurs when he no longer tries to craft a participatory curriculum but instead spontaneously shares his own enjoyment of a high-modernist text utterly alien to her experience. On an idyllic road trip through Vermont, he recites Yeats's "Leda and the Swan" after they have made love. He fears that the poem merely draws attention to the "chasm" that lies between them: "I am smart and you are dumb" (*PC*, 192). However, once Alexander explains the poem's mythological context, it provokes an erotic response, making her "pussy all wet" (*PC*, 194). The Monkey, Roth suggests, can transcend her straitened upbringing only when she confronts and gains pleasure from a challenging art object on its own terms. At this moment, a transfiguration occurs that mirrors Leda's congress with the swan; she is penetrated by something completely other. A similar confluence of art and class uplift takes place in Roth's first novella, *Goodbye, Columbus*, when the book's protagonist, Neil Klugman, finds a job as an assistant librarian. Discovering a young black child lurking in the stacks, he guides him to the art section and facilitates his enthusiasm for a volume of Gauguin reproductions, against the wishes of librarian administrators.[11] Like Alexander when he reads "Leda and the Swan," Neil provides the conditions that allow the child to pursue his education on his own terms.[12] In Ross Posnock's terms, Neil facilitates the child's entry into "'the kingdom of culture,' free of racial and class barriers,"[13] a concept that

Posnock uses to situate Roth in a transnational humanist tradition extending from W. E. B. Du Bois to Milan Kundera.

This antiprocess conception of autonomous cultural education lies at the heart of Roth's satire of the postmodern academy in *The Human Stain*. In this novel, Roth develops a model of the university that parallels his modernist, object-oriented conception of the literary text. *The Human Stain* tells the story of the rise and fall of Coleman Silk, who disguises his black working-class origins to pass as a secular Jew. Coleman's rise depends on the kind of humanist education that Klugman tries to make available to the black child in *Goodbye, Columbus*. Growing up in East Orange in the 1940s and 1950s, he is immersed in a black bourgeois family that values humanistic education; his father sees to it "that the children learned not just to speak properly but to think logically, to classify, to analyze, to describe, to enumerate, to learn not only English but Latin or Greek" (*HS*, 317). This education, for the Silks, is not always enough to ward off the effects of discrimination; although he is trained as an optician, Coleman's father can find work only as a Pullman porter. Nevertheless, education allows the Silks to act as if racism does not affect them while they acquire the knowledge and skills that will eventually benefit their children. When Coleman's father comes home after being insulted by one of his customers, he transmutes his rage into "pedagogical" lessons for his children (*HS*, 103). Eschewing physical violence, he disciplines his children "with words. With speech. With what he called 'the language of Chaucer, Shakespeare, and Dickens'" (*HS*, 92). Instead of taking them to the prizefights, he takes them "to the Metropolitan Museum of New York to see the armor" (*HS*, 94). Humanistic education is both a weapon and armor for poor minorities, allowing them to successfully make their way in a discriminatory society. In Coleman's case, the culture he assimilates from his family, and from New York and New Jersey's public institutions, enables him to shed his racial particularity. He rejects the "they" of racist whites and the "oppressive we" of race-conscious African Americans to become "the greatest of the great *pioneers* of the I" (*HS*, 108). In so doing, he becomes an institutional caretaker of the universalist culture he revered as a child: a classics professor who teaches Greek and Latin to a new generation of youth.

By way of contrast, the novel excoriates the politics of those who condescend to lower-class minorities, attempting to incorporate them into educational institutions on the basis of their particularistic identities. Roth's academic satire focuses on two issues: affirmative action and the liberalization of the arts curriculum. Staking out opposing positions on these issues, the novel pits Coleman, an old-fashioned humanist, against an array of postmodern, feminist, and critical race scholars. For Coleman, admissions should be restricted to those with an aptitude for learning, regardless of their race or ethnicity, and the curriculum should be restricted to the best texts in the Western canon. The faculty who oppose him want to bring more minority students to Athena, even if they are unprepared. Delphine Roux, Coleman's faculty nemesis, thus defends Coleman's black student accusers throughout the spooks affair. One of the accusers, she explains, fails to attend class because she is "too intimidated by the racism emanating from her white professors to work up the courage to go to class" (*HS*, 17). Opening admissions also entails changing the curriculum, introducing new courses that feature minority writers, and changing the old courses so that they appeal to newer students. Indeed, Coleman suggests that the entire spooks incident is driven by the faculty's desire to make the institution more inclusive: "more black students, more black professors. Representation—that was the issue" (*HS*, 17). The problem, the novel insists, extends throughout the educational system. "In my parents' day and into yours and mine," Coleman's sister Ernestine explains to Nathan about the inner-city high school students she teaches, "it used to be the person who fell short. Now it's the discipline. Reading the classics is too difficult, therefore it's the classics that are to blame. Today the student asserts his incapacity as a privilege" (*HS*, 330–331). This rejection of difficulty leads to a revised curriculum that teaches students only what they already know. Ernestine complains about the impact of Black History month on inner-city schools: her students will "only read a biography of a black by a black" (*HS*, 329). The problem with this participatory openness to new students and new subject matter is that it disguises a more fundamental educational closure. Students like Coleman's accusers and Ernestine's inner-city teenagers are closed to the education that universities and high schools offer. They are like the naïve, affective readers that Wimsatt and Beardsley exclude from literary criticism in "The Affective Fallacy"; they cannot respond to that education on its own terms. Meanwhile, politically correct professors are in turn closed to their students; like Alexander Portnoy when he draws up his educational program for The Monkey, they interpellate students as "humiliated minorities."

This antiprocess critique of affirmative action and multicultural education means that *The Human Stain* closely tracks conservative jeremiads against the postmodern academy such as Allan Bloom's *The Closing of the American*

Mind (1987).[14] Bloom similarly presented himself as a beleaguered Jewish classics professor, trained in the 1950s, now facing what Coleman calls "the dumbest generation in American history" (*HS*, 192). Like Roth, Bloom explored the apparent paradox that the American academy's increasing openness—to new subject matter and to new students—leads to cultural, political, and intellectual closure. Multicultural education that teaches students to respect other cultures, he argued, produces thoughtless conformism, instructing students that "the rest of the world is a drab diversity," while robbing them of any understanding of their own cultural tradition. Affirmative action policies, meanwhile, institutionalize "the worst aspects of separatism," turning black students into a lower-ranked caste whose accomplishments will always be suspect. Both multiculturalism and affirmative action, he argued, mask an underlying contempt for the students they try to accommodate. However, disciplines such as classics "necessarily look closed and rigid," insofar as they are genuinely alien to students and teach them to question their present-day prejudices. Bloom contrasted the generation of students he taught in the 1980s with that which passed through the academy between the 1940s and early 1960s. The earlier generation, which usually entered the academy without much prior learning, was radically open to the university's traditional curriculum; they were driven by a "boundless thirst for significant awareness."[15] The later generation combined ignorance with a profound disinterest in learning anything other than the commonplaces they absorbed from popular culture.

For both Roth and Bloom, the question is not one of excluding all cultural outsiders; Bloom was the son of Jewish social workers, while Coleman is a middle-class African American passing as a working-class Jew. Rather, the point is to admit students whose selective openness matches that of the university itself. Roth allegorizes this match between professor, pupil, and institution through his misogynist caricature of Delphine, the French feminist who spearheads the campaign to disgrace Coleman. Delphine begins her academic career in France as a student with the right kind of openness. Her animus against Coleman is driven by her repressed admiration for his traditional humanism, which makes "her sometimes feel shallow" because "the humanist is the very part of her own self that she sometimes feels herself betraying" (*HS*, 266). In particular, Coleman reminds her of her classics professor at the lycée, with whom she has an undergraduate affair. The affair's educational impact is symbolized by the ring that Delphine's professor gives her. It depicts "Danäe receiving Zeus as a shower of gold" (*HS*, 186), another image, like Leda and the Swan, of impregnation by something completely other. At Athena, in contrast, Delphine becomes closed—especially to the underprivileged students whom she attempts to bring into the academy. In particular, she reveals her closure through her fear of dating minorities. As she sits down to write a personal ad, she is paralyzed, worried that she might attract the wrong kind of person: "What if he had AIDS," she asks, "what if he was violent, vicious, married, or on Medicare? . . . And what about race?" (*HS*, 261). As a result of this closure, in America, Delphine's love life is barren; she is terrified of attracting anyone different from herself. The key, Roth suggests, is for the academy to choose its lovers carefully—to act like a passionate but selective mistress and not like a prostitute or prude.

Strategic Conservatism

However, if Roth incorporates cultural conservatism into his work, he does so to preserve the liberalism that he identifies with the New Deal welfare state. *The Human Stain*'s concern with admitting the right kinds of students to the university has little to do with the actual problems facing elite liberal arts colleges like Athena in the 1990s, where low-income minority students were few and far between and were becoming scarcer thanks to rising tuition.[16] Rather, like his characterization of The Monkey, Roth's portrait of Coleman's black accusers gestures toward a broader critique of the Great Society–era impulse to encompass the particularistic politics of Black Power and other identity movements. Roth's central project, throughout the American trilogy that concludes with *The Human Stain*, is to trace the evolution of post–World War II liberalism. In Sean McCann's terms, the trilogy "offers an intensely disenchanted view of the course of postwar liberalism—a history that Roth views, as his frequent references to Shakespeare and Sophocles emphasize, as a tragic tale of great aspiration leading to terrible self-destruction."[17] In particular, the trilogy follows the decline of the New Deal coalition that propelled the Democrats to victory in the 1930s and 1940s. Each novel explores a moment of crisis for that coalition as it struggles to fend off challenges from the left: *I Married a Communist* charts the collapse of Popular Front culture in the 1940s and 1950s; *American Pastoral* explores the radicalism of the 1960s; and *The Human Stain* engages with academic political correctness. One of Roth's anxieties is that these challenges will transform the party and the liberalism it espouses, to the point that they dissolve the nexus between Jewish ethnicity and Democratic affiliation at the core of his nostalgic fiction. When Nathan attends his forty-fifth high school reunion near the opening of *American Pastoral*, he discovers that many of his Jewish schoolmates now vote Republican. Alan Meisner, whose father had a "rotogravure picture of FDR framed on the wall" (*AP*, 57) of his dry cleaning shop, is now a Republican-appointed superior court judge.

One of the reasons for this decline is the Vietnam War, which features centrally in both *American Pastoral* and *The Human Stain*. However, the primary challenge facing the Democratic coalition is the same one that faces Roth's childhood neighborhood of Weequahic, New Jersey, which transforms over the course of the trilogy from a vibrant, multiethnic community into a black slum: how to accommodate the changing demographics of the Great Migration. In *I Married a Communist*, Jewish and African American relations are relatively unproblematic. Nathan Zuckerman's political awakening begins in high school at a stage reenactment of the Lincoln-Douglas debates, where he leads his fellow students in booing Douglas's defense of white supremacy. By the 1960s, the relationship has soured. *American Pastoral* charts Swede Levov's bewilderment over the growing radicalism of urban African Americans, especially after the 1967 Newark riots. While young Nathan idolizes Paul Robeson in *I Married a Communist*, shaking hands with him at a rally for Henry Wallace, Swede and other 1960s liberal Jews find nothing to admire in their era's black radicals. Swede's father complains that the family business, a Newark-based glove manufacturing company, "is going down the drain because of that son of a bitch LeRoi Jones" (*AP*, 163), while Swede engages in imaginary debates with a hallucination of Angela Davis. The problem, for Roth, is that the nature of black protest has changed. In the 1940s, Nathan can identify with a black Communist like Robeson because he presents his politics as transracially American; Robeson leads a protest against the 1948 Mundt-Nixon Bill by singing "Ol' Man River" at the foot of the Washington Monument.[18] In the 1960s, in contrast, the new generation of black leaders rejects America as a nation and symbol in favor of racial particularism. Swede, in particular, is troubled by black radicals' rejection of the ideal that motivated his parents: the idea of America as a place of unlimited opportunity for those who work hard. Angela Davis and other black and New Left radicals instead perceive America as an imperialist power that has imposed its rule on African Americans at home and colonial subjects abroad.

Faced with this ideological challenge, Jewish American liberals like Swede have no choice but to amend their political creed. In Swede's case, the problem is especially acute, since his daughter Merry, identifying with black radicals at home and the Viet Cong abroad, becomes a New Left terrorist. What Swede must abandon, the novel suggests, is his "tolerant respect for every position," which prevents him from wholly condemning individuals and political groups that want to destroy him. "Sure, it's 'liberal,'" his brother explains, "I know, a liberal father. But what does that mean? What is at the center of it?" (*AP*, 279). To survive as a manufacturer and as a Democrat, Swede must extricate himself from Newark's black working class and from the radical ideologies that incite that class to riot. The problem he faces, however, is that there is no institutionalized alternative to his centerless liberalism, which by the late 1960s has become that of the Democratic Party itself. *American Pastoral* concludes with a dinner party that Swede holds for his father and several of his liberal friends in the summer of 1973. Conversation revolves around Watergate and *Deep Throat*, the X-rated pornographic movie that became a surprise mainstream hit. While Watergate is the product of Republican corruption, *Deep Throat*, one of Swede's friends suggests, is a film that mostly appeals to "McGovernites" (*AP*, 344). Just as McGovern's candidacy signals the Democrats' openness to all of the various groups that challenged the party from the left throughout the 1960s, *Deep Throat* signals his voters' openness to "the permissiveness. Abnormality cloaked as ideology. The perpetual protest" (*AP*, 347) that characterized the 1960s.

In *The Human Stain*, finally, the permissive liberalism of the 1960s lives on in the halls of academe, which has assimilated the demands of black radicals and other 1960s protesters in the form of multicultural education, affirmative action, and postmodern theory. In their relationship to students like Coleman's black accusers, Athena's faculty accept the ideology of radicals like Angela Davis, affirming their duty to make amends for the nation's history of racism. Even as Roth highlights the hothouse isolation of academic political correctness, his novel draws much of its pathos from an implicit homology between academic and national politics. As John Guillory observes, this homology was a pervasive feature of the 1980s and 1990s canon wars between cultural conservatives and multiculturalists; both sides assumed that "the process of *selection*, by which certain works are designated canonical, others noncanonical," could be mapped onto "the process of *exclusion*, by which socially defined minorities are excluded from the exercise of power or from political representation."[19] Roth underscores this homology by linking Coleman's plight to that of President Bill Clinton. Coleman's one-man fight against the forces threatening the academy, the novel suggests, is an extension of Clinton's strategic employment of cultural conservatism to refashion his party's liberalism. The DLC's rise to prominence was driven by the need to reconstruct the New Deal coalition, reintegrating white ethnic and working-class voters who fled the party in the 1970s and 1980s.[20] This strategy was central to Clinton's 1992 presidential campaign, in which he promised to get tough on crime and "end welfare as we know it," while distancing himself from black leaders like Jesse Jackson who articulated the demands of lower-class African Americans and black activists like Sister Souljah who espoused ideas offensive to white voters.

In particular, in the distinctions it draws between deserving and undeserving minority students, *The Human Stain* echoes the kind of underclass discourse that the DLC employed throughout the 1990s in the lead-up to welfare reform. Roth's racial politics in *The Human Stain* have divided critics since the book was published. As most readers have noted, the novel posits an antiessentialist notion of race, in which, as one critic puts it, whiteness is "a fluid state, a state one can perform too well."[21] For Coleman, race is something one chooses to perform, rather than an identity ascribed at birth. At the same time, the American trilogy's overall representation of black characters has struck many readers as problematic. Larry Schwartz, the trilogy's harshest critic, argues that Roth draws on "race-inflected shibboleths" about inner-city crime to depict Newark's decline.[22] *American Pastoral*'s Swede Levov flees the city after being carjacked by a black gang, while *I Married a Communist*'s Murray Ringold leaves after a black mugger kills his wife. Roth, in fact, tends to dichotomize his black characters, distinguishing between those, like Coleman, who transcend their race to join a transracial professional elite, and those, like his accusers, who remain trapped in their poverty and racial particularity. Coleman, as one character puts it, is a "model Negro" (*HS*, 86) by virtue of his work ethic and facility for humanistic learning. His accusers, however, are unable to assert themselves against adverse circumstances. Delphine explains that one of them fails to attend class because "she is from a rather difficult background, in that she separated from her immediate family in tenth grade and lived with relatives" (*HS*, 18). Throughout the American trilogy, nonmodel African Americans demand access to educational and consumer goods, without the capacity for disciplined hard work that makes those goods possible. Hiding in his factory during the Newark riot, Swede observes that the black rioters are taking illicit shortcuts, indulging in the American "appetite for ownership" by looting Newark's stores (*AP*, 268). This demand for immediate gratification transforms Newark from "the city where they manufactured everything" into "the car-theft capital of the world" (*AP*, 24).

The underclass discourse that Clinton and the DLC employed in the years leading up to the Personal Responsibility and Work Opportunity Act similarly distinguished between model and not-so-model minorities. Beginning with *The Negro Family*, this discourse routinely differentiated the black underclass from the black bourgeoisie; the black community, Moynihan cautioned, is "dividing between a stable middle-class group that is steadily growing stronger and more successful, and an increasingly disorganized and disadvantaged lower-class group."[23] More generally, underclass theory distinguished between entire races based on their cultural proximity to the white middle class, extending a model minority discourse traceable back to nineteenth-century texts like *How the Other Half Lives*. Clinton, in his June 3, 1992, appearance on the *Arsenio Hall Show*, offered a typical example of this distinction. Linking the recent Rodney King riots to the disappearance of Los Angeles manufacturing jobs since the 1970s, he distinguished between two minority responses to that disappearance. Whereas Korean immigrants' "entrepreneurial culture" helped them establish small businesses, black migrants failed to adjust to the new, postindustrial order: "When the manufacturing jobs went away, there was only small business, and nobody stepped in and said, here's how you get a loan, we're going to make sure that the loans are made in this community, we're going to make sure you learn to manage these businesses and create markets." African Americans, Clinton suggested, needed to be culturally reconditioned to adapt to globalization in a fashion that Asian immigrants had already accomplished on their own. The Personal Responsibility and Work Opportunity Act was one of the tools that Clinton, in collaboration with a Republican-controlled Congress, used to achieve this reconditioning. The act took aim at AFDC, the primary New Deal program that benefited low-income women, replacing it with Temporary Assistance for Needy Families (TANF), which permitted a maximum of five years of benefits within each recipient's lifetime and required her to find work within two years of receiving aid. TANF's goal was to instill in low-income Americans a responsible work ethic, thereby creating a disciplined labor force. Welfare mothers, Republican and Democratic legislators insisted, needed "tough love" to wean them off their dependency on welfare.[24]

In the American trilogy, Roth similarly extols the value of disciplined manual labor as a counterpoint to the cultural professionalism enabled by the university. In explaining the reasons behind his decision to close his Newark factory, Swede blames "the erosion of workmanship, which had deteriorated steadily since the riots" (*AP*, 24). In contrast, he praises the workers in his Puerto Rican factory, who exhibit a humble work ethic largely absent in Newark. In *The Human Stain*, Faunia Farley, the white, thirty-four-year-old janitress who becomes Coleman's lover after his academic disgrace and wife's death, similarly functions as a figure for the disciplined laboring class that knows and accepts its own place. Coleman and Faunia's affair revisits the cross-class sexual dynamics of Alexander's relationship with The Monkey in *Portnoy's Complaint*. She is the object of the same kind of condescending solicitude that Alexander directs toward his lover and that Delphine directs toward Coleman's accusers. Attempting to intimidate Coleman, Delphine writes him an anonymous note, accusing him of "sexually exploiting an abused, illiterate woman half your age" (*HS*, 38). However, Nathan, who imaginatively reconstructs the affair after the lovers' deaths in a car crash, imagines them as coequals. This equality is grounded in Faunia's refusal to be educated: "I can't learn! I don't learn! I don't *want* to learn! Stop fucking teaching me—it won't work!" (*HS*, 234). This refusal is a choice, much like Coleman's decision to change his race and become a classics professor. Faunia's claim that she "can't learn" derives from her supposed illiteracy. However, as Nathan learns from Faunia's father at her funeral, she has a diary; her illiteracy "had been an act, something she decided her situation demanded" (*HS*, 297). By pretending not to read, the condition of possibility for all forms of educational capital, Faunia abandons any claim to membership in the professional class that the university engenders. While Coleman's accusers implicitly affirm the value of a university education by enrolling in college, even if they lack the discipline to succeed, Faunia never aspires to be anything other than a janitress. She rejects higher learning in favor of what Nathan calls "a knowledge that is stronger and prior" (*HS*, 297).

This knowledge, the novel insists, is rooted in the physical labor that she performs. Indeed, the novel fetishizes Faunia's work; in two erotically charged scenes, Coleman watches Faunia milk cows at a feminist organic dairy and relax during a break from her janitorial duties on campus. At Faunia's funeral, she is eulogized by Sally, one of the dairy's owners, and Smoky Hollenbeck, the supervisor of Athena's physical plant. Both extol her selfless devotion to work. Faunia's work with the cows, Sally suggests, is a spiritual exercise, an extension of her love for humanity: "Her God was nature, and her worship of nature extended to her love for our little herd of cows, for all cows really, for that most benevolent of creatures who is foster mother of the human race" (*HS*, 286). Smoky, similarly, describes Faunia as a maternal figure who cares for the students and instills in them a sense of responsibility for their dormitory rooms. In both cases, Faunia's labor materially reproduces the institutions that she serves. She makes no claim on the farm's profits (she is not a shareholder), and she does not participate in the production of academic knowledge. Nevertheless, she makes both of these larger aims possible; her dormitories, Smoky explains, are "conducive to good productivity, to learning and living and to feeling a part of the Athena community" (*HS*, 287). Like the cows that she cares for, Faunia becomes a foster mother who nurtures the future professional class. By juxtaposing Coleman and Faunia, Roth constructs an idealized vision of the division of labor within the university, and by extension within America. Coleman becomes a disinterested scholar, eschewing the physical labor that his father performed. Faunia accepts her status as a pure laborer, with no interest in the university's higher functions.

The Neoliberal Academy

Saving the New Deal welfare state, then, depends on delimiting the boundaries of both the Democratic coalition and the new class. This salvation is crucial for Roth, since the meritocratic kingdom of culture that he evokes throughout his fiction is imbricated within the institutions of that state. Ross Posnock underscores this imbrication when he argues that the kingdom of culture is potentially open to anyone, since all it "requires is a good library."[25] Good libraries, however, are fragile institutions, dependent on community support and state funding. Roth underscored this fragility in a 1969 letter to the *New York Times*, in which he protested the closure of the Newark Public Library because of the city's shrinking tax base after the Great Migration. When he was a child, the library taught him "about the rules of civilized life." Most important, as Mary Esteve observes, the library taught him one of the basic tenets of welfare liberalism: the value of public as opposed to private goods.[26] Roth's chief pleasure as a child was "to carry home across the city and even into bed at night a book with a local lineage of its own, a family tree of Newark readers to which one's name had now been added." The sign-out card, for Roth, is a concrete emblem of the kingdom of culture; it materializes a community defined by separate, autonomous acts of reading. At the same time, the card marks the book as public property. Although Roth reads the book alone, "beyond the reach of parent or school," it instills in him "the idea of communal ownership, property held in common for the common good."[27] Indeed, the community created by the card is dependent on public ownership; as a class and cultural outsider, the young Roth can enter the kingdom of culture only through institutions that makes its objects available to anyone, regardless of his or her race or income. As Roth's letter underscores, these institutions are the products of specific historical and sociological circumstances, which existed for his generation of Jews in the 1940s and 1950s but were disappearing for the new generation of African Americans who dominated the city in the 1960s.

This recognition of the kingdom of culture's institutional dependence complicates the Allan Bloom–style cultural conservatism that *The Human Stain* uses to distinguish between those who do and do not belong in the academy, and by extension, the political demands that can and cannot be adopted by the Democratic Party. According to John Guillory, by conflating academic and national politics, both sides in the canon wars overlooked a deeper crisis that informed both of their positions: the ongoing devaluation of humanistic education as a form of cultural capital. Traditional humanists like Bloom and his multicultural opponents were fighting over diminishing returns; the "category of literature," Guillory argues, "names the cultural capital of the old bourgeoisie, a form of capital increasingly marginal to the social function of the present educational system."[28] Coleman is both the benefactor and victim of this devaluation of humanistic cultural capital. His passing is enabled by his rigorous at-home education in Greek, Latin, and Shakespeare, the traditional form of learning acquired by gentlemen in the nineteenth- and early twentieth-century academy to help distinguish them from men of other classes. Coleman's education is already a symptom of the humanities' loss of value in comparison to other kinds of knowledge; the fact that a black family like the Silks has access to the classics is a product of the democratic dissemination of humanistic education through projects such as Charles Eliot's Harvard Classics collection. Moreover, Coleman benefits from the fact that he enters the academy in the 1950s—a period of unprecedented university expansion, when colleges still perceived the classics as a valuable tool for instructing first-generation university students. Coleman's pedagogy is entirely shaped by this democratizing moment in American education. His goal is to make the classics accessible by emphasizing their universal content. His survey course in ancient Greek literature attracts students because of his "direct, frank, and unacademically forceful" comportment, and he begins his first lecture by describing *The Iliad* as being as "basic as a barroom brawl. [Agamemnon and Achilles] are quarreling over a woman. A girl, really" (*HS*, 4). Coleman's pedagogy, in his day, is as promiscuously open as Delphine's pedagogy is in hers. It is simply open to a different group of students. Coleman's narrative about Western literature beginning with an "offense against the phallic entitlement, the phallic *dignity*, of a powerhouse of a warrior" (*HS*, 5) appeals to the first-generation student body of the 1950s—mostly white, mostly male, many of them former warriors studying under the GI Bill. It is less appealing to the somewhat less white but decidedly more female student body of the 1990s.

Coleman's problem is that the traditional humanistic learning that facilitated his passing in the 1950s is not as valuable anymore. Indeed, as Athena's dean, he plays a key role in devaluing that learning. When Coleman begins his tenure as dean, Athena is a "gentleman's farm" (*HS*, 5), run by "senior professors who were the scions of the old county families who'd founded and originally endowed the place" (*HS*, 8). The university embodies liberal arts education in its traditional form: a static system of classic texts and ideas passed on from generation to generation. Coleman sets out to reform this system, instituting what the younger faculty call a "revolution of quality" (*HS*, 9); he eradicates faculty governance, introduces publish or perish as criteria for advancement and tenure, punishes faculty who recycle their lecture notes, and pushes senior professors into early retirement. Most crucially in terms of his future at Athena, Coleman marginalizes the humanities, especially his own discipline. When Coleman first begins to teach, he is the junior instructor in Athena's Classics Department; when he steps down from the deanship to resume teaching, he returns to an amalgamated Languages and Literature Department as its sole classics professor. Under Coleman's deanship, classics shrinks to a minor specialty in a department that emphasizes cultural plurality. For the older faculty, all of these changes mark Coleman as a dangerous outsider; he introduces base economic calculation into the liberal arts. "He brought in competition, he made the place competitive," one faculty member observes, which "is what Jews do" (*HS*, 9). When Delphine complains that Coleman's pedagogy is "fossilized" and that he insists on "the so-called humanist approach to Greek tragedy [he had] been taking since the 1950s" (*HS*, 193), she extends the educational revolution that Coleman himself initiates: the introduction of creative destruction into a previously rigid arts curriculum. Delphine, the novel suggests, will herself become another victim of this process. Already, most of the campus feminists find Delphine's version of French feminism too old fashioned. She is "so passé, such a parody of Simone de Beauvoir" (*HS*, 269).

Coleman's participation in his own obsolescence highlights contradictions in 1990s New Democrats' conception of the flexible, globalized workforce they hoped to foster through policies like welfare reform. As part of their effort to reclaim white working-class voters, New Democrats reiterated many Republican talking points about family values. Strong families and the traditional values that they instill are what differentiate middle-class Americans from the underclass. At the same time, New Democrats also extolled the value of creative destruction. America, the DLC argued in one policy document, should cultivate a "flexible" and "self-adapting" labor force capable of adjusting "rapidly to today's environment of faster economic change, wide dispersals of information, and instantaneous global communication." According to New Democrats, these two features of their ideology were one and the same. A flexible workforce can be shored up only in a nation composed of traditional, two-parent families: "As Americans struggle to master new, knowledge-based work and attain and maintain a middle-class living standard while getting less support from big institutions, they must turn to a strong, functioning family as the primary source of the security, socialization, and investment necessary to prepare the next generation and sustain the present one."[29] Families are perfect neoliberal institutions: a decentralized, flexible network of centers for education and social control. Part of the problem with the underclass, as Clinton made clear in his *Arsenio Hall Show* comments on the Watts riot, is that lacking strong families, they also lack self-reliance and discipline and are unable to adapt to the disappearance of manufacturing jobs. Part of the impetus for welfare reform was to shore up lower-class families. Title I of the Personal Responsibility and Work Opportunity Act began by stating, "Marriage is the foundation of a successful society," and labeled out-of-wedlock pregnancy "the crisis in our Nation."[30] The family, however, was threatened by the very market forces that it was supposed to shield against, and New Democrats had no real solution for preserving it. As the DLC outlined in policy documents like *The New Progressive Declaration* (1996), many of the key features of the postindustrial economy—the stagnation of middle-class wages, the growing insecurity of work, the requirement that virtually all families have two wage earners—contributed to the growing incidence of broken families that they deplored.

This pattern of traditional institutions giving rise to modernizing changes that ultimately destroy them is the structuring principle of Coleman's tragedy in *The Human Stain* and of the nation's decline in the American trilogy as a whole. The lessons and values that Coleman's family instills in him facilitate his upward mobility, transforming him into a self-reliant individualist. This mobility, however, entails rejecting that family and any institutions that resemble it. Reflecting on his dissatisfaction with Howard University, which he attends for a year before he starts to pass as white, Coleman realizes that the institution's problem is that it is too much like his family: "You finally leave home, the Ur of we, and you find *another* we? Another place that's just like that, the *substitute* for that?" (*HS*, 108). Coleman's subsequent success as Athena's dean of arts relies on this same distrust of familial ties; he uproots all of the professors whose positions depend on their blood relation to the institution's founders. On a larger scale, Roth suggests, the disintegration of familial bonds is reshaping America itself. The Silks' ability to refashion themselves as model Negroes rests on a unique set of historical circumstances. In 1945, the Silks' neighborhood is populated by "families of professional men, mainly, of teachers, doctors, and dentists" (*HS*, 123). These black families are following the path to upward mobility that Chicago school theorists in the 1930s and 1940s claimed was the American norm; they are leaving behind segregated ghettos, migrating into stable, middle-class neighborhoods formerly populated by previous immigrants.[31] East Orange's role as a nursery for the black bourgeoisie, however, is disrupted by market-driven urban reforms. The 280 freeway, designed to accelerate the flow of workers and capital through New Jersey, cuts through the center of the black community, eradicating many of its better houses. In its wake come the chain stores, which replace the old, family-owned department stores. This transformation of the city, Ernestine suggests, goes hand in hand with the cultural degeneration that she observes in the schools where she once taught: "I often wrestle," she complains, "with what everything used to be. What education used to be. What East Orange High used to be. What East Orange used to be" (*HS*, 311). The distinction between the deserving and the undeserving turns out to be a fragile one; the cultural values that fashion and sustain model minorities are threatened by the economic and institutional changes that these minorities help unleash.

The same pattern structures *American Pastoral*'s vision of Newark's decline into a black slum. Long stretches of the novel document the history of Swede's glove-making company, Newark Maid, which Roth uses as a synecdoche for midcentury American industry. Beginning in the 1930s as a small, family-owned business, the factory flourishes in the 1940s thanks to wartime government contracts. Its success enables the company to open a Puerto Rican factory in 1958 and move all operations offshore in the 1970s. The Levov family's transformation from working-class immigrants into industrialists depends on what David Harvey calls the "embedded liberalism" of the post–World War II period, a form of political-economic organization in which "market processes and entrepreneurial and corporate activities were surrounded by a web of social constraints and a regulatory environment that sometimes restrained but in other instances led the way in economic and industrial strategy."[32] The success of companies like Newark Maid contributes to Newark's deindustrialization; industrial flight closes off the city's engine of upward mobility just as the Second Great Migration brings tens of thousands of African Americans to the city. Throughout the novel, Swede complains about his black workers' deficient work ethic in comparison with that of his Puerto Rican workers or his father's generation of working-class Jews. As the history of Newark Maid underscores, however, African Americans cannot pursue the same path to upward mobility as their Jewish forebears; the conditions that made that mobility possible no longer exist.

More fundamentally, as Coleman discovers in *The Human Stain*, creative destruction imperils the very possibility of meritocracy itself, threatening the antiprocess academy that he wants to institute at Athena. When Coleman becomes the object of his colleagues' ire, he seems like Swede's African American workers in *American Pastoral*: someone who lacks the flexibility needed to adapt to changing working conditions. He adopts the language of victimhood that the American trilogy attributes to these workers and the radicals who speak for them; when Nathan visits Coleman after the spooks incident, he raves against the injustice of his expulsion from Athena and seems "completely unhinged" (*HS*, 11). Part of Coleman's problem is that the flexibility required by the modernized academy is impossible; given the time required to build up humanist cultural capital, professors cannot retrain when their approach or entire discipline falls out of academic fashion. The pathos of Coleman's career is that, after having spent his life instituting and defending meritocratic criteria, he falls into the category of those who do not belong. For most of his colleagues, he becomes the most abject figure within the discourse of political correctness: the white male oppressor. Rumors circulate that Coleman sexually and physically abuses Faunia, forcing her to have an abortion and ultimately killing her in a murder-suicide. An anonymous Listserv posting highlights the community's sense that Coleman represents an atavistic intrusion of prepolitically correct values into their community. His reasons for tormenting Faunia are unfathomable to "those who have made their peace with the restraints imposed by civilization on what is raw and untrammeled in us all" (*HS*, 293). Nathan underscores the pathos of this accusation through his comparison between Coleman's affair and the Monica Lewinsky scandal. For the Republicans who led the impeachment proceedings against Clinton, the affair similarly seemed like an intrusion of the undeserving into America's highest office. Toni Morrison captured the logic of the Republican attack when she referred to Clinton as "our first black President," who was born into a single-parent home and whose blackness became evident when "his unpoliced sexuality became the focus of the persecution."[33] The irony of this persecution was that Clinton himself perpetuated the policing of lower-class black sexuality as part of his effort to distinguish between those who do and do not belong in the New Democratic coalition; the Personal Responsibility and Work Opportunity Act included measures forcing single mothers on welfare to identify the fathers of their children.[34]

As *The Human Stain* repeatedly reminds its readers, Coleman and Clinton's accusers are driven by a "purity binge" (*HS*, 2) aimed at punishing members of their community who fail to live up to its standards. Coleman imagines this binge as a specific product of contemporary right- and left-wing versions of political correctness. Roth, however, insists that Coleman and Clinton's accusers are enacting something much more ancient, what "Hawthorne . . . identified in the incipient country of long ago as 'the persecuting spirit'" (*HS*, 2). Americans continually distinguish between the deserving and undeserving, and they inevitably interpret this distinction in moralistic terms. The neoliberal ideology that the DLC embraced in the 1990s was the ultimate manifestation of this impulse; neoliberalism insists that all human beings should be rational, responsible risk takers capable of adapting to an ever-changing market economy. Welfare reform was part of this fantasy; it assumed that responsibility must be inculcated in the poor and that those who cannot adapt should suffer. In *The Human Stain*, Roth embodies neoliberalism's fantasy of absolute personal responsibility in another Athena faculty member, a visiting economist named Arthur Sussman who once worked in the Ford administration. Underscoring the economic consensus linking New Democrats and Republicans, Arthur hates Clinton "for proposing the Democratic version of everything he wanted." What Arthur wants, more than anything else, is to dismantle the New Deal welfare state—the entity that made possible Coleman and Roth's humanist careers. His economic philosophy is rooted in a conception of "radical personal liberty that, in his thinking, is reduced to a radical sovereignty in the market" (*HS*, 268). The problem with this philosophy, as Coleman and Clinton's downfalls demonstrate, is that radical sovereignty is impossible. The welfare state, designed to compensate for individual citizens' incapacity for total economic mastery, is a system that acknowledges the persistence of the human stain in a way that free-market capitalism cannot.

Roth's American trilogy thus identifies a series of quandaries, built into the New Deal welfare state, that imperil both that state and the cultural institutions that it fosters. For Roth, the New Deal welfare state provides equal opportunities for talented racial and class outsiders to enter the professional class. At the same time, it ennobles the work of satisfied laborers like Coleman's lover, Faunia Farley. However, the actual historical trajectory of the welfare state endangers both groups, rendering professional and manual labor increasingly insecure. Ironically, in *The Human Stain*, Coleman's career is not really threatened by the inclusion of untalented students into the academy through his colleagues' participatory professionalism; rather, it is threatened by the devaluation of his own academic labor, which renders him exchangeable with the low-skilled working class. For Roth, this threat finally encompasses literature itself. In interviews before his retirement in 2012, Roth predicted the novel's extinction in the United States: "People will always be reading [novels], but it will be a small group of people. Maybe more people than now read Latin poetry, but somewhere in that range." Part of the problem lies with the degeneration of reading culture; in an age of movies, television, and the Internet, readers no longer have the "concentration and focus and attentiveness" required by serious writers like himself.[35] However, as the comparison to Latin poetry underscores, the problem also lies in literature's devaluation in the marketplace of cultural commodities. Roth's antiprocess aesthetic culminates in his prediction of literature's total closure, as it no longer finds the audience capable of responding to it on its own terms.

Conclusion

Working-Class Community Action

The 2016 election, which left Republicans in control of the White House, Senate, House of Representatives, and two-thirds of America's governorships, highlighted the long-term legacy of the conservative assault on the War on Poverty. Donald Trump won the Electoral College after running a populist, right-wing campaign that targeted two abject figures linked in the American imagination since the 1960s: poor minorities and urban elites. Pretending to appeal to black voters while speaking to crowds of white supporters, Trump asked them, "What have you got to lose?" by voting Republican. For Trump, liberals had politically and materially benefited by transforming urban minorities into a permanent client population. He would fix the situation by expelling illegal immigrants and encouraging police to stop and frisk young black men, thereby restoring law and order to the cities. His tax measures and economic protectionism, meanwhile, would ensure prosperity for all. The explicit racism that Trump infused into this campaign seemed new to presidential politics, but its underlying themes were not. Since the late 1960s, Republicans have attracted traditionally Democratic, white working-class voters by making similar claims.[1]

In the aftermath of Trump's victory, many liberals tried to understand Trump's appeal to these voters by turning to the class culture paradigm that conservatives had successfully employed for decades. In an interview with *Washington Post* reporter Jeff Guo, political scientist Kathy Cramer, drawing on her ethnographic work with Wisconsin rural voters, explained how Trump spoke to their deep-grained sense of resentment. This resentment derives from the economic insecurity generated by neoliberal policies promoted by both major political parties, policies that eradicate older forms of job security while cutting away the last vestiges of the welfare security net. However, white rural voters tend not to channel that resentment toward rich entrepreneurs like Donald Trump. Rather, they channel it toward those they perceive as not working hard enough—groups who get "more than their fair share." This category encompasses minorities, whom these voters incorrectly identify as privileged recipients of government largesse. It also encompasses anyone who does professional work. Cramer described her subjects' resentment toward her own class status:

> When people are talking about those people in the city getting an "unfair share," there's certainly a racial component to that. But they're also talking about people like me [a white, female professor]. They're asking questions like how often do I teach, what am I doing driving around the state of Wisconsin when I'm supposed to be working full time in Madison, like, *what kind of job is that, right*?[2]

Cramer's interview highlights the dilemma faced by the Democratic Party after the 2016 election. While both parties have embraced policies that create social insecurity, Republicans are best adapted to benefit from it. Since the 1970s, they have fashioned a cultural politics that turns the victims of globalization against each other. They have also waged a successful campaign against the notion of professional expertise, undermining the legitimacy of professions like journalism that might help those victims understand their plight.

Analyses like Guo's and Cramer's point to the path that the Democratic Party might take to regain white working-class voters that the party first began to lose in 1968: a program oriented toward establishing or restoring welfare state programs that benefit all Americans, regardless of their income. However, the interview also highlights one of the War on Poverty's most problematic legacies: the tendency to think that different classes inhabit ontologically distinct cultures. According to Cramer, white rural voters' animus toward expertise has become part of their "tribal identity."[3] Her description of that identity closely tracks accounts of white working-class culture that conservatives offered in the late 1960s. In *The Unheavenly City*, Edward Banfield located the working class in the second-lowest tier of his hierarchy of class cultures, just above the underclass. For Banfield, the working class rejects the extreme future orientation characteristic of the upper and middle classes. This rejection makes the typical member of that class naturally conservative, with "less confidence in his ability to shape the future" and a tendency toward intolerance. The working class channels this intolerance toward other classes, especially those it believes work less hard than it does: "To the working class, the middle class appears somewhat lacking in masculinity, and the upper class—a male member of which may even weep under stress—appears decidedly feminine or queer."[4] Banfield applauded this natural conservatism as a necessary brake on the reformist impulses of upper- and middle-class liberals. After the 2016 election, liberals bemoaned this same cultural tendency as a social illness that must be understood in order to contain authoritarian populists like Donald Trump. For Cramer, it is not enough for liberals to attend to the working class's economic needs; they also need to cross the cultural divide between themselves and the white rural poor: "That's partly about listening, and that's partly about spending time with people from a different walk of life, from a different perspective."[5]

What are the consequences of thinking of the white working class as a "tribe" culturally defined by its animus toward professional elites? Given this premise, is it even feasible to imagine that class embracing a progressive politics? One of the few authors who has fully worked out the implications of imagining the white working class in these terms is Carolyn Chute, best known for her best-selling first novel, *The Beans of Egypt, Maine* (1985). Most of Chute's novels are set in her fictional county of Egypt, Maine, and all of them explore the rural, working-class culture that is the object of Cramer's research. Chute self-consciously inhabits this culture; she lives off the grid in rural Maine with her illiterate husband in a ramshackle house. She is also the founder of the Second Maine Militia, a no-wing organization dedicated to preserving Second Amendment rights and fighting corporate interests. Over the course of her career, she has written increasingly ambitious and complex works that imagine Maine's rural white residents as a tribe culturally at odds with urban professionals. At the same time, she has struggled to imagine that tribe cultivating indigenous forms of expertise compatible with a progressive politics. These efforts culminate in her two most recent novels, *The School on Heart's Content Road* (2008) and *Treat Us like Dogs and We Will Become Wolves* (2014),[6] two parts of a projected tetralogy that Chute began writing in 1993. In both novels, Chute turns to community action and participatory art to reconcile the contradictions between tribal identity and progressive politics she sets out in her early work; in so doing, she echoes many of the concerns about class culture that animated process artists and War on Poverty liberals in the 1960s.

Chute's animus toward urban professionals has been a constant feature of her work since *The Beans of Egypt, Maine*, and it has shaped her critical reception. Although *Beans* helped pioneer the genre of "grit lit" that culminated in books like Daniel Woodrell's *Winter's Bone* (2006) and Jesmyn Ward's *Salvage the Bones* (2011), critics often overlook the novel in favor of Dorothy Allison's *Bastard out of Carolina* (1992) as the paradigmatic example of rural, white working-class fiction. Discussing the reasons for this neglect, Cynthia Ward argues that *Beans* resists middle-class reading practices, specifically the "mechanism by which readers identify with imaginary characters and sympathize with imaginary others." Both *Bastard out of Carolina* and *Beans* tell the story of young girls (Bone and Earlene) growing up in poverty. In *Bastard*, however, Bone is a bookworm and storyteller, and Allison suggests she will escape her environment to become someone like her professionally trained readers. *Beans* resists this identification; Earlene turns her back on her family's middle-class pretensions to join the violent and sexually promiscuous Bean clan. The novel provides "no easy reassurance to middle-class readers that their behavior models and values offer salvation."[7]

As Laura Browder points out, this resistance to middle-class models of professional salvation is central to Chute's version of working-class identity politics. Her novels promote "a vision of authentic folk, unsullied by education, living in a barter economy."[8] Chute envisages Maine's white working class in essentialist terms, as a timeless tribe bound together by culture and blood ties. This culture encompasses beliefs and folkways passed down from generation to generation, including many that are offensive to most professionals, such as a traditional conception of gender roles. According to Browder, Chute's novels usually code fertile, stay-at-home mothers as authentically working class in contrast with university-educated feminists. She also imagines gun ownership as a fundamental part of working-class culture incomprehensible to middle-class liberals; asked about her defense of Second Amendment rights, Chute explained, "Rednecks love guns, always have. It's our *culture.*"[9] Most fundamentally, Chute is hostile toward schooling, at least as embodied in the formal education system. One of her "Revolutionary Abby" pamphlets, which she wrote for the Second Maine Militia, encouraged its readers to "burn down the schools. These are the total institutions of industrialism and capitalism."[10] In Chute's novels, the school system humiliates most working-class students. Those who succeed do so at the expense of the contextualized know-how they learn from their working-class parents.[11] Commenting on the home computer that the school pressures him to buy for his son, one of Chute's characters complains that the boy has withdrawn entirely from the family, becoming "*theirs*, just the way they like it . . . the school, the companies an' all those other fuckers."[12] In contrast,

Chute encourages the working class to recover the practical skills that the education system has tried to stifle, skills rooted in their traditional culture. "How many survival skills do your children have?" a visiting activist minister asks a group of unemployed men in *Merry Men* (1994); "how many kids today can provide for themselves food, tools, clothing, warmth . . . from the elements?"[13]

Chute's authorship performatively contradicts this identity politics; in particular, as Browder points out, Chute's gender essentialism "creates a dilemma for her as a woman writer."[14] As a novelist whose work is directed to an audience composed of the very middle-class types she caricatures, Chute transgresses the social roles she celebrates. In interviews, she often downplays her own education, presenting herself as an outsider artist, with no literary influences. "There is one bookshelf in the front room of the Chute house at Gag Corner," the *Washington Post* reported in a profile published after the success of *Beans*; "it is half full and stands against a wall. Chute estimates that she has read about 30 books in her life, mostly things friends recommend."[15] In spite of her off-the-grid lifestyle, Chute's career is thoroughly imbricated in what Mark McGurl calls the Program Era. She began work on *Beans* shortly after completing a 1975 creative writing workshop with Ken Rosen at the University of Southern Maine. Her association with creative writing institutions led her to push against many beliefs integral to working-class Maine culture. Chute came up with the idea for the Second Maine Militia while listening to Noam Chomsky's taped lectures at the prestigious MacDowell artists' colony; she wanted to "bring his message to the people she knew back home."[16] Her no-wing militia rejects the racism, misogyny, and homophobia of other militias and promotes solar energy and environmental sustainability—ideas, she acknowledged, that "may not be typical working-class ones."[17] In her fiction and activism, Chute wants to preserve working-class Maine culture, which she imagines as a timeless essence, while challenging it with critical consciousness derived from her professional connections as a novelist and public intellectual.

In *The School on Heart's Content Road* and *Treat Us like Dogs*, Chute tries to resolve this contradiction. She does so through the medium of community action and participatory art, which allows her to imagine how Maine's working class might be educated without experiencing the damaging effects of formal education. The two novels were originally parts of a twenty-six hundred–page manuscript that Chute began writing in 1993. Both take place in 2000 and tell the story of the Settlement, a countercultural commune, alternative school, and polygamous compound run by the charismatic Gordon St. Onge, a "redneck philosopher" (*S*, 234). Both novels purport to offer the reader an alternative history of the Settlement left out of the official history books; *The School on Heart's Content Road* begins by announcing that in the year 2000, "Big things happened in America. But you never heard about some of them. They were erased" (*S*, 9). This historiography, however, rejects the practices of professional historians; both novels are multiperspectival, and some of these perspectives are impossible: sections of *Treat Us like Dogs* are narrated by a transdimensional alien species. At the same time, the novels present themselves as examples of folk art at odds with the serious literature marketed to university-educated readers. Each novel is broken down into short chapters preceded by icons that indicate which of the book's narrative perspectives are being used. The icons look crude and hand drawn, and each novel begins with a message welcoming the reader, followed by an invitation to turn to the character list at the end: "I, myself, love character lists because I like to refresh myself on how characters look. Maybe you do too" (*S*, 1). The novels, in other words, welcome affective reading practices of the kind excluded from fiction in the modernist tradition.

This formal evocation of folk expertise is crucial to the novels' didactic project, which is to imagine alternative professional practices that can be realized within working-class communities. The Settlement embodies the political ideals that Chute tried to realize in her activism on behalf of the Second Maine Militia; it draws most of its energy from solar panels and windmills, grows its own crops, and barters for resources and services with other cooperatives. It also embodies Chute's critique of formal education as a system that destroys working-class culture. The Settlement has no grading system or classrooms. Instead, students discuss history and philosophy in informal symposia directed by older students and learn trade and agricultural skills from adults in the community's workshops. This education draws on rather than disrupts working-class patterns of family socialization, ensuring that all of the knowledge it teaches remains contextualized. The Settlement obliterates distinctions between school and family, between learning and doing. In this way, like the novel itself, it aims at creating homegrown, working-class expertise shielded from the influence of urban professionals. As Gordon explains to a group of visitors, "We aren't less intelligent than the experts. We just aren't experts . . . yet" (*S*, 305). Both the books and the Settlement they depict radicalize community action and process art's promise to eradicate divisions between professionals and their lower-class clients. They do so without involving professionals at all, instead creating organic communities of working-class experts.

At the same time, the Settlement resolves the gender contradiction that plagues Chute's work: the contradiction between her feminine authorship and her idealization of patriarchal families as authentically working class. She resolves this contradiction through Gordon's polygamy. The Settlement is a direct democracy, in which policy is determined through discussions and voting by all members above the age of twelve. It is also a patriarchy headed by Gordon, who owns the land and fathers many of the students. Chute imagines polygamy as an institution that allows the female residents of the Settlement to simultaneously inhabit conventionally feminine gender roles and exert forms of agency unavailable to women in the outside world. Parenting is shared among the women, so no one has to take sole responsibility for her own children. At the same time, the women's numerical superiority means that Gordon's power is diffuse and subject to feminine veto; whenever he wants to shape the Settlement's policy, he begins a one-on-one process of sexual persuasion: "He acts silly, wags his head, covers his ears or leaves them for later, for bed, where they are more easily influenced" (*T*, 432). As one of the novel's characters comments when he observes the wives' authority, Gordon "isn't really a man with a harem. He's a man with a problem" (*S*, 249). This polygamous agency is best exemplified by Gordon's first wife, Claire St. Onge, a Passamaquoddy Indian who works as an adjunct history instructor at the nearby University of Southern Maine and who might be the folk historian who compiles the two novels' narrative fragments after the Settlement's demise. Shuttling back and forth between Egypt and the university, Claire embodies the contradictions that inform Chute's career as a writer who has taught creative writing classes on several college campuses. Claire's extended Settlement family allows her to resist the decontextualized feminism of her female colleagues. Noticing her department chairwoman's hostility toward the working class, Claire comments that she would hate real-life Native Americans, most of whom have redneck views. "But of *course*, I like Indians!" her chair replies; "Claire, you know that given a chance, Native Americans wouldn't think like that. Education would enlighten them" (*T*, 202). Claire's home in the Settlement, where she helps guide the students' history symposia, inoculates her against the educational processing that her chair extols, allowing her to maintain her redneck and Passamaquoddy identity intact.

The Settlement, however, does not much resolve as displace the contradictions that troubled 1960s writers who struggled with community action and participatory art. The two novels trace the disastrous collision between Gordon St. Onge and another charismatic working-class leader, Rex York, the captain of the right-wing Border Mountain Militia. The two men, who are childhood friends, reenact the tension between tradition and critical consciousness supposedly resolved within the Settlement. This tension is reflected in their respective positions on marriage and the Constitution. For Rex, both are God-given institutions, not subject to alteration by human beings. He continues to wear his wedding band, even though his wife has remarried, since "God does not recognize divorce" (*S*, 150). Gordon, however, perceives marriage as a mutable institution to be reimagined to suit the needs of those who enter into it. Rex believes that his militia's mission is to defend the Constitution, which "is written by the hand of divinity itself and can never be erased or obscured by mortal power" (*S*, 162). Like his wedding ring, the Constitution is an object that Rex venerates even after others have abandoned it. For Gordon, the Constitution is "only a pile of old paper" (*S*, 158), already compromised by commercial interests in the eighteenth century and now interpreted beyond recognition by more than a century of pro-corporate Supreme Court decisions. More generally, the two men differ in their tendency toward the intolerance that class culture theorists like Banfield attribute to the working class. For Rex, all of the problems facing America are created by a corrupt federal government that infringes on constitutional rights. The men in his militia are prone to paranoia, creating abject categories like blacks, gays, liberals, communists, and feminists that embody their grievances against a government that seems indifferent to white working-class men. Gordon sees the government as a puppet entity, overshadowed by the "octopus" (*S*, 122) of global capitalism, and he resists exclusionary thinking, welcoming people of color and homosexuals into his community.

Gordon and Rex try to overcome these differences to form a coalitional working-class politics, capable of addressing that class's economic needs while also embodying its cultural biases. In terms of the 2016 election, the two men try to synthesize the left- and right-wing populisms that culminated in the unlikely candidacies of Bernie Sanders and Donald Trump. Gordon appropriates the Border Mountain Militia's style, dressing up in its uniform and incorporating gun rights into the Settlement's ideology. Rex's militia, meanwhile, comes to respect the Settlement's push toward economic independence, especially its windmills and radio transmitter, which might be useful in the apocalyptic times they see coming ahead. The tension between Rex's traditionalism and Gordon's transgressive modernism, however, drives the two men apart, threatening the survival of their respective communities. Both novels culminate in Rex's savage beating of Gordon, which leaves Gordon disfigured and brain damaged. The beating is precipitated by Gordon's drunken outdoor orgy with Rex's troubled twenty-year-old daughter, Glory. By having sex with Glory, Gordon betrays the brotherhood he imagines that the two men share. This brotherhood was, in fact, always rooted in the same conflict between tradition and transgression that divides the two men's political philosophies. For Gordon, their friendship evokes two memories from his young manhood. In the first, Gordon and Rex help Rex's aunt haul ancient tombstones from her barn back to Egypt's graveyard; her ancestors stole them a hundred years ago. The two men rectify an ancient theft and reestablish an intergenerational continuity forgotten by most of the county's residents. In the second memory, Gordon and Rex take turns watching each other perform cunnilingus on a stripper at a local fair—a transgressive homosocial experience that prefigures Gordon's experiments in communal marriage.

At the same time, the Settlement reinscribes another problem that troubled 1960s and 1970s accounts of community action: the problem of government patronage. The Settlement's virtues derive from its independence from government and big business. This independence separates its model of working-class expertise from that of the professional class. As a visiting anarchist explains about the difference between blue-collar workers and professionals, professionals are essentially "honor students . . . they're still looking for that gummy star on the forehead from the big hand. They were always plastered with those and that feeling of pleasure carries through into their adult lives" (*T*, 618–619). Professionals have been indoctrinated by the school system and absorbed into an ideological state apparatus that serves corporations. As a result, they betray working-class interests: "Ratting on us bad kids was part of how they became teacher's pets *then* . . . and now" (*T*, 619). The Settlement, however, can never entirely be free from that apparatus. Financially, in spite of its bartering with other cooperatives, the Settlement is dependent on Gordon, who provides the initial capital for the venture from his family business, a big contracting company that builds schools and banks in the 1970s. Politically, the Settlement is dependent on Gordon's government connections, left over from the family business. His family, an old acquaintance explains, was political "in the way any good-sized successful, monied contracting outfit looks after its interests. Friends in Augusta. Family in the House and Senate. Connections all over the place. And hired lobbyists" (*T*, 215). Gordon uses these connections to shield the Settlement from social workers and school officials who would like to investigate conditions there.

In *The School on Heart's Content Road* and *Treat Us like Dogs*, Chute backs away from her early primitivist vision of Maine's working class, imagining the conditions under which that class might acquire a complex version of cultural capital that is a natural outgrowth of their practical skills. However, she clings to the notion that the differences between the working and professional classes are cultural rather than economic, and she continues to imagine rural Mainers as a folk tribe bound together by geography, culture, and blood. Indeed, the Settlement is the vehicle that the residents of Egypt use to realize their tribal essence: residents eat in collective kitchens, share the products of their labor, and celebrate pagan rituals like the solstice. In conceiving rural Mainers as a tribal folk at odds with the professional middle class, Chute echoes the cultural binaries that have fissured literary, social scientific, and public policy representations of poverty since the 1960s. In particular, she echoes Oscar Lewis's culture of poverty thesis. For Lewis, the slum dwellers of Mexico City and San Juan were peasant folk pushed into modernity; the culture of poverty most frequently results "from imperial conquest in which the native social and economic structure is smashed and the natives are maintained in a servile colonial status, sometimes for many generations. It can also occur in the process of detribalization, such as that now going on in Africa."[18] Chute conceives of the people of Egypt in the same way—as a peasant folk undergoing modernization, losing their traditions and succumbing to disorganization as they are assimilated into America's low-wage service class. Chute's disagreement with Lewis and other poverty theorists lies in her insistence that these traditions can be recovered in small-scale communities like the Settlement and through her own literary folk art. However, as she explores the obstacles facing the Settlement and similar experiments in tribal living, she despairs. Trying to imagine the Settlement's future in the face of global capitalism, hostile federal agents, and the news media, Gordon always comes up against the "bricked-up end of the universe" (*S*, 161).

Chute's impasse in *The School on Heart's Content Road* and *Treat Us like Dogs* mirrors that of the liberals she claims to despise. It is an impasse derived from the binary model of class culture that informed the War on Poverty in the 1960s and has continued to inform the War on Welfare from the 1980s to the present day. The participatory professionalism of the 1960s attempted to bridge the cultural gap between professionals and the poor, but its proponents all too readily accepted the idea that the gap could or should not be closed. Like Chute, they conceived of professionals and the poor as separate tribes with different customs. Ultimately, the culture of poverty thesis contributed to efforts to discipline and contain the poor through workfare and mass incarceration—the very features of the American polity that Chute condemns in her work. The persistence of the idea of class culture is unfortunate, for the expertise of public-sector professionals like doctors, social workers, and educators remains a crucial resource that must be freely accessible to everyone. Universally accessible expertise is a defining feature of the welfare state. Its absence in the United States highlights the extent to which the nation has embraced the practice and ideology of neoliberalism.

Notes

Introduction: Maximum Feasible Participation

1. By 1965, HARYOU had merged with Adam Clayton Powell's Associated Community Teams (ACT) to form the new hybrid organization HARYOU-ACT.

2. Herbert Krosney, *Beyond Welfare: Poverty in the Supercity* (New York: Holt, Rinehart & Winston, 1966), 83.

3. Amiri Baraka, *The Autobiography of LeRoi Jones / Amiri Baraka* (1984; repr., Chicago: Lawrence Hill Books, 1997), 211.

4. Robert Levine, *The Poor Ye Need Not Have with You: Lessons from the War on Poverty* (Cambridge, MA: MIT Press, 1970), 55.

5. Paul A. Fino, Republican congressman from New York, complained that BARTS's plays "advocated Negro revolution and murder of white people." Quoted in Erik Nielson, "White Surveillance of the Black Arts," *African American Review* 47, no. 1 (2014): 174.

6. As Kenneth Clark announced in his proposal for HARYOU, its purpose was to cultivate "the strength of personality, the stability of character, and confidence which are required to achieve, and to function effectively within, a non-segregated society." Harlem Youth Opportunities Unlimited, *Youth in the Ghetto: A Study of the Consequences of Powerlessness and a Blueprint for Change* (New York: Harlem Youth Opportunities Unlimited, 1964), 9–10.

7. Karen Ferguson, *Top Down: The Ford Foundation, Black Power, and the Reinvention of Racial Liberalism* (Philadelphia: University of Pennsylvania Press, 2013), 1.

8. J. Phillip Thompson III, *Double Trouble: Black Mayors, Black Communities, and the Call for a Deep Democracy* (Oxford: Oxford University Press, 2006), 148.

9. K. Ferguson, *Top Down*, 17–18. See also Devin Fergus, *Liberalism, Black Power, and the Making of American Politics, 1965–1980* (Athens: University of Georgia Press, 2009), which similarly explores connections between liberalism and black nationalism.

10. See Roderick Ferguson, *The Reorder of Things: The University and Its Pedagogies of Minority Difference* (Minneapolis: University of Minnesota Press, 2012), for a recent account of the institutionalization of Black Power and other cultural nationalist movements within the post-1960s university.

11. Geneviève Fabre, *Drumbeats, Masks, and Metaphor: Contemporary Afro-American Theatre*, trans. Melvin Dixon (Cambridge, MA: Harvard University Press, 1983), 20.

12. K. Ferguson, *Top Down*, 7.

13. Amiri Baraka, *Conversations with Amiri Baraka*, ed. Charlie Reilly (Jackson: University Press of Mississippi, 1994), 20–21.

14. Lyndon Johnson, "Remarks upon Signing the Economic Opportunity Act," August 20, 1964, in *The American Presidency Project*, ed. Gerhard Peters and John T. Woolley, available at http://www.presidency.ucsb.edu/ws/?pid=26452.

15. "The Economic Opportunity Act of 1964," Public Law 88-452, August 20, 1964, available at http://www.gpo.gov/fdsys/pkg/STATUTE-78/pdf/STATUTE-78-Pg508.pdf.

16. For an account of changes taking place within social work in the 1960s, see John Ehrenreich, *The Altruistic Imagination: A History of Social Work and Social Policy in the United States* (Ithaca, NY: Cornell University Press, 1985), 187–208. I discuss the emergence of Legal Services, the Community Action Program's network of legal aid offices, in Chapter 3. For a history of the free clinic movement among medical professionals, see Robert Castel, Françoise Castel, and Anne Lovell, *The Psychiatric Society*, trans. Arthur Goldhammer (New York: Columbia University Press, 1982), 214–255.

17. Charles Olson, *Collected Prose*, ed. Donald Allen and Benjamin Friedlander (Berkeley: University of California Press, 1997), 240. For an account of the centrality of ideas of process to post–World War II avant-garde poetry, see William Watkin, *In the Process of Poetry: The New York School and the Avant-Garde* (Lewisburg, PA: Bucknell University Press, 2001).

18. Lisa Siraganian, *Modernism's Other Work: The Art Object's Political Life* (Oxford: Oxford University Press, 2012), 6.

19. Amiri Baraka, *Home: Social Essays* (1966; repr., Hopewell, NJ: Ecco Press, 1998), 173.

20. Paul Ylvisaker, quoted in Peter Marris and Martin Rein, *Dilemmas of Social Reform: Poverty and Community Action in the United States* (New York: Atherton Press, 1969), 42, 44.

21. Harlem Youth Opportunities Unlimited, *Youth in the Ghetto*, 349.

22. Mark McGurl, *The Program Era: Postwar Fiction and the Rise of Creative Writing* (Cambridge, MA: Harvard University Press, 2009), ix.

23. For an overview of the massive literature on the professional-managerial class, see John Frow, *Cultural Studies and Cultural Capital* (Oxford: Oxford University Press, 1995), 89–130. See also Stephen Schryer, *Fantasies of the New Class: Ideologies of Professionalism in Post–World War II American Fiction* (New York: Columbia University Press, 2011).

24. McGurl, *The Program Era*, 59.

25. The Works Progress Administration (WPA) was founded in 1935 to carry out public works projects, including arts projects. Michael Szalay explores the WPA's impact on 1930s literature in *New Deal Modernism: American Literature and the Invention of the Welfare State* (Durham, NC: Duke University Press, 2000). In her account of the Ford Foundation's interest in 1960s black theater, Karen Ferguson provides a sense of the massive number of minority artists funded through War on Poverty–related programs.

She focuses on Robert Macbeth's New Lafayette Theatre and Douglas Turner Ward's Negro Ensemble Company, both located in New York. These two theaters alone were "hothouses for cultivating African American artists, producing hundreds who joined and enriched the American cultural mainstream." *Top Down*, 209.

26. Madhu Dubey, *Signs and Cities: Black Literary Postmodernism* (Chicago: University of Chicago Press, 2003), 5.

27. Michael Fried's "Art and Objecthood" (1967) was one of the first texts to characterize postmodern art in terms of its incorporation of audience response. Disparaging contemporary art trends as "theatrical," he argued that by depending on audience engagement, they negate the "absorption" and "presentness" that characterizes modern painting. *Art and Objecthood: Essays and Reviews* (Chicago: University of Chicago Press, 1998). As Michael Szalay notes, this concept offered critics "a way to map the distinction between a modernist, politically apathetic formalism on the one hand, and a proto-postmodern, proactive commitment to 'the performative' on the other." *New Deal Modernism: American Literature and the Invention of the Welfare State* (Durham, NC: Duke University Press, 2000), 261. Other early critics defined postmodernism as an art form that challenges modernist conceptions of literary expertise. Leslie Fiedler famously characterized postmodern novels as "anti-art" that try "to straddle the border, if not quite close the gap between high culture and low, *belles lettres* and pop art." "Cross the Border—Close That Gap: Post-modernism," in *Postmodernism and the Contemporary Novel: A Reader*, ed. Brian Nicol (Edinburgh: Edinburgh University Press, 2002), 163, 164.

28. Schryer, *Fantasies of the New Class.*

29. As Sargent Shriver's deputy, Adam Yarmolinsky, later reflected, "It was less expensive to prepare people for jobs than to create jobs for people." Quoted in Michael Katz, *The Undeserving Poor: From the War on Poverty to the War on Welfare* (New York: Pantheon Books, 1989), 93. According to Alice O'Connor, the federal government's embrace of community action was an effort to sidestep the structural demands of the civil rights movement, which was "building toward their own version of a 'domestic Marshall Plan' that would come to include job creation and income guarantees as well as more specifically race-targeted measures to combat segregation, discrimination, and the absence of capital in black urban communities." *Poverty Knowledge: Social Science, Social Policy, and the Poor in Twentieth-Century U.S. History* (Princeton, NJ: Princeton University Press, 2001), 149.

30. Steven Brint, *In an Age of Experts: The Changing Role of Professionals in Politics and Public Life* (Princeton, NJ: Princeton University Press, 1994), 2.

31. For an account of how post–World War II writers helped the Democratic Party imaginatively synthesize its two new constituencies, see Michael Szalay, *Hip Figures: A Literary History of the Democratic Party* (Stanford, CA: Stanford University Press, 2012).

32. For an overview of American social scientific theories of poverty throughout the twentieth century, see Katz, *The Undeserving Poor*; and O'Connor, *Poverty Knowledge*. Critics interested in connections between mid-century American literature and social

science have mostly focused on the sociology of race. See in particular Carlo Rotella, *October Cities: The Redevelopment of Urban Literature* (Berkeley: University of California Press, 1998); Roderick Ferguson, *Aberrations in Black: Toward a Queer of Color Critique* (Minneapolis: University of Minnesota Press, 2004); and Thomas Heise, *Urban Underworlds: A Geography of Twentieth-Century American Literature and Culture* (New Brunswick, NJ: Rutgers University Press, 2011).

33. Michael Harrington, *The Other America: Poverty in the United States, with a New Introduction* (1962; repr., New York: Macmillan, 1969), 8, 10.

34. Harrington borrowed this conception of poverty from John Kenneth Galbraith's *The Affluent Society* (1958; repr., New York: Houghton Mifflin, 1998), where Galbraith distinguished between case and insular poverty, the two kinds of poverty that he claimed persisted after World War II. Case poverty "is commonly and properly related to some characteristic of the individuals so afflicted." Insular poverty is restricted to islands of poverty where "everyone or nearly everyone is poor" due to "some factor common to their environment" (236).

35. Harrington, *The Other America*, 1, 6, 11, 18.

36. Oscar Lewis, *La Vida: A Puerto Rican Family in the Culture of Poverty—San Juan and New York* (New York: Random House, 1966), xlvi, xlv.

37. Richard Cloward and Lloyd Ohlin, *Delinquency and Opportunity: A Theory of Delinquent Gangs* (New York: Free Press, 1960).

38. James Sundquist, "Origins of the War on Poverty," in *On Fighting Poverty: Perspectives from Experience*, ed. James Sundquist (New York: Basic Books, 1969), 7.

39. Marris and Rein, *Dilemmas of Social Reform*, 22.

40. O. Lewis, *La Vida*, xlviii.

41. As Charles Valentine complained in an early critique of Lewis, the culture of poverty thesis was used "to justify programs designed to inculcate middle-class values and virtues among the poor and especially their children, rather than changing the conditions of their existence." "The 'Culture of Poverty': Its Scientific Significance and Its Implications for Action," in *The Culture of Poverty: A Critique*, ed. Eleanor Burke Leacock (New York: Simon & Schuster, 1971), 213.

42. Szalay, *Hip Figures*, 4.

43. Jack Kerouac, *On the Road* (1957; repr., New York: Penguin Books, 1999), 169–170.

44. Olson, *Collected Prose*, 158.

45. Werner Sollors, *Amiri Baraka / LeRoi Jones: The Quest for a "Populist Modernism"* (New York: Columbia University Press, 1978), 25.

46. Jerry Watts, *Amiri Baraka: The Politics and Art of a Black Intellectual* (New York: New York University Press, 2001), 118.

47. Madhu Dubey, *Black Women Novelists and the Nationalist Aesthetic* (Bloomington: Indiana University Press, 1994), 17. Roderick Ferguson also notes this connection between black nationalism and the Moynihan report: "Black nationalist groups, while they contested Moynihan's argument about the state being the appropriate catalyst to

masculine agency, agreed with Moynihan's thesis about the emasculating effects of black women and the need for black men to resume their role as patriarchs." *Aberrations in Black*, 123.

48. Amiri Baraka and Edward Dorn, *Amiri Baraka & Edward Dorn: The Collected Letters*, ed. Claudia Moreno Pisano (Albuquerque: University of New Mexico Press, 2013), 208.

49. Kenneth Marshall, cited in Daniel Moynihan, *Maximum Feasible Misunderstanding: Community Action in the War on Poverty* (New York: Free Press, 1969), 130.

50. Moynihan, *Maximum Feasible Misunderstanding*, 21, 24.

51. See Barry Bruce-Briggs, ed., *The New Class?* (New Brunswick, NJ: Transaction Books, 1979), a collection of a series of essays outlining the neoconservative theory of the new class. See also Schryer, *Fantasies of the New Class*, 111–139.

52. Kenneth Clark, *Dark Ghetto: Dilemmas of Social Power* (New York: Harper & Row, 1965), xvi.

53. Joyce Ladner, ed., *The Death of White Sociology: Essays on Race and Culture* (1973, repr.; Baltimore: Black Classics Press, 1998). Other social scientists criticized Oscar Lewis's specific formulation of the culture of poverty thesis throughout the 1960s. Eleanor Burke Leacock edited an anthology of these critiques, *The Culture of Poverty*.

54. In African American studies, the most influential critique of Moynihan is Hortense Spillers's "Mama's Baby, Papa's Maybe: An American Grammar Book," *Diacritics* 17, no. 2 (1987): 64–81. Latino/Latina writers' critical response to Oscar Lewis's work is addressed in Marta Sánchez, *"Shakin' Up" Race and Gender: Intercultural Connections in Puerto Rican, African American, and Chicano Narratives and Culture (1965–1995)* (Austin: University of Texas Press, 2005); and John Alba Cutler, *Ends of Assimilation: The Formation of Chicano Literature* (Oxford: Oxford University Press, 2015).

55. Gavin Jones, *American Hungers: The Problem of Poverty in U.S. Literature, 1840–1945* (Princeton, NJ: Princeton University Press, 2008), 15.

56. Walter Benn Michaels, *The Shape of the Signifier: 1967 to the End of History* (Princeton, NJ: Princeton University Press, 2004), 180.

57. Gates, writes Warren, "has been all too ready to posit the idea of an underclass desperately in need of leadership from the talented fifteenth of black America," while Baker proffers "a Moynihanesque remedy for black impoverishment." *So Black and Blue: Ralph Ellison and the Occasion of Criticism* (Chicago: University of Chicago Press, 2003), 92, 98.

58. Ruth Benedict, *Patterns of Culture* (1934; repr., Boston: Houghton Mifflin, 2005), 46. Susan Rigdon explores Benedict's impact on Lewis in *The Culture Facade: Art, Science, and Politics in the Work of Oscar Lewis* (Urbana: University of Illinois Press, 1988), 6–15.

59. O. Lewis, *La Vida*, xv, xliv.

60. Oscar Lewis, *Five Families: Mexican Case Studies in the Culture of Poverty* (New York: Basic Books, 1959), 2.

61. Lewis's confusion of class and culture is evident in the catalog of traits he associated with the culture of poverty, which includes female-headed families (arguably a cultural trait) but also "poor housing conditions" and "the use of second-hand clothing and furniture." *La Vida*, xlvi. As Anthony Leeds notes about Lewis's inclusion of "pawning" in his lists of traits, "this is a structural response to needs, usually rational and problem-solving, under extremely difficult conditions, rather than a specific trait of a postulated subculture." "The Concept of the 'Culture of Poverty': Conceptual, Logical, and Empirical Problems, with Perspectives from Brazil and Peru," in Leacock, *The Culture of Poverty*, 250.

62. O. Lewis, *La Vida*, xxiv, lii. By insisting on the culture of poverty's thinness, Lewis echoed 1960s psychiatrists, who drew on sensory-deprivation studies to argue that the poor suffer from "cultural deprivation." For more on this psychiatric trend and its impact on the War on Poverty, see Mical Raz, *What's Wrong with the Poor? Psychiatry, Race, and the War on Poverty* (Chapel Hill: University of North Carolina Press, 2013).

63. This same reductio ad absurdum of anthropological relativism featured centrally in the work of liberal social scientists whom Lewis influenced, such as Daniel Moynihan. In *The Negro Family: The Case for National Action* (Washington, DC: US Department of Labor, 1965), Moynihan gestured toward cultural relativism. "There is, presumably," he admitted, "no special reason why a society in which males are dominant in family relationships is to be preferred to a matriarchal arrangement" (29). Nevertheless, Moynihan went on to describe lower-class black families as pathological aberrations from a white middle-class norm, citing research demonstrating that children from female-centered families are more likely to suffer from mental illness than those from patriarchal homes.

64. O. Lewis, *La Vida*, li.

65. Kerouac, *On the Road*, 91.

66. Oswald Spengler, *The Decline of the West*, trans. Charles Francis Atkinson (New York: Alfred A. Knopf, 1926), 170–171.

67. Olson, *Collected Prose*, 158.

68. Thomas Pynchon, *The Crying of Lot 49* (1966; repr., New York: Harper & Row, 1986), 103, 105, 149, 150.

69. J. Kerry Grant, *A Companion to "The Crying of Lot 49"* (Athens: University of Georgia Press, 1994), 125.

70. Pynchon, *The Crying of Lot 49*, 103.

71. Sean McCann and Michael Szalay, "Do You Believe in Magic? Literary Thinking after the New Left," *Yale Journal of Criticism* 18, no. 2 (2005): 436.

72. Pynchon, *The Crying of Lot 49*, 102.

73. Edward Banfield, *The Unheavenly City: The Nature and Future of Our Urban Crisis* (Boston: Little, Brown, 1970), 46, 48.

74. Key texts that developed the concept of the underclass in the 1980s include Doug Glasgow, *The Black Underclass* (San Francisco: Jossey Bass, 1980); Ken Auletta, *The Un-*

derclass (New York: Random House, 1982); and Lawrence Mead, *Beyond Entitlement: The Social Obligations of Citizenship* (New York: Free Press, 1986). By the mid-1980s, the term had gained traction among liberal as well as conservative writers; William Julius Wilson used it in *The Truly Disadvantaged: The Inner City, the Underclass, and Public Policy* (Chicago: University of Chicago Press, 1987).

75. Banfield, *The Unheavenly City*, 127.

76. Adolph Reed Jr., *Stirrings in the Jug: Black Politics in the Post-segregation Era* (Minneapolis: University of Minnesota Press, 1999), 180.

77. O. Lewis, *La Vida*, li.

78. Moynihan, *The Negro Family*, 5–6.

79. Loïc Wacquant, *Punishing the Poor: The Neoliberal Government of Social Insecurity* (Durham, NC: Duke University Press, 2009), 15, 4.

80. Until the mid-1960s, this figure was not necessarily black. The typical delinquent imagined by politicians and depicted in popular films like *The Wild One* (1953) and *West Side Story* (1961) was just as likely to be white ethnic or Puerto Rican.

81. "The Economic Opportunity Act of 1964."

82. In particular, the Woodlawn Organization, a Chicago-based Community Action Agency, came under fire for paying salaries to the Blackstone Rangers.

83. Johnson, "Remarks upon Signing the Economic Opportunity Act."

84. Much of this rise can be attributed to the migration of African Americans and Puerto Ricans to the city, rather than to the activities of the welfare rights movement. However, the movement was instrumental in pushing the city to increase welfare grants, which rose "in real terms by more than 37 percent while average wages were nearly stagnant." Felicia Kornbluh, *The Battle for Welfare Rights: Politics and Poverty in Modern America* (Philadelphia: University of Pennsylvania Press, 2007), 92.

85. Norman Mailer, *Advertisements for Myself* (1959; repr,, Cambridge, MA: Harvard University Press, 1992), 340, 347.

86. Natalie Moore and Lance Williams, *The Almighty Black P Stone Nation: The Rise, Fall, and Resurgence of an American Gang* (Chicago: Lawrence Hill Books, 2011), 59.

87. John Fry, cited in ibid., 52.

88. Keith Gandal, *The Virtues of the Vicious: Jacob Riis, Stephen Crane, and the Spectacle of the Slum* (New York: Oxford University Press, 1997), 123.

89. Jacob Riis, *How the Other Half Lives* (1890; repr., Boston: Bedford / St. Martin's, 1996), 222.

90. See, for example, Sapphire's description of a typical meal eaten by Claireece Precious Jones and her abusive mother, Mary: "collard greens and ham hocks, corn bread, fried apple pies, and macaroni 'n cheese," consumed until Claireece is "so full I could bust." *Push* (New York: Vintage, 1996), 19, 20. It is not clear how the two women can afford this amount of food on the money they get from AFDC; at this moment in the text, Sapphire reinforces right-wing discourse about welfare queens. More generally, Sapphire splits her depiction of welfare mothers between the two women, echoing

conventional distinctions between the deserving and undeserving poor. In spite of her two illegitimate children (the result of incestuous rape), Claireece is a would-be middle-class subject, as evidenced by her pursuit of literacy and desire to go to college. Mary, in contrast, grotesquely embodies all of the negative stereotypes associated with AFDC recipients.

91. In a climactic moment in Baraka's *Madheart*, BLACK MAN slaps BLACK WOMAN. She responds, "I am your woman, and you are the strongest of God. Fill me with your seed." *Madheart*, in *Black Drama: 1850 to Present*, ed. James V. Hatch, Will Whalen, and Jeremy Caleb Johnson (Chicago: Alexander Street Press, 2015), 17, available at http://alexanderstreet.com.

92. Riis, in *How the Other Half Lives*, provides his readers with an early example of a welfare queen—a woman who begs for money alongside her famished child. She turns out to be a "pauper capitalist" (223) with three thousand dollars in savings—in today's money, about seventy-five thousand. Riis appears unaware that this example problematizes his distinction between the pauper and the tough; by deliberately committing fraud, the pauper exhibits the same character as the tough. This anecdote prefigures Ronald Reagan's use of grotesque exaggeration. During his 1976 presidential campaign, Reagan described a Chicago woman arrested for welfare fraud: "She has eighty names, thirty addresses, twelve Social Security cards and is collecting veteran's benefits on four non-existing deceased husbands. And she is collecting Social Security on her cards. She's got Medicaid, getting food stamps, and she is collecting welfare under each of her names. Her tax-free cash income is over $150,000." "'Welfare Queen' Becomes Issue in Reagan Campaign," *New York Times*, February 15, 1976, 51.

93. Apart from excluding most African Americans from Social Security, the New Deal also helped enforce and extend urban segregation. The New Deal adopted another two-track system for dealing with the housing problems of whites and blacks. The Federal Housing Administration provided low-cost mortgages for whites buying suburban houses, while the United States Housing Authority built public housing for inner-city minorities. Racial discrimination was also built into AFDC. The states determined most eligibility requirements, which meant that many states, especially in the South, included rules that excluded women of color from receiving support. See Jill Quadagno, *The Color of Welfare: How Racism Undermined the War on Poverty* (Oxford: Oxford University Press, 1996).

94. See in particular Linda Gordon, *Pitied but Not Entitled: Single Mothers and the History of Welfare, 1890–1935* (New York: Free Press, 1994); and Gwendolyn Mink, *The Wages of Motherhood: Inequality in the Welfare State, 1917–1942* (Ithaca, NY: Cornell University Press, 1996). See also Brandon Gordon, "Professions of Sentiment: Culture, Poverty, and the Social Work of American Literature" (PhD diss., University of California, Irvine, 2012), which traces AFDC's impact on a sentimental tradition of American fiction stretching from the 1930s to the 1960s; and Susan Edmunds, *Grotesque Relations: Modernist Domestic Fiction and the U.S. Welfare State* (New York: Oxford University

Press, 2008), which situates New Deal–era domestic fiction in the context of the gender-bifurcated welfare state.

95. Moynihan, *The Negro Family*, 30, 34, 28. Moynihan's feminist critics argue that he fundamentally misunderstands black family structure. In particular, beginning with Carol Stack's *All Our Kin: Strategies for Survival in a Black Community* (1974; repr., New York: Basic Books, 2013), feminist social scientists have shown that black communities exhibit extended female kin networks that offer a viable alternative to the American patriarchal nuclear family.

96. While Moynihan promoted work training programs for African American men, he was one of the Community Action Program's most outspoken Democratic critics. The program, he claimed, raised expectations it could never fulfill, pushing hitherto quiescent lower-class minorities into open conflict with society. The unanswered question of Community Action "is whether the poor are ever to be politicized save in terms of conflict and fear and the creation of hate objects." *Maximum Feasible Misunderstanding*, 163.

97. Moynihan, *The Negro Family*, 42.

Chapter 1: Jack Kerouac's Delinquent Art

1. Jack Kerouac, *Conversations with Jack Kerouac*, ed. Kevin Hayes (Jackson: University Press of Mississippi, 2005), 12.

2. Kerouac, *On the Road*. All page references to this novel are to the 1999 Penguin edition and are noted parenthetically in the text as *OR*.

3. Jack Kerouac, *The Portable Jack Kerouac*, ed. Ann Charters (New York: Viking, 1995), 559.

4. Norman Podhoretz, "The Know-Nothing Bohemians," in *Beat Down to Your Soul: What Was the Beat Generation?*, ed. Ann Charters (New York: Penguin, 2001), 492. See also John Ciardi: "The fact is that the Beat Generation is not only juvenile but certainly related to juvenile delinquency through a common ancestor whose best name is Disgust. The street gang rebellion has gone for blood and violence. The Beats have found their kicks in an intellectual pose, in drugs . . . and in wine, Zen, jazz, sex, and a carefully mannered jargon." "Epitaph for the Dead Beats," in *A Casebook on the Beats*, ed. Thomas Parkinson (New York: Thomas Y. Crowell, 1968), 257.

5. David Steritt, *Mad to Be Saved: The Beats, the '50s, and Film* (Carbondale: Southern Illinois University Press, 1998), 164. As Steritt documents, a spate of Hollywood exploitation films emerged in the late 1950s and early 1960s that depicted Beat artists as murderers and rapists.

6. Rotella, *October Cities*, 225.

7. Ibid., 242.

8. In 1950s delinquency discourse, both species were male. Paul Goodman explained delinquency theorists' exclusive focus on young men in his best-selling *Growing Up Absurd*: "The problems I want to discuss in this book belong primarily, in our

society, to the boys: how to be useful and make something of oneself. A girl does not *have* to, she is not expected to, 'make something' of herself. Her career does not have to be self-justifying, for she will have children, which is absolutely self-justifying, like any other natural or creative act." *Growing Up Absurd: Problems of Youth in the Organized Society* (New York: Vintage, 1960), 13. Delinquency discourse was a crucial component of Cold War gender ideology, which reacted against women's entry into the workforce during World War II by reinscribing nineteenth-century divisions between the masculine and feminine domestic spheres. For a classic social history of this ideology, see Elaine Tyler May, *Homeward Bound: American Families in the Cold War Era* (New York: Basic Books, 1999).

9. Émile Durkheim, *Suicide: A Study in Sociology*, trans. John A. Spaulding and George Simpson (Glencoe, IL: Free Press, 1951), 250, 254.

10. Goodman, *Growing Up Absurd*, 163. The idea that anomic delinquents secretly want to become middle class informed many popular representations of lower-class youth, especially László Benedek's *The Wild One* (1953). The film stages a confrontation between two rival gangs of hip motorcyclists and the residents of a square, middle-class town. As the film emphasizes, this cultural conflict has already been decided in favor of square values, which the delinquent bikers, including Johnny Strabler (Marlon Brando), secretly covet. In an early scene, Johnny's gang descends on a respectable motorcycle race and steals the second-class trophy—a middle-class prize conquered through illegitimate means. The trophy, which Johnny carries with him throughout the film, becomes a symbol of his frustrated middle-class aspirations.

11. Frederic Thrasher, *The Gang: A Study of 1313 Gangs in Chicago* (Chicago: University of Chicago Press, 1936), 7, 22, 217. Other major studies of juvenile delinquency by Chicago school sociologists include Clifford Shaw, *The Natural History of a Delinquent Career* (Chicago: University of Chicago Press, 1931); Clifford Shaw, Frederick Zorbaugh, Henry McKay, and Leonard Cottrell, *Delinquency Areas: A Study of the Geographical Distribution of School Truants, Juvenile Delinquents, and Adult Offenders in Chicago* (Chicago: University of Chicago Press, 1929); Clifford Shaw and Henry McKay, *Juvenile Delinquency in Urban Areas: A Study of Rates of Delinquency in Relation to the Differential Characteristics of Local Communities in American Cities* (Chicago: University of Chicago Press, 1969); and Edwin Sutherland, *The Professional Thief* (Chicago: University of Chicago Press, 1937).

12. William F. Whyte, *Street Corner Society: The Social Structure of an Italian Slum* (Chicago: University of Chicago Press, 1943), 97.

13. In particular, 1950s observers sometimes lamented the displacement of the early twentieth-century urban political machines by the bureaucratic institutions of the welfare state. According to Cloward and Ohlin in *Delinquency and Opportunity*, the political machines had been "an important integrating structure and a significant channel for social ascent" (207) within immigrant communities. One of their chief recommendations was for the federal government to refashion local welfare bureaus so that they would

take on some of the functions of these older institutions. This recommendation helped inspire the Community Action Program.

14. Galbraith, *The Affluent Society*, 253.

15. Robert Holton, "Kerouac among the Fellahin: *On the Road* to the Postmodern," *Modern Fiction Studies* 41, no. 2 (1995): 265–283. Other critics who explore the Fellahin's centrality to Kerouac's fiction include Mark Richardson, "Peasant Dreams: Reading *On the Road*," *Texas Studies in Literature and Language* 13, no. 2 (2001): 218–242; Brendon Nicholls, "The Melting Pot That Boiled Over: Racial Fetishism and the *Lingua Franca* of Jack Kerouac's Fiction," *Modern Fiction Studies* 49, no. 3 (2003): 524–549; and Manuel Luis Martinez, *Countering the Counterculture: Rereading Postwar American Dissent from Jack Kerouac to Tomás Rivera* (Madison: University of Wisconsin Press, 2003).

16. Spengler, *The Decline of the West*, 170–171.

17. As Lisa Siraganian notes, breath was central to the bodily aesthetics of Olson and other process writers. Through its emphasis on breath, Olson's poetry "aims to represent—or more accurately capture—the body's trace, condensing the essence of the poet's historical specificity for the reader to read and thus perform—a literal manifestation of the poet's bodily response to the world." *Modernism's Other Work*, 141.

18. Jack Kerouac, "Essentials of Spontaneous Prose," in *The Portable Beat Reader*, ed. Ann Charters (New York: Viking, 1992), 484. Kerouac originally published this manifesto in *Black Mountain Review*.

19. Spengler, *The Decline of the West*, 185.

20. Jack Kerouac, *Vanity of Duluoz: An Adventurous Education, 1935–1946* (New York: Coward-McCann, 1968), 273. All page references to this novel are hereafter noted parenthetically in the text as *VD*. The original publication date of this and other novels does not correspond to the year when Kerouac wrote it. Kerouac produced most of his work in an outpouring of creativity in the early to mid-1950s, immediately after the breakthrough he accomplished with *On the Road*. None of this work was published until after he became a literary celebrity in the late 1950s.

21. Jack Kerouac, *Desolation Angels* (1965; repr., New York: Riverhead, 1995), 341, 343.

22. Jack Kerouac, *Maggie Cassidy* (1959; repr., New York: Penguin Books, 1993). All page references are to this edition and are hereafter noted parenthetically in the text as *MC*.

23. Nancy McCampbell Grace, "A White Man in Love: A Study of Race, Gender, Class, and Ethnicity in Jack Kerouac's *Maggie Cassidy, The Subterraneans*, and *Tristessa*," in *The Beat Generation: Critical Essays*, ed. Kostas Myrsiades (New York: Peter Lang, 2002), 93–120.

24. Ralph Ellison, *Invisible Man* (1952; repr., New York: Vintage, 1995), 266. This opposition between Jackie's Faustian ambitions and Maggie's Fellahin rootedness simplifies the cultural dynamics of working-class communities. In particular, one of the puzzling features of *Maggie Cassidy* is that it is set in the 1930s but entirely ignores the labor conflicts that transformed industrial towns like Lowell. The Textile Workers Union

of America–CIO were actively organizing Lowell workers in the 1930s and 1940s. Laurence Gross, "The Game Is Played Out: The Closing Decades of the Boott Mill," in *The Continuing Revolution: A History of Lowell, Massachusetts*, ed. Robert Weible (Lowell, MA: Lowell Historical Society, 1991), 291. The Depression-era proletariat, in other words, had little in common with the static peasantry that Kerouac idealizes in his fiction. Rather, workers like Maggie's brothers were involved in their own Faustian project of self- and social transformation.

25. Kerouac began his first book, a short story collection titled *Atop an Underwood*, shortly after leaving Columbia University. See Gerald Nicosia, *Memory Babe: A Critical Biography of Jack Kerouac* (Berkeley: University of California Press, 1994), 90–91.

26. Kerouac, "Essentials of Spontaneous Prose," 485.

27. Christina Klein, *Cold War Orientalism: Asia in the Middlebrow Imagination, 1945–1961* (Berkeley: University of California Press, 2003), 64.

28. Pierre Bourdieu, *Distinction: A Social Critique of the Judgment of Taste*, trans. Richard Nice (Cambridge, MA: Harvard University Press, 1984), 294.

29. Norman Podhoretz outlined this parallel in "The Know-Nothing Bohemians," in which he compared the Beats to delinquents. Whereas the avant-garde of the 1920s challenged bourgeois art "in the name of civilization," the Beats, have few "intellectual interests" and worship "primitivism, instinct, energy, 'blood'" (484).

30. Cloward and Ohlin, *Delinquency and Opportunity*, 106–107.

31. C. Wright Mills, *White Collar: The American Middle Classes* (London: Oxford University Press, 1956), xvii.

32. Talcott Parsons, *Essays in Sociological Theory* (Glencoe, IL: Free Press, 1954), 306.

33. The most famous 1950s film about juvenile delinquency, *Rebel without a Cause* (1955), depicts youth criminality as a middle-class pathology. The film attributes the seemingly irrational behavior of its teenage characters to dysfunctions within their relatively affluent families. This is especially true of the film's central figure, Jim Stark (played by James Dean). His rebellion is a response to his domineering mother and effeminate father. The latter, in particular, provokes a psychological crisis when Stark discovers him wearing the mother's apron. At the core of the film is the question that Stark repeatedly asks his father: "What do you do when you have to be a man?"

34. Albert Cohen, *Delinquent Boys: The Culture of the Gang* (New York: Free Press, 1955), 165.

35. Moynihan, *The Negro Family*, 29, 35.

36. James Jones, *Jack Kerouac's Duluoz Legend: The Mythic Form of an Autobiographical Fiction* (Carbondale: Southern Illinois University Press, 1999), 91.

37. The original scroll version of *On the Road* begins with Leo Kerouac's death: "I met Neal not long after my father died. . . . I had just gotten over a serious illness that I won't talk about except that it really had to do with my father's death and my awful feeling that everything was dead." Jack Kerouac, *On the Road: The Original Scroll*, ed. Howard Cunnell (New York: Penguin Books, 2007), 109.

38. Jack Kerouac, *Dr. Sax: Faust Part III* (1959; repr., New York: Grove Press, 1987). All page references are to this edition and are hereafter noted parenthetically in the text as *DS*.

39. Nicholls links Jackie's Oedipal desire in *Dr. Sax* to the racial fetishism that runs throughout Kerouac's fiction. Jones interprets the Freudian symbolism of the novel's fantasy sections.

40. J. Jones, *Jack Kerouac's Duluoz Legend*, 43.

41. Malcolm Cowley, *The Literary Situation* (New York: Viking, 1954), 43, 45, 52–53, 50.

Chapter 2: Black Arts and the Great Society

1. Gwendolyn Brooks, *Conversations with Gwendolyn Brooks*, ed. Gloria Wade Gayles (Jackson: University Press of Mississippi, 2003), 69.

2. Brooks completed a two-year degree at Wilson Junior College. See George Kent, *A Life of Gwendolyn Brooks* (Lexington: University Press of Kentucky, 1990), 33. Baraka dropped out of Howard University, an experience that he described in many of his autobiographical texts.

3. See Julius E. Thompson, *Dudley Randall, Broadside Press, and the Black Arts Movement in Detroit, 1960–1995* (Jefferson, NC: McFarland, 1999).

4. Raymond Malewitz, "'My Newish Voice': Rethinking Black Power in Gwendolyn Brooks's Whirlwind," *Callaloo* 29, no. 2 (2006): 532.

5. Baraka, *Conversations*, 21.

6. Amiri Baraka, *The System of Dante's Hell*, in *The Fiction of LeRoi Jones / Amiri Baraka*, ed. Greg Tate (Chicago: Lawrence Hill Books, 2000), 15–125. All subsequent page references are to this edition and are noted parenthetically in the text.

7. Gwendolyn Brooks, *In the Mecca*, in *The World of Gwendolyn Brooks* (New York: Harper & Row, 1971), 371–426. All subsequent page references to this book are noted parenthetically in the text.

8. Baraka's use of multiple names highlights his sense that the narrator is fragmented into many selves, an idea that he would explore at greater length in *6 Persons*, a work of fiction that he completed in 1974 but did not publish until 2000. In *The System of Dante's Hell*, this fragmented conception of the self is especially evident in "THE EIGHTH DITCH (IS DRAMA," an experimental play that Baraka includes as one of his chapters. In the play, an older man named 64 seduces and sodomizes a teenage boy named 46 at a summer camp. Both Sollors, *Amiri Baraka/LeRoi Jones*, 95–102, 139–146; and Kimberly Benston, *Baraka: The Renegade and the Mask* (New Haven, CT: Yale University Press, 1976), 10–30, suggest that the two characters may be different versions of the novel's narrator: a naïve middle-class black teenager and an older, disillusioned black bohemian. In Baraka's terms, the play is a "foetus drama" (77) in which the writer impregnates his younger self. For the sake of convenience, I refer to the narrator as "Roi," the name used in the novel's last chapter, "Heretics."

9. As many of Baraka's critics have pointed out, his attempt to free himself from his parents' class aspirations is a motif that runs through all phases of his career. Watts, in

particular, highlights this dimension of Baraka's work in *Amiri Baraka*. Initially, Baraka "considered his emergence in the bohemian subculture of the Beat community as a negation of the lifestyle of the black bourgeoisie to which he had been exposed at Howard and had always been expected to join" (29). Later, he successively denounced both Beat bohemianism and black cultural nationalism as bourgeois social movements.

10. Baraka, *Conversations*, 100.

11. For a detailed account of the rich intertextuality of *The System of Dante's Hell*, see Lloyd Brown, "Jones (Baraka) and His Literary Heritage in *The System of Dante's Hell*," in *Imamu Amiri Baraka (LeRoi Jones): A Collection of Critical Essays*, ed. Kimberly Benston (Englewood Cliffs, NJ: Prentice-Hall, 1978), 71–83. The novel, he argues, exemplifies the extent to which Baraka's art depends on the Western literary tradition that he seeks to repudiate: "The rejected tradition continues to function in the artist's work for the simple reason that a conscious act of repudiation does not necessarily constitute an expunging" (72).

12. See Andrew Epstein, *Beautiful Enemies: Friendship and Postwar American Poetry* (Oxford: Oxford University Press, 2006), 194–219, which underscores *The System of Dante's Hell*'s indebtedness to the New American Poetry movement. Epstein focuses, in particular, on Baraka's friendship with Frank O'Hara, to whom Baraka alludes throughout the novel.

13. According to Baraka, "In the various bohemias and near bohemias there is a kind of openness about the white man's (and woman's) needs, hence such normally hidden or reversed image of the black man as superstud for white women (as that image is projected by both black and white) is not only given large currency, but taken literally by both black and white." *Home*, 227.

14. Amiri Baraka, *Blues People: Negro Music in White America* (1963; repr., New York: HarperCollins, 2002), 7.

15. Baraka, *Home*, 183.

16. Brown, "Jones (Baraka) and His Literary Heritage," 77.

17. O. Lewis, *La Vida*, xlvi.

18. E. Franklin Frazier's influence on Baraka has been well documented. Watts, in particular, complains that Baraka's work is marred by his "uncritical reliance on E. Franklin Frazier's distorted polemic *The Black Bourgeoisie* as a primary source of knowledge." *Amiri Baraka*, 486.

19. E. Franklin Frazier, *Black Bourgeoisie: The Rise of a New Middle Class* (1957; repr., New York: Free Press, 1965), 195, 229.

20. Benston, *Baraka*, 30.

21. Amiri Baraka, *Four Black Revolutionary Plays, All Praises to the Black Man* (Indianapolis, IN: Bobbs-Merrill, 1969), 23.

22. Amiri Baraka, "Columbia, the Gem of the Ocean," in *Black Drama, 1850 to Present*, ed. James V. Hatch, Will Whalen, and Jeremy Caleb Johnson (Chicago: Alexander Street Press, 2015), 2, available at http://alexanderstreet.com.

23. Amiri Baraka, *Kawaida Studies: The New Nationalism* (Chicago: Third World Press, 1972), 12.

24. Baraka, *Conversations*, 20.

25. Amiri Baraka and Fundi (Billy Abernathy), *In Our Terribleness (Some Elements and Meaning in Black Style)* (Indianapolis, IN: Bobbs-Merrill, 1970).

26. Quoted in Kent, *A Life of Gwendolyn Brooks*, 74.

27. Gwendolyn Brooks, "Poets Who Are Negroes," *Phylon* 11, no. 4 (1950): 312.

28. For more on the New Poetry, see Edward Brunner, *Cold War Poetry* (Urbana: University of Illinois Press, 2001).

29. Larry Neal, "The Black Arts Movement," *TDR: The Drama Review* 12, no. 4 (1968): 29.

30. Baraka, *Home*, 106, 108, 112–113.

31. See Judith Saunders, "The Love Song of Satin-Legs Smith: Gwendolyn Brooks Revisits Prufrock's Hell," *Papers on Language & Literature* 36, no. 1 (2000): 3–18, which explores the poem's indebtedness to Eliot's "The Love Song of J. Alfred Prufrock." See also Karen Ford, "The Sonnets of Satin-Legs Brooks," *Contemporary Literature* 48, no. 3 (2007): 345–373. Ford argues that Brooks develops a "zoot-suit aesthetic" (349) that mediates her relationship with Eliot's poem. Just as the zoot suit worn by Brooks's title character parodies a white man's suit, "The Sundays of Satin-Legs Smith" parodies a white man's poem.

32. For an in-depth account of Chicago's Black Arts network, see Kinohi Nishikawa, "Between the World and *Nommo*: Hoyt W. Fuller and Chicago's Black Arts Magazines," *Chicago Review* 59/60, no. 4/1 (2016): 143–163.

33. Brooks, *Conversations*, 68.

34. Gwendolyn Brooks, "Class Notes—Madison, Wisconsin," Box 107C, Gwendolyn Brooks Archive, Rare Book & Manuscript Library, University of Illinois, Urbana-Champaign.

35. Brooks, "Blackstone Rangers Teaching Materials," Box 107C, Gwendolyn Brooks Archive. Brooks also assigned *Paris Review* interviews by William Faulkner and Ernest Hemingway and read excerpts from E. M. Forster.

36. Brooks, *Conversations*, 55.

37. Amiri Baraka and Larry Neal, eds., *Black Fire: An Anthology of Afro-American Writing* (New York: William Morrow, 1968).

38. Brooks, "Class notes—Northeastern—Black Literature—May 7, Mondays and Wednesdays (1969)," Writings: Personal Files 2, Gwendolyn Brooks Archives.

39. Ibid. Brooks's statement about art's relationship to the materials of the world recurs in her coauthored pedagogical manifesto: Gwendolyn Brooks, Keorapetse Kgositsile, Haki Madhubuti, and Dudley Randall, *A Capsule Course in Black Poetry Writing* (Detroit, MI: Broadside Press, 1975), 11.

40. Brooks published poems commemorating the deaths of John F. Kennedy and Adlai Stevenson in the *Chicago Sun-Times* and *Negro Digest*. On October 24, 1965, she

read excerpts from both poems in a speech for Vice President Hubert Humphrey. See Kent, *A Life of Gwendolyn Brooks*, 184.

41. D. H. Melhem, *Gwendolyn Brooks: Poetry and the Heroic Voice* (Lexington: University Press of Kentucky, 1987), 180.

42. Brooks's response to the Wall, for instance, differs dramatically from Haki Madhubuti's poem, "The Wall," which similarly contrasts Picasso's Chicago sculpture with the *Wall of Respect*. Madhubuti insists on the identification of artist, artwork, and community through his use of repetition:

> we got black artists
> who paint black art
> the mighty black wall
> negroes from south shore &
> hyde park coming to check out
> a black creation
> black art, of the people,
> for the people,
> art for people's sake
> black people
> the mighty black wall

"The Wall," *The Wall of Respect*, Mary and Leigh Block Museum of Art, 1967, available at http://www.blockmuseum.northwestern.edu/wallofrespect/main.htm. Brooks challenges this simple identification through her use of ambiguity. She also refuses Madhubuti's characterization of the community as "black," instead insisting on the multiplicity of the Wall's audience. Those who listen to Brooks's speech in her poem have "black ears, brown ears, reddish-brown / and ivory ears" (414).

43. Amiri Baraka, *Black Magic: Collected Poetry, 1961–1967* (Indianapolis, IN: Bobbs-Merrill, 1969), 225.

44. Melhem, *Gwendolyn Brooks*, 176.

45. For detailed accounts of Mecca Flats's history in relation to Brooks's poem, see Daniela Kukrechtova, "The Death and Life of a Chicago Edifice: Gwendolyn Brooks's 'In the Mecca,'" *African American Review* 43, no. 2–3 (2009): 457–472; C. K. Doreski, *Writing America Black: Race Rhetoric in the Public Sphere* (Cambridge: Cambridge University Press, 1998), 119–144; and John Lowney, "'A Material Collapse That Is Construction': History and Counter-memory in Gwendolyn Brooks's 'In the Mecca,'" *MELUS* 23, no. 3 (1998): 3–20.

46. According to Cheryl Clarke, "At times his relationship to the narrator evokes younger black poets' relationship to Brooks; at other times Alfred seems to be a persona for Brooks, apprenticing herself to the younger (male) poets." "The Loss of Lyric Space and the Critique of Traditions in Gwendolyn Brooks's 'In the Mecca,'" *Kenyon Review* 17, no. 1 (1995): 140.

47. Gwendolyn Brooks, *Report from Part One* (Detroit, MI: Broadside Press, 1972), 183.

48. Because of these twin allusions to Amiri Baraka and Haki Madhubuti, critics have interpreted the poem's conception of what it means to write black poetry in terms influenced by the Black Arts movement itself. In particular, they have read the poem in light of Brooks's repeated claims after 1967 that she was in the process of abandoning the lyric in favor of colloquial free verse. Cheryl Clarke, for example, reads the poem as an elegy for the lyric, which cannot survive in the "apocalyptic . . . black political climate of the sixties." "The Loss of Lyric Space," 144. Karen Ford, in contrast, draws attention to the persistence of the lyric in the poem, arguing that "In the Mecca" makes a case for the continuing survival of Brooks's early poetics in her later work. Brooks's renunciation of the lyric "does not prevent the Meccans—or, apparently, the poem itself—from longing for beauty." "The Last Quatrain: Gwendolyn Brooks and the Ends of Ballads," *Twentieth-Century Literature* 56, no. 3 (2010): 385.

49. Ferdinand de Saussure, *Course in General Linguistics*, trans. Roy Harris (La Salle, IL: Open Court, 1983), 112.

50. Sheila Hughes, "A Prophet Overheard: A Juxtapositional Reading of Gwendolyn Brooks's 'In the Mecca,'" *African American Review* 38, no. 2 (2004): 270.

51. Quoted in Melhem, *Gwendolyn Brooks*, 214.

52. Craig Hansen Werner, *Playing the Changes: From Afro-Modernism to the Jazz Impulse* (Urbana: University of Illinois Press, 1994), 148.

53. Ibid., 159.

54. Melhem, *Gwendolyn Brooks*, 162.

55. Brooks, *Report from Part One*, 39.

Chapter 3: Legal Services and the Cockroach Revolution

1. Oscar Zeta Acosta, *Autobiography of a Brown Buffalo* (1972; repr., New York: Vintage, 1989). All subsequent page references are to the 1989 Vintage edition and are noted parenthetically in the text as *A*.

2. Oscar Zeta Acosta, *The Revolt of the Cockroach People* (1973; repr., New York: Vintage, 1989). All subsequent page references are to the 1989 Vintage edition and are noted parenthetically in the text as *R*. Following the lead of Michael Hames-García, *Fugitive Thought: Prison Movements, Race, and the Meaning of Justice* (Minneapolis: University of Minnesota Press, 2004), I refer to the historical Oscar Zeta Acosta as Acosta, the protagonist of *The Autobiography of a Brown Buffalo* as Oscar, and that of *The Revolt of the Cockroach People* as Brown.

3. In the interests of historical accuracy, I use the term "Mexican American" to refer to Americans of Mexican descent. I use the more specific cultural nationalist terms "Chicano" and "Chicana" to refer to Mexican Americans involved in the Brown Power movement of the late 1960s / early 1970s.

4. The most notable of these militants was Rodolfo "Corky" Gonzalez, the professional boxer–turned Democratic insider–turned Chicano activist and poet, whom Brown defends against weapons charges in *Revolt*. Carlos Muñoz Jr. describes Commu-

nity Action Agencies as "training grounds" for many of the Mexican American students who became Chicano activists. *Youth, Identity Power: The Chicano Movement* (London: Verso, 1989), 73.

5. For a reading of *Autobiography* as a response to *On the Road*, see Marci Carrasquillo, "Oscar 'Zeta' Acosta's American Odyssey," *MELUS* 35, no. 1 (2010): 77–97.

6. Earl Johnson Jr., *Justice and Reform: The Formative Years of the OEO Legal Services Program* (New York: Russell Sage, 1974), 73.

7. Ramón Saldívar, *Chicano Narrative: The Dialectics of Difference* (Madison: University of Wisconsin Press, 1990), 97.

8. Acosta's interests in politics began with Kennedy's presidential campaign. "I am a RED HOT DEMOCRAT," he declared to Betty Davis Acosta in 1960. "Really, I've been reading voraciously on politics for the past two months. After the convention next month when they start campaigning here in SF I am going to join the Young Democrat Movement." Letter to Betty Davis Acosta, June 30, 1960, Oscar Zeta Acosta Papers, CEMA 1, Box 2, Folder 7, University of California, Santa Barbara Library.

9. Community Progress, Inc.'s law office opened on January 2, 1963, and closed on February 27, 1963. For more on the New Haven experience, see E. Johnson, *Justice and Reform*, 22–23.

10. Ibid., 13.

11. Edgar Cahn and Jean Cahn, "The War on Poverty: A Civilian Perspective," *Yale Law Journal* 73, no. 8 (1964): 1320, 1332, 1335, 1334.

12. Ibid., 1346, 1321.

13. Philip Hannon commented on the failure of Legal Services lawyers to enact the Cahns' vision: "Most lawyers are familiar with the more mundane of the legal problems of the poor. If need be, they can process divorces and bankruptcies on a volume basis, but few if any know how to go about achieving that vague something called law reform." "The Leadership Problem in the Legal Services Program," *Law and Society Review* 4 (1969–1970): 246.

14. For histories of the welfare rights movement, see Kornbluh, *The Battle for Welfare Rights*; Premilla Nadasen, *Welfare Warriors: The Welfare Rights Movement in the United States* (New York: Routledge, 2005); and Annelise Orleck, *Storming Caesars Palace: How Black Mothers Fought Their Own War on Poverty* (Boston: Beacon Press, 2005).

15. Edward Sparer, the lawyer and legal theorist who established Columbia University's Center on Social Welfare Policy and Law, mapped out an ambitious legal plan for the NWRO, one that he hoped would establish a constitutional "right to live." He explained this right in his 1971 essay, "The Right to Welfare," in *The Rights of Americans: What They Are—What They Should Be*, ed. Norman Dorsen (New York: Pantheon Press, 1971), 65–93. See also Martha Davis, *Brutal Need: Lawyers and the Welfare Rights Movement, 1960–1973* (New Haven, CT: Yale University Press, 1993), 37–38. Although the welfare rights movement scored some early victories, it was ultimately unsuccessful in effecting constitutional change.

16. Hames-García, *Fugitive Thought*, 71.

17. Peter Stallybrass and Allon White, *The Politics and Poetics of Transgression* (Ithaca, NY: Cornell University Press, 1989).

18. Quoted in Davis, *Brutal Need*, 120.

19. Carl Gutiérrez-Jones offers the most widely cited analysis of Acosta's misogyny, focusing on the homosocial bonds that Brown forms with the Chicano militants in *Revolt*. These bonds depend on the transformation of Chicanas into sexual capital exchanged between men. *Rethinking the Borderlands: Between Chicano Culture and Legal Discourse* (Berkeley: University of California Press, 1995), 130. Carrasquillo, meanwhile, focuses directly on Oscar/Brown's representation of women in both novels. Referring specifically to Oscar's flight in *Autobiography*, she argues that he "does not fully consider how the combined forces of his class status and gender enable his mobility as surely as his female clients' gender and class restrict theirs." "Oscar 'Zeta' Acosta's American Odyssey," 82. Other critics who address Acosta's misogyny include Hames-García, *Fugitive Thought*, 64–70; and Sarah Deutsch, "Gender, Labor History, and Chicano/a Ethnic Identity," *Frontiers* 14, no. 2 (1994): 13–14.

20. Héctor Calderón, "To Read Chicano Narrative: Commentary and Metacommentary," *Mester* 11 (May 1982): 7.

21. Gutiérrez-Jones, *Rethinking the Borderlands*, 135–136. Gutiérrez-Jones notes that Brown eroticizes the Chicano handshake, turning it into a symbol of anal rape. During an encounter between Brown and Liberace, Brown teaches the gesture to "the world famous fag": "He reaches for my hand. I clasp his thumb. 'This is the Chicano Handshake,' I say. He blushes and squeezes" (*R*, 163).

22. Some of the more prominent critiques of Brown Power machismo by Chicana theorists include Ana Castillo, *Massacre of the Dreamers: Essays on Xicanisma* (New York: Plume, 1995), 21–41; Alma García, ed., *Chicana Feminist Thought: The Basic Historical Writings* (New York: Routledge, 1997); and Vicki Ruiz, *From out of the Shadows: Mexican Women in Twentieth-Century America* (New York: Oxford University Press, 1998), 99–146.

23. For more on professionalism and the New Left, see Schryer, *Fantasies of the New Class*, 141–166; and McCann and Szalay, "Do You Believe in Magic?," 451–460. Within the legal profession, violations of professional norms became common among activist lawyers associated with both the welfare rights and civil rights movements. Poverty lawyers working for New York's Mobilization for Youth, for example, "believed that their clients were more important than their professionalism; they would violate court etiquette and the bounds of professional good taste by, for example, interrupting opposing counsel or following a judge into chambers to argue a case if it might mean a better result for their client." Davis, *Brutal Need*, 31. These violations were generally more effective than the conflict-free advocacy typical of pre-1960s Legal Aid.

24. Hames-García, *Fugitive Thought*, 74–75. In developing this extramural critique, Acosta again echoes the strategies of the lawyers who helped establish Legal Services. Up

until the mid-1960s, most lawyers associated with the Legal Aid movement made no connection between economic deprivation and legal injustice. The law itself, they believed, was blind to class. As Reginald Herber Smith, one of the movement's founders, expressed in 1919, "The legal disabilities of the poor in nearly every instance result from defects in the machinery of the law and are not created by any discriminations of the substantive law against them." Quoted in E. Johnson, *Justice and Reform*, 13. In contrast, when Edward Sparer planned out a long-term strategy for reforming welfare laws, he drew on the work of Charles Reich and other legal theorists who emphasized the American legal system's inherent bias toward the propertied classes. In "The New Property," *Yale Law Journal* 73, no. 5 (1964): 733–787, Charles Reich argued that the welfare state had transformed the nature of American wealth so that most wealth took the form of government largesse. The law, however, had not yet recognized this shift, allowing the government to exert tyrannical rule by granting or withholding benefits; the new wealth "was linked to class; the lower on the totem pole you are, the fewer rights you have." Quoted in Davis, *Brutal Need*, 85. For Reich and Sparer, the solution was to redefine welfare as property rather than gratuity, subject to the constitutional protections surrounding property rights.

25. Brown describes three defenses in *Revolt*, loosely modeled after cases that Acosta fought between 1968 and 1971. The first is his defense of the East L.A. Thirteen, charged with inciting a riot during the East L.A. Walkouts. The second is his defense of the St. Basil Twenty-One, a group of militants who interrupted a service at St. Basil's Cathedral in protest against Cardinal McIntyre's racist policies against Mexican American parishioners. Brown's third case is his defense of the Tooner Flats Seven, arrested during the 1970 Chicano Moratorium march, an anti–Vietnam War protest. This last case is an amalgam of two of Acosta's actual cases: his defense of Rodolfo "Corky" Gonzalez and Albert Gurule against weapons charges and his defense of the Biltmore Ten, accused of trying to set fire to the Biltmore Hotel during a 1969 speech by Governor Ronald Reagan. For a detailed account of these four trials and Acosta's strategies in them, see Ian Haney-López, *Racism on Trial: The Chicano Fight for Justice* (Cambridge, MA: Harvard University Press, 2003); and Burton Moore, *Love and Riot: Oscar Zeta Acosta and the Great Mexican American Revolt* (Northridge, CA: Floricanto Press, 2003).

26. Hames-García, *Fugitive Thought*, 76.

27. Roland Zanzibar is a thinly veiled allusion to the journalist Rubén Salazar, who was killed by a police tear-gas canister during the Chicano Moratorium. His death became a rallying cry for Chicano militants and a symbol of police violence against Mexican Americans.

28. The version of the chapter published in *La Gente* can be found in Oscar Zeta Acosta, *Oscar "Zeta" Acosta: The Uncollected Works*, ed. Ilan Stavans (Houston: Arte Público, 1996), 177–190.

29. Ibid., 282.

30. Louis Gerard Mendoza, *Historia: The Literary Making of Chicana and Chicano History* (College Station: Texas A&M University Press, 2001), 205.

31. Mendoza observes that the lone student among the East L.A. Thirteen in *Revolt* is likely a thinly veiled portrait of the future movement historian, Carlos Muñoz Jr. (192).

32. Hunter S. Thompson, *Fear and Loathing in America: The Brutal Odyssey of an Outlaw Journalist* (New York: Simon & Schuster, 2000), 446.

33. Oscar Zeta Acosta, "Letter to Helen Brann," January 1974, Oscar Zeta Acosta Papers, CEMA 1, Box 2, Folder 38, University of California, Santa Barbara Library.

Chapter 4: Writing Urban Crisis after Moynihan

1. Joyce Carol Oates, *them* (New York: Fawcett Crest, 1969). All subsequent page references to this book are to this edition and noted parenthetically in the text.

2. See Sidney Fine, *Violence in the Model City: The Cavanagh Administration, Race Relations, and the Detroit Riot of 1967* (East Lansing: Michigan State University Press, 2007). Most of the 1960s riots similarly began with unplanned confrontations between police and ghetto residents. None were orchestrated events.

3. Moynihan fashioned this book out of a series of articles that he published in the *Public Interest* throughout the late 1960s. In this period, the *Public Interest* was the best-known vehicle for neoconservative critiques of the Great Society.

4. Moynihan, *Maximum Feasible Misunderstanding*, 24, 163.

5. Ibid., 192.

6. O'Connor, *Poverty Knowledge*, 209.

7. See Clark, *Dark Ghetto*; Elliot Liebow, *Tally's Corner: A Study of Negro Streetcorner Men* (1967; repr., Washington, DC: Rowman & Littlefield, 2003); and Lee Rainwater, *Behind Ghetto Walls: Black Families in a Federal Slum* (Chicago: Aldine Transaction, 1970).

8. O'Connor, *Poverty Knowledge*, 213–241.

9. Quoted in ibid., 209.

10. Tom Wolfe, *Radical Chic & Mau-Mauing the Flak Catchers* (1970; repr., New York: Bantam Books, 1999). All subsequent page references to this book are to this edition and noted parenthetically in the text.

11. Émile Zola, *The Experimental Novel and Other Essays*, trans. Belle M. Sherman (New York: Cassell, 1893), 18.

12. Jude Davies, "Naturalism and Class," in *The Oxford Handbook of American Literary Naturalism*, ed. Keith Newlin (Oxford: Oxford University Press, 2011), 307.

13. Joyce Carol Oates, *Conversations with Joyce Carol Oates*, ed. Lee Milazzo (Jackson: University Press of Mississippi, 1989), 4.

14. McGurl, *The Program Era*, 301.

15. Galbraith, *The Affluent Society*, 236.

16. Since Donald Pizer's *Realism and Naturalism in Nineteenth-Century American Literature* (Carbondale: Southern Illinois University Press, 1984), critics have rejected the notion that American literary naturalists merely applied deterministic theories to their fiction. Pizer instead discovers an active tension in naturalist fiction: "The naturalist often describes his characters as though they are conditioned and controlled by envi-

ronment, heredity, instinct or chance. But he also suggests a compensating humanistic value in his characters or their fates which affirms the significance of the individual and of his life" (11). Oates's novel embodies a similar tension; in spite of the setbacks they suffer, many of their own making, the Wendalls keep on striving for a better life.

17. Many of *them*'s early critics questioned whether the novel demonstrates the kind of determinism characteristic of classic naturalist novels. For Steven Barza, the novel affirms "the importance of individual caprice. The Uncertainty Principle has arrived at the human laboratory." "Joyce Carol Oates: Naturalism and the Aberrant Response," *Studies in American Fiction* 7, no. 2 (1979): 142. Ellen Friedman similarly calls attention to the apparent randomness of the novel's events: "Rather than describing an environment that willfully oppresses the poverty-stricken, Oates is describing a universe of pure accident, in which contingency dominates." *Joyce Carol Oates* (New York: Frederick Ungar, 1980), 81. However, even as critics have characterized the Wendalls' history as random, they have also underscored its cyclical regularity. As Joanne Creighton points out, there is a "recurrent sameness to their lives a disturbing replay of experiences in the lives of succeeding generations." *Joyce Carol Oates* (Boston: Twayne, 1979), 65.

18. Joanne Creighton and Kori Binette argue that Loretta's unstated desire to see Maureen repeat her own traumatic entry into womanhood exemplifies a recurring pattern in Oates's depiction of mother/daughter relationships: "The mother passes on her acceptance of female subjugation to the next generation," initiating her daughter "into a world where men are all-powerful and women are the victims." "'What Does It Mean to Be a Woman?': The Daughter's Story in Oates's Novels," *Studies in the Novel* 38, no. 4 (2006): 444.

19. Davies, "Naturalism and Class," 308. June Howard similarly observes that although authors and readers of naturalist fiction "explore determinism, we are never submerged in it and ourselves become the brute." *Form and History in American Literary Naturalism* (Chapel Hill: University of North Carolina Press, 1985), 104.

20. Reed, *Stirrings in the Jug*, 17.

21. Susana Araújo, "Space, Property, and the Psyche: Violent Topographies in Early Oates Novels," *Studies in the Novel* 38, no. 4 (2006): 404.

22. In an interview, Oates agreed that her "most inspired area for long fiction" can be summed up by Gyorgi Lukács's account of realism's "exploration of the links between individual destinies and large historical events." Gavin Cologne-Brooks, "Written Interviews and a Conversation with Joyce Carol Oates," *Studies in the Novel* 38, no. 4 (2006): 550.

23. Greg Johnson, *Invisible Writer: A Biography of Joyce Carol Oates* (New York: Penguin, 1998), 155.

24. McGurl, *The Program Era*, 317.

25. This pattern is especially clear in two of Oates's later novels that address American race relations: *Because It Is Bitter, and Because It Is My Heart* (New York: Plume, 1990); and *Black Girl / White Girl* (New York: Harper Perennial, 2006).

26. Lerone Bennett Jr., "Nat's Last White Man," in *William Styron's Nat Turner: Ten Black Writers Respond*, ed. John Henrik Clarke (Boston: Beacon Press, 1968), 8, 9.

27. G. Johnson, *Invisible Writer*, 396, quoted in McGurl, *The Program Era*, 318.

28. For many of Wolfe's readers, the book outed him as a social conservative. Wolfe's stylistic eccentricities, one reviewer commented, masked the fact that he was an "old-fashioned moralist." Quoted in Thomas Hartshorne, "Tom Wolfe on the 1960's," in *Tom Wolfe*, ed. Harold Bloom (Broomall, PA: Chelsea House, 2001), 86. Meanwhile, *Radical Chic* found an appreciative audience among conservatives, who claimed Wolfe as their own; William Buckley's *National Review* published two positive reviews (ibid.).

29. Tom Wolfe, *The Kandy-Kolored Tangerine-Flake Streamline Baby* (New York: Farrar, Straus and Giroux, 1965), xiv.

30. Tom Wolfe, *The Pump House Gang* (New York: Farrar, Straus & Giroux, 1968), 6, 11.

31. Tom Wolfe, *Mauve Gloves & Madmen, Clutter & Vine* (1976; repr., New York: Bantam Books, 1977), 105.

32. Before *Radical Chic*, Wolfe wrote only one profile of a black celebrity: an article on Cassius Clay ("The Marvelous Mouth"). He later acknowledged that this was one of his weakest pieces. *Conversations with Tom Wolfe*, ed. Dorothy M. Scura (Jackson: University Press of Mississippi, 1990), 11.

33. Wolfe, *Pump House Gang*, 14, 23.

34. Wolfe, *Mauve Gloves*, 184.

35. Wolfe, *Pump House Gang*, 19.

36. Ibid., 9.

37. Wolfe, *Conversations*, 21.

38. James Stull, "The Cultural Gamesmanship of Tom Wolfe," *Journal of American Culture* 14, no. 3 (1991): 26.

39. Tom Wolfe, "The New Journalism," in *The New Journalism, with an Anthology*, ed. Tom Wolfe and E. W. Johnson (New York: Harper & Row, 1973), 34.

40. Wolfe, *Conversations*, 260.

41. Thomas Hartshorne similarly observes Wolfe's reliance on a process aesthetic. His 1960s work calls attention to "writing as performance" and exhibits "an improvisational quality . . . that puts him in tune with the sensibility of the 1960's in its emphasis on the importance of immediate inspiration." "Tom Wolfe on the 1960's," 86.

42. Tom Wolfe, *The Electric Kool-Aid Acid Test* (1968; repr., New York: Bantam Books, 1999).

43. Wolfe, *Conversations*, 212. This method acting technique, Daniel Lehman argues, opens up an "epistemological break" in Wolfe's reportage, one that he tries to arrest by insisting on the objectivity of his work. "'Split Flee Hide Vanish Disintegrate': Tom Wolfe and the Arrest of New Journalism," *Prospects* 21 (October 1996): 399.

44. Wolfe, "The New Journalism," 40, 28.

45. Wolfe, *Kandy-Kolored*, 79.

46. Wolfe, "The New Journalism," 25, 35.

47. Tom Wolfe, *The Bonfire of the Vanities* (New York: Picador, 1987).

48. Joshua Masters, "Race and the Infernal City in Tom Wolfe's *Bonfire of the Vanities*," in *Tom Wolfe*, ed. Harold Bloom (Broomall, PA: Chelsea House, 2001), 183, 184.

49. Auletta, *The Underclass*, 28.

Chapter 5: Civil Rights and the Southern Folk Aesthetic

1. Cornel West, *Race Matters* (1994; repr., New York: Vintage, 2001), 15–16.

2. Quoted in Evelyn White, *Alice Walker: A Life* (New York: W. W. Norton, 2004), 122.

3. Dubey, *Signs and Cities*, 165.

4. Warren, *So Black and Blue*, 82.

5. Alice Walker, *Meridian* (1976; repr., New York: Simon & Schuster, 1986); Toni Cade Bambara, *The Salt Eaters* (1980; repr., New York: Vintage, 1992). All subsequent references to these books are to these editions and are noted parenthetically in the text. Other critics have noted the similarities between these two books. Melissa Walker, in particular, reads the novels as retrospective historical fictions about the civil rights movement. *Down from the Mountaintop: Black Women's Novels in the Wake of the Civil Rights Movement, 1966–1989* (New Haven, CT: Yale University Press, 1991), 167–198.

6. Alice Walker, *In Search of Our Mothers' Gardens: Womanist Prose* (New York: Harcourt Brace Jovanovich, 1983), 138, 130, 132, 31.

7. Ibid., 131, 28, 237, 240.

8. Alice Walker, *The World Has Changed: Conversations with Alice Walker*, ed. Rudolph P. Byrd (New York: New Press, 2010), 58.

9. Many of the novel's critics have outlined the novel's allusions to the SNCC. As Susan Danielson points out, the novel is dedicated to SNCC leaders Staughton Lynd and John Lewis; its title is taken from the Mississippi town where three SNCC workers, James Chaney, Andrew Goodman, and Michael Schwerner, were murdered in 1964; and its events loosely coincide with significant dates in the history of SNCC. "Alice Walker's *Meridian*, Feminism, and the 'Movement,'" *Women's Studies* 16, no. 3–4 (1989): 318–319. Other critics who discuss the novel's account of movement politics include Lauren Cardon, "From Black Nationalism to the Ethnic Revival: *Meridian*'s Lynne Rabinowitz," *MELUS* 36, no. 3 (2011): 159–185; Paul Tewkesbury, "Keeping the Dream Alive: *Meridian* as Alice Walker's Homage to Martin Luther King and the Beloved Community," *Religion and the Arts* 15, no. 5 (2011): 603–627; Mab Segrest, "Rebirths of a U.S. Nation: Race and Gendering of the Nation State," *Mississippi Quarterly* 67, no. 1 (2003–2004): 27–40; Roberta Hendrickson, "Remembering the Dream: Alice Walker, *Meridian* and the Civil Rights Movement," *MELUS* 24, no. 3 (1999): 111–128; and Karen Stein, "*Meridian*: Alice Walker's Critique of Revolution," *Black American Literature Forum* 20, no. 1/2 (1986): 129–141.

10. Danielson, "Alice Walker's *Meridian*," 321.

11. Wesley Hogan, *Many Minds, One Heart: SNCC's Dream for a New America* (Chapel Hill: University of North Carolina Press, 2007), 167.

12. Andrew Lewis, *The Shadows of Youth: The Remarkable Journey of the Civil Rights Generation* (New York: Hill & Wang, 2009), 181.

13. Quoted in Clayborne Carson, *In Struggle: SNCC and the Black Awakening of the 1960s* (Cambridge, MA: Harvard University Press, 1995), 155, 143, 142.

14. In Roderick Ferguson's terms, even as historically black colleges mandated "a racial formation that conforms to heteronormativity, that formation can never elude nonheteronormative elements." *Aberrations in Black*, 61.

15. The culture of critical discourse "forbids reliance upon the speaker's person, authority, or status in society to justify his claims. As a result, [this culture] de-authorizes all speech grounded in traditional societal authority." Alvin Gouldner, *The Future of Intellectuals and the Rise of the New Class: A Frame of Reference, Theses, Conjectures, Arguments, and an Historical Perspective on the Role of Intellectuals and Intelligentsia in the International Class Contest of the Modern Era* (New York: Seabury Press, 1979), 29.

16. Cardon, "From Black Nationalism," 172.

17. Walker, *In Search*, 121, 122, 125.

18. Keith Byerman, *Fingering the Jagged Grain: Tradition and Form in Recent Black Fiction* (Athens: University of Georgia Press, 1985), 105.

19. The student civil rights organization that Meridian joins similarly eschews the black church. Unlike older civil rights organizations like the Southern Christian Leadership Conference, the SNCC was predominantly secular.

20. Gunnar Myrdal, *An American Dilemma: The Negro Problem and Modern Democracy* (1944; repr., New York: Pantheon Books, 1972).

21. William Graham Sumner, *Folkways: A Study of the Sociological Importance of Usages, Manners, Customs, Mores, and Morals* (1907; repr., New York: Dover, 1959), 5.

22. For more on Ellison's negotiation with Myrdal and Sumner's theories of culture, see Warren, *So Black and Blue*, 63–64; and Schryer, *Fantasies of the New Class*, 66–69.

23. Carson, *In Struggle*, 142.

24. Walker, *The World Has Changed*, 60. Ralph Ellison offered an influential assessment of the tension between figurative folk art and abstract expressionism in Bearden's 1960s work. His art expresses an "irremediable conflict between his identity as a member of an embattled social minority and his freedom as an artist." Ralph Ellison, "Romare Bearden: Paintings and Projections," *Crisis* 77 (March 1970): 82.

25. Dubey, *Black Women Novelists*, 140.

26. Walker, *The World Has Changed*, 66, 273.

27. Toni Cade Bambara, *Conversations with Toni Cade Bambara*, ed. Thabiti Lewis (Jackson: University Press of Mississippi, 2012), 42, 81, 34.

28. This erasure was central to Bambara's theory of revolution. "Revolution," she claimed, "begins with the self, in the self. The individual, the basic revolutionary unit, must be purged of poison and lies that assault the ego and threaten the heart, that haz-

ard the next larger unit—the couple or pair, that jeopardize the still larger unit—the family or cell, that put the entire movement in peril." "On the Issue of Roles," in *The Black Woman: An Anthology*, ed. Toni Cade Bambara (New York: Signet, 1970), 109.

29. Bambara, *Conversations*, 109–110.

30. Ibid., 8.

31. Byerman, *Fingering the Jagged Grain*, 128. Susan Willis similarly comments on the town's enduring divisions; racial community "never comes together during the space of the novel; rather, we feel its lack in the hectic sites where cacophony prevails." *Specifying: Black Women Writing the American Experience* (Madison: University of Wisconsin Press, 1987), 132.

32. In particular, the reader must decide whether to attribute the thunder to spiritual or human-made causes. The thunder may be the physical manifestation of Minnie's healing; alternatively, it may be an explosion at the nuclear plant that adjoins the town.

33. Bambara, *Conversations*, 50.

34. Linda Holmes, *A Joyous Revolt: Toni Cade Bambara, Writer and Activist* (Santa Barbara, CA: Praeger, 2014), 84.

35. Toni Cade Bambara, *Gorilla, My Love* (1972; repr., New York: Vintage, 1981). All subsequent references to this book are noted parenthetically in the text as *G*.

36. The two forces are complementary; most of Punjab's clients seek him out for bail money.

37. Dubey, *Signs and Cities*, 165.

38. Courtney Thorsson, *Women's Work: Nationalism and Contemporary African American Women's Novels* (Charlottesville: University of Virginia Press, 2013), 56.

39. Ibid., 58.

40. Bambara, *Conversations*, 34.

Chapter 6: Who Belongs in the University?

1. Philip Roth, *The Human Stain* (New York: Vintage, 2000). All subsequent page references are noted parenthetically in the text as *HS*.

2. Philip Roth, *The Plot Against America* (New York: Vintage, 2004).

3. Philip Roth, *American Pastoral* (New York: Vintage, 1997). All subsequent page references are noted parenthetically in the text as *AP*.

4. Al From, William Galston, Will Marshall, and Doug Ross, *The New Progressive Declaration: A Political Philosophy for the Information Age* (Washington, DC: Progressive Policy Foundation, 1996), 6.

5. Philip Roth, *Portnoy's Complaint* (1969, repr.; New York: Vintage, 1994). All subsequent page references are noted parenthetically in the text as *PC*.

6. Philip Roth, "Introduction," in *Conversations with Philip Roth*, ed. George Searles (Jackson: University Press of Mississippi, 1992), ix.

7. Diana Trilling, in her review, describes *Portnoy's Complaint* as "the latest offensive in our escalating literary-political war upon society." "The Uncomplaining Homo-

sexuals," *Harper's Magazine*, August 1969, available at http://harpers.org/archive/1969/08/the-uncomplaining-homosexuals/.

8. Philip Roth, *Conversations*, 177, 36.

9. Ross Posnock similarly makes a case for Roth's career-long commitment to modernism. In novels that seem to draw on postmodern, metafictional techniques, like *The Counterlife* (1986) and *Operation Shylock* (1993), Roth "was proving over and over how much power to unsettle, how much audacity, remained both in the genre dedicated to the new—the novel—and in the modernist (Poundian) dictum to 'make it new.'" *Philip Roth's Rude Truth: The Art of Immaturity* (Princeton, NJ: Princeton University Press, 2006), xvii.

10. Cahn and Cahn, "The War on Poverty," 1332.

11. Philip Roth, *Goodbye, Columbus* (1959, repr.; New York: Bantam, 1970), 25.

12. Mary Esteve offers an extended reading of Neil's interaction with the black boy in light of Roth's engagement with Kantian aesthetics and midcentury sociological theories of happiness. Acting as a "creatively conscientious bureaucrat," Neil facilitates "the development of the boy's self-sourced faculty of imagination." "Postwar Pastoral: The Art of Happiness in Philip Roth," in *American Literature's Aesthetic Dimensions*, ed. Cindy Weinstein and Christopher Looby (New York: Columbia University Press, 2012), 341.

13. Posnock, *Philip Roth's Rude Truth*, 6.

14. After Roth published *American Pastoral*, critics began to reassess his politics. Louis Menand argues that the novel is "about the corruption of American life by the culture of liberal permissiveness." "The Irony and the Ecstasy: Philip Roth and the Jewish Atlantis," *New Yorker*, May 19, 1997, 64. Neoconservative critic Norman Podhoretz hails the "liberation" of Philip Roth's "mind from the stifling orthodoxies of the politically correct liberal faith of his youth." "The Adventures of Philip Roth," *Commentary*, October 1998, 36. Apart from *The Closing of the American Mind*, other texts that formed part of the conservative backlash against the humanities include Alvin Kernan, *The Death of Literature* (New Haven, CT: Yale University Press, 1990); Roger Kimball, *Tenured Radicals: How Politics Has Corrupted Our Higher Education* (New York: Harper & Row, 1990); and Dinesh D'Souza, *Illiberal Education: The Politics of Race and Sex on Campus* (New York: Free Press, 1991).

15. Allan Bloom, *The Closing of the American Mind: How Higher Education Has Failed Democracy and Impoverished the Souls of Today's Students* (New York: Simon & Schuster, 1987), 34, 96, 42, 48.

16. William Bowen and Matthew Chingos find that youth from the highest income bracket are almost five times more likely than youth from the lowest income bracket to graduate with a bachelor's degree. *Crossing the Finish Line: Completing College at America's Public Universities* (Princeton, NJ: Princeton University Press, 2009), 22. See also Peter Sachs, who similarly links socioeconomic status with high school and university graduation rates. Sachs calculates that students from the poorest quartile are 6 per-

cent more likely to graduate from college, compared to 26.8 percent from the wealthiest quartile. *Tearing Down the Gates: Confronting the Class Divide in American Education* (Berkeley: University of California Press, 2007), 118. The rising cost of tuition has much to do with the exclusion of low-income students from the university. In the 1970s and 1980s, college tuition largely kept pace with inflation; "beginning in the 1990s—for reasons not well explained—the price of a degree began rising faster than the cost of other goods and services." John Schoen, "Why Does a College Degree Cost So Much?," CNBC, June 16, 2015, available at http://www.cnbc.com/2015/06/16/why-college-costs-are-so -high-and-rising.html.

17. Sean McCann, *A Pinnacle of Feeling: American Literature and Presidential Government* (Princeton, NJ: Princeton University Press, 2008), 187.

18. Philip Roth, *I Married a Communist* (New York: Vintage, 1998), 22.

19. John Guillory, *Cultural Capital: The Politics of Literary Canon Formation* (Chicago: University of Chicago Press, 1993), 6.

20. See Kenneth Baer, *Reinventing Democrats: The Politics of Liberalism from Reagan to Clinton* (Lawrence: University Press of Kansas, 2000), who documents the disintegration of the New Deal coalition in the 1970s and the emergence of the DLC in the 1980s.

21. Jennifer Glaser, "The Jew in the Canon: Reading Race and Literary History in Philip Roth's *The Human Stain*," *PMLA* 123, no. 5 (2008): 1469. Roth's performative conception of race is central to most critical commentary on *The Human Stain*. Amy Hungerford, for example, argues that Roth acknowledges "the need of individuals to join themselves to others without making the individual subordinate" to "coercive group identities." *The Holocaust of Texts: Genocide, Literature, and Personification* (Chicago: University of Chicago Press, 2003), 123. Other critics who focus on the novel's passing narrative include Michele Elam, "Passing in the Post-race Era: Danny Senza, Philip Roth, and Colson Whitehead," *African American Review* 41, no. 4 (2007): 749–768; Julia Faisst, "'Delusionary Thinking, Whether White or Black or in Between': Fictions of Race in Philip Roth's *The Human Stain*," *Philip Roth Studies* 2, no. 2 (2006): 121–137; Brett Ashley Kaplan, "Anatole Broyard's *Human Stain*: Performing Postracial Consciousness," *Philip Roth Studies* 1, no. 2 (2005): 125–144; Mark Maslan, "The Faking of Americans: Passing, Trauma, and National Identity in Philip Roth's *The Human Stain*," *Modern Language Quarterly* 66, no. 3 (2005): 365–389; and Patrice Rankine, "Passing as Tragedy: Philip Roth's *The Human Stain*, the Oedipus Myth, and the Self-Made Man," *Critique* 47, no. 1 (2005): 101–112.

22. Larry Schwartz, "Roth, Race, and Newark," *Cultural Logic* (2005), available at http://clogic.eserver.org/2005/schwartz.html.

23. Moynihan, *The Negro Family*, 5–6. This distinction between the underclass and black bourgeoisie is central to William Julius Wilson's *The Declining Significance of Race* (1978, repr.; Chicago: University of Chicago Press, 1980), the most influential statement of underclass theory for centrist Democrats in the 1980s and 1990s.

24. Quoted in Holloway Sparks, "Queens, Teens, and Model Mothers: Race, Gender,

and the Discourse of Welfare Reform," in *Race and the Politics of Welfare Reform*, ed. Sanford F. Schram, Joe Soss, and Richard C. Fording (Ann Arbor: University of Michigan Press, 2010), 178.

25. Posnock, *Philip Roth's Rude Truth*, 5.

26. Esteve argues, "In Roth's hands the public library becomes one of the 'new symbols of happiness' that . . . John Kenneth Galbraith hoped to see Americans invest in." "Postwar Pastoral," 44. Galbraith distinguished between private and public goods in *The Affluent Society*. The problem with post–World War II America is that it privileges the former at the expense of the latter: "The line which divides our area of wealth from our area of poverty is roughly that which divides privately produced and marketed goods and services from publicly rendered services" (198).

27. Philip Roth, *Reading Myself and Others* (New York: Farrar, Straus & Giroux, 1975), 176.

28. Guillory, *Cultural Capital*, x.

29. From et al., *The New Progressive Declaration*, 5, 16.

30. "Personal Responsibility and Work Opportunity Reconciliation Act of 1996," Public Law 104-193, August 22, 1996, available at https://www.congress.gov/104/plaws/publ193/PLAW-104publ193.pdf.

31. In Robert Park, Ernest Burgess, R. D. McKenzie, and Louis Wirth, *The City* (1925, repr.; Chicago: University of Chicago Press, 1967), Park and Burgess argued that cities grow in concentric circles, with new influxes of poor immigrants filling up the central manufacturing districts and pushing previous immigrant generations outward to the suburbs, where they disappear into the American melting pot. Roth echoes this conception of urban migration in *Goodbye, Columbus*. Neil imagines that Jews and African Americans are successive waves in an inevitable process of urban migration leading to the integration of all races and ethnicities in the suburbs: "The old Jews like my grandparents had struggled and died, and moved further and further west, towards the edge of Newark, and then out of it, and up the slope of the Orange Mountains, until they had reached the crest and started down the other side, pouring into Gentile territory as the Scotch-Irish had poured through the Cumberland Gap. Now, in fact, the Negroes were making the same migration, following the steps of the Jews" (64).

32. David Harvey, *A Brief History of Neoliberalism* (Oxford: Oxford University Press, 2007), 11.

33. Toni Morrison, *What Moves at the Margin: Selected Nonfiction*, ed. Carolyn Denard (Jackson: University Press of Mississippi, 2008), 152.

34. See Gwendolyn Mink, *Welfare's End* (Ithaca, NY: Cornell University Press, 1998), for a detailed account of welfare reform's impact on the privacy rights of lower-class women.

35. Alison Flood, "Philip Roth Predicts Novel Will Be Minority Cult within 25 Years," *The Guardian*, October 26, 2009, available at https://www.theguardian.com/books/2009/oct/26/philip-roth-novel-minority-cult.

Conclusion: Working-Class Community Action

1. As Eric Sasson points out, while the "white working class was instrumental in delivering Trump the White House," journalists should also focus on "middle-class and wealthy suburban whites, who also came out in droves for Trump and who make up a larger part of his coalition." "Blame Trump's Victory on College-Educated Whites, Not the Working Class," *New Republic*, November 15, 2016, available at https://newrepublic .com/article/138754/blame-trumps-victory-college-educated-whites-not-working-class ?utm_source=social&utm_medium=facebook&utm_campaign=sharebtn.

2. Jeff Guo, "A New Theory for Why Trump Voters Are So Angry—That Actually Makes Sense," *Washington Post*, November 8, 2016, available at https://www.washing tonpost.com/news/wonk/wp/2016/11/08/a-new-theory-for-why-trump-voters-are-so -angry-that-actually-makes-sense/?postshare=121478883323950 &tid=ss_fb.

3. Ibid.

4. Banfield, *The Unheavenly City*, 52.

5. Guo, "A New Theory."

6. Carolyn Chute, *The School on Heart's Content Road* (New York: Grove Press, 2008); and *Treat Us like Dogs and We Will Become Wolves* (New York: Grove Press, 2014). All subsequent references to these two novels are noted parenthetically in the text as *S* and *T*.

7. Cynthia Ward, "From Suwanee to Egypt, There's No Place like Home," *PMLA* 115, no. 1 (2000): 76, 83.

8. Laura Browder, *Her Best Shot: Women and Guns in America* (Chapel Hill: University of North Carolina Press, 2006), 199.

9. Carolyn Chute, "An Interview with Carolyn Chute," *New Democracy Newsletter*, March–April 2000, available at http://newdemocracyworld.org/old/chute.htm.

10. Peter Carlson, "Ask Questions First: Novelist Carolyn Chute's Militia Aims to Be Different," *Washington Post*, January 3, 2000, C01, available at http://www.washington post.com/wp-srv/WPcap/2000-01/03/039r-010300-idx.html.

11. According to Ward, Chute's critique of formal education echoes that of ethnolinguists like Shirley Heath who study working- and middle-class styles of socialization. Heath argues that working-class families "encourage their children to contextualize experience through participation in an ongoing panorama of verbal games and role playing," while middle-class families "teach their children to decontextualize and value experience according to abstract categories of time and place." The school system bases its "skill hierarchies on middle-class learning patterns," discouraging working-class children "whose skills do not map so neatly onto these patterns." "From the Suwanee to Egypt," 78.

12. Carolyn Chute, *Snow Man* (New York: Harcourt, Brace, 1999), 144.

13. Carolyn Chute, *Merry Men* (New York: Harcourt, Brace, 1994), 618.

14. Browder, *Her Best Shot*, 201.

15. Mary Battiata, "Carolyn Chute, Voice of Poverty," *Washington Post*, February 10,

1985, F1-5, available at https://www.washingtonpost.com/archive/lifestyle/1985/02/10/carolyn-chute-voice-of-poverty/93827a1b-86b4-4088d9a44bd37c3fb7/.

16. Carlson, "Ask Questions First."

17. David Connerty-Marin, "Author Hopes 'Militia' Will Lead to Change," *Portland Press Herald*, January 24, 1996, quoted in Browder, *Her Best Shot*, 198.

18. O. Lewis, *La Vida*, xlv.

Bibliography

Acosta, Oscar Zeta. *The Autobiography of a Brown Buffalo*. 1972. Reprint, New York: Vintage, 1989.

———. Letter to Betty Davis Acosta. June 30, 1960. MS. Oscar Zeta Acosta Papers, CEMA 1, Box 2, Folder 7. University of California, Santa Barbara Library.

———. Letter to Helen Brann. January 1974. MS. Oscar Zeta Acosta Papers, CEMA 1, Box 2, Folder 38. University of California, Santa Barbara Library.

———. *Oscar "Zeta" Acosta: The Uncollected Works*. Ed. Ilan Stavans. Houston: Arte Público, 1996.

———. *The Revolt of the Cockroach People*. 1973. Reprint, New York: Vintage, 1989.

Araújo, Susana. "Space, Property, and the Psyche: Violent Topographies in Early Oates Novels." *Studies in the Novel* 38, no. 4 (2006): 397–413.

Auletta, Ken. *The Underclass*. New York: Random House, 1982.

Baer, Kenneth. *Reinventing Democrats: The Politics of Liberalism from Reagan to Clinton*. Lawrence: University Press of Kansas, 2000.

Bambara, Toni Cade. *The Black Woman: An Anthology*. New York: Signet, 1970.

———. *Conversations with Toni Cade Bambara*. Ed. Thabiti Lewis. Jackson: University Press of Mississippi, 2012.

———. *Gorilla, My Love*. 1972. Reprint, New York: Vintage, 1981.

———. *The Salt Eaters*. 1980. Reprint, New York: Vintage, 1992.

———. *The Sea Birds Are Still Alive*. 1977. Reprint, New York: Vintage, 1982.

Banfield, Edward. *The Unheavenly City: The Nature and Future of Our Urban Crisis*. Boston: Little, Brown, 1970.

Baraka, Amiri. *The Autobiography of LeRoi Jones / Amiri Baraka*. 1984. Reprint, Chicago: Lawrence Hill Books, 1997.

———. *Black Magic: Collected Poetry, 1961–1967*. Indianapolis, IN: Bobbs-Merrill, 1969.

———. *Blues People: Negro Music in White America*. 1963. Reprint, New York: Harper-Collins, 2002.

———. "Columbia, the Gem of the Ocean." In *Black Drama, 1850 to Present*, ed. James V. Hatch, Will Whalen, and Jeremy Caleb Johnson. Chicago: Alexander Street Press, 2015. Available at http://alexanderstreet.com.

———. *Conversations with Amiri Baraka.* Ed. Charlie Reilly. Jackson: University Press of Mississippi, 1994.

———. *The Fiction of LeRoi Jones / Amiri Baraka.* Ed. Greg Tate. Chicago: Lawrence Hill Books, 2000.

———. *Four Black Revolutionary Plays, All Praises to the Black Man.* Indianapolis, IN: Bobbs-Merrill, 1969.

———. *Home: Social Essays.* 1966. Reprint, Hopewell, NJ: Ecco Press, 1998.

———. *Kawaida Studies: The New Nationalism.* Chicago: Third World Press, 1972.

———. *Madheart.* In *Black Drama, 1850 to Present*, ed. James V. Hatch, Will Whalen, and Jeremy Caleb Johnson. Chicago: Alexander Street Press, 2015. Available at http://alexanderstreet.com.

———. *The System of Dante's Hell.* In *The Fiction of LeRoi Jones / Amiri Baraka,* ed. Greg Tate, 15–125. Chicago: Lawrence Hill Books, 2000.

Baraka, Amiri, and Edward Dorn. *Amiri Baraka & Edward Dorn: The Collected Letters.* Ed. Claudia Moreno Pisano. Albuquerque: University of New Mexico Press, 2013.

Baraka, Amiri, and Fundi (Billy Abernathy). *In Our Terribleness (Some Elements and Meaning in Black Style).* Indianapolis, IN: Bobbs-Merrill, 1970.

Baraka, Amiri, and Larry Neal, eds. *Black Fire: An Anthology of Afro-American Writing.* New York: William Morrow, 1968.

Barza, Steven. "Joyce Carol Oates: Naturalism and the Aberrant Response." *Studies in American Fiction* 7, no. 2 (1979): 141–151.

Battiata, Mary. "Carolyn Chute, Voice of Poverty." *Washington Post*, February 10, 1985, F1–5. Available at https://www.washingtonpost.com/archive/lifestyle/1985/02/10/carolyn-chute-voice-of-poverty/93827a1b-86b4-4088-8d95-a44bd37c3fb7/.

Benedict, Ruth. *Patterns of Culture.* 1934. Reprint, Boston: Houghton Mifflin, 2005.

Bennett, Lerone, Jr. "Nat's Last White Man." In *William Styron's Nat Turner: Ten Black Writers Respond,* ed. John Henrik Clarke, 3–16. Boston: Beacon Press, 1968.

Benston, Kimberly. *Baraka: The Renegade and the Mask.* New Haven, CT: Yale University Press, 1976.

Bloom, Allan. *The Closing of the American Mind: How Higher Education Has Failed Democracy and Impoverished the Souls of Today's Students.* New York: Simon & Schuster, 1987.

Bourdieu, Pierre. *Distinction: A Social Critique of the Judgment of Taste.* Trans. Richard Nice. Cambridge, MA: Harvard University Press, 1984.

Bowen, William, and Matthew Chingos. *Crossing the Finish Line: Completing College at America's Public Universities.* Princeton, NJ: Princeton University Press, 2009.

Brint, Steven. *In an Age of Experts: The Changing Role of Professionals in Politics and Public Life.* Princeton, NJ: Princeton University Press, 1994.

Brooks, Gwendolyn. "Blackstone Rangers Teaching Materials." Box 107C. Gwendolyn Brooks Archive. The Rare Book & Manuscript Library. University of Illinois, Urbana-Champaign.

———. "Class Notes—Madison, Wisconsin." Box 107C. Gwendolyn Brooks Archive. The Rare Book & Manuscript Library. University of Illinois, Urbana-Champaign.

———. "Class Notes—Northeastern—Black Literature—May 7, Mondays and Wednesdays (1969)." Writings: Personal Files 2. Gwendolyn Brooks Archive. The Rare Book & Manuscript Library. University of Illinois, Urbana-Champaign.

———. *Conversations with Gwendolyn Brooks.* Ed. Gloria Wade Gayles. Jackson: University Press of Mississippi, 2003.

———. *In the Mecca.* In *The World of Gwendolyn Brooks*, 371–426. New York: Harper & Row, 1971.

———. "Poets Who Are Negroes." *Phylon* 11, no. 4 (1950): 312.

———. *Report from Part One.* Detroit, MI: Broadside Press, 1972.

———. *The World of Gwendolyn Brooks.* New York: Harper & Row, 1971.

Brooks, Gwendolyn, Keorapetse Kgositsile, Haki Madhubuti, and Dudley Randall. *A Capsule Course in Black Poetry Writing.* Detroit, MI: Broadside Press, 1975.

Browder, Laura. *Her Best Shot: Women and Guns in America.* Chapel Hill: University of North Carolina Press, 2006.

Brown, Lloyd. "Jones (Baraka) and His Literary Heritage in *The System of Dante's Hell.*" In *Imamu Amiri Baraka (LeRoi Jones): A Collection of Critical Essays*, ed. Kimberly Benston, 71–83. Englewood Cliffs, NJ: Prentice-Hall, 1978.

Bruce-Briggs, Barry, ed. *The New Class?* New Brunswick, NJ: Transaction Books, 1979.

Brunner, Edward. *Cold War Poetry.* Urbana: University of Illinois Press, 2001.

Byerman, Keith. *Fingering the Jagged Grain: Tradition and Form in Recent Black Fiction.* Athens: University of Georgia Press, 1985.

Cahn, Edgar, and Jean Cahn. "The War on Poverty: A Civilian Perspective." *Yale Law Journal* 73, no. 8 (1964): 1317–1352.

Calderón, Héctor. "To Read Chicano Narrative: Commentary and Metacommentary." *Mester* 11 (May 1982): 3–14.

Cardon, Lauren. "From Black Nationalism to the Ethnic Revival: *Meridian*'s Lynne Rabinowitz." *MELUS* 36, no. 3 (2011): 159–185.

Carlson, Peter. "Ask Questions First: Novelist Carolyn Chute's Militia Aims to Be Different." *Washington Post*, January 3, 2000, C01. Available at http://www.washington post.com/wp-srv/WPcap/2000-01/03/039r-010300-idx.html.

Carrasquillo, Marci. "Oscar 'Zeta' Acosta's American Odyssey." *MELUS* 35, no. 1 (2010): 77–95.

Carson, Clayborne. *In Struggle: SNCC and the Black Awakening of the 1960s.* Cambridge, MA: Harvard University Press, 1995.

Castel, Robert, Françoise Castel, and Anne Lovell. *The Psychiatric Society.* Trans. Arthur Goldhammer. New York: Columbia University Press, 1982.

Castillo, Ana. *Massacre of the Dreamers: Essays on Xicanisma.* New York: Plume, 1995.

Chute, Carolyn. "An Interview with Carolyn Chute." *New Democracy Newsletter*, March–April 2000. Available at http://newdemocracyworld.org/old/chute.htm.

————. *Merry Men.* New York: Harcourt, Brace, 1994.

————. *The School on Heart's Content Road.* New York: Grove Press, 2008.

————. *Snow Man.* New York: Harcourt, Brace, 1999.

————. *Treat Us like Dogs and We Will Become Wolves.* New York: Grove Press, 2014.

Ciardi, John. "Epitaph for the Dead Beats." In *A Casebook on the Beats*, ed. Thomas Parkinson, 257–265. New York: Thomas Y. Crowell, 1968.

Clark, Kenneth. *Dark Ghetto: Dilemmas of Social Power.* New York: Harper & Row, 1965.

Clarke, Cheryl. "The Loss of Lyric Space and the Critique of Traditions in Gwendolyn Brooks's *In the Mecca.*" *Kenyon Review* 17, no. 1 (1995): 135–147.

Cloward, Richard, and Lloyd Ohlin. *Delinquency and Opportunity: A Theory of Delinquent Gangs.* New York: Free Press, 1960.

Cohen, Albert K. *Delinquent Boys: The Culture of the Gang.* New York: Free Press, 1955.

Cologne-Brookes, Gavin. "Written Interviews and a Conversation with Joyce Carol Oates." *Studies in the Novel* 38, no. 4 (2006): 547–565.

Connerty-Marin, David. "Author Hopes 'Militia' Will Lead to Change." *Portland Press Herald*, January 24, 1996.

Cowley, Malcolm. *The Literary Situation.* New York: Viking, 1954.

Creighton, Joanne. *Joyce Carol Oates.* Boston: Twayne, 1979.

Creighton, Joanne, and Kori Binette. "'What Does It Mean to Be a Woman?': The Daughter's Story in Oates's Novels." *Studies in the Novel* 38, no. 4 (2006): 440–456.

Cutler, John Alba. *Ends of Assimilation: The Formation of Chicano Literature.* Oxford: Oxford University Press, 2015.

Danielson, Susan. "Alice Walker's *Meridian*, Feminism, and the 'Movement.'" *Women's Studies* 16, no. 3–4 (1989): 317–330.

Davies, Jude. "Naturalism and Class." In *The Oxford Handbook of American Literary Naturalism*, ed. Keith Newlin, 307–321. Oxford: Oxford University Press, 2011.

Davis, Martha. *Brutal Need: Lawyers and the Welfare Rights Movement, 1960–1973.* New Haven, CT: Yale University Press, 1993.

Deutsch, Sarah. "Gender, Labor History, and Chicano/a Ethnic Identity." *Frontiers* 14, no. 2 (1994): 1–22.

Doreski, C. K. *Writing America Black: Race Rhetoric in the Public Sphere.* Cambridge: Cambridge University Press, 1998.

D'Souza, Dinesh. *Illiberal Education: The Politics of Race and Sex on Campus.* New York: Free Press, 1991.

Dubey, Madhu. *Black Women Novelists and the Nationalist Aesthetic.* Bloomington: Indiana University Press, 1994.

————. *Signs and Cities: Black Literary Postmodernism.* Chicago: University of Chicago Press, 2003.

Durkheim, Émile. *Suicide: A Study in Sociology.* Ed. George Simpson. Trans. John A. Spaulding and George Simpson. Glencoe, IL: Free Press, 1951.

"The Economic Opportunity Act of 1964." Public Law 88-452, August 20, 1964. Available at http://www.gpo.gov/fdsys/pkg/STATUTE-78/pdf/STATUTE-78-Pg508.pdf.

Edmunds, Susan. *Grotesque Relations: Modernist Domestic Fiction and the U.S. Welfare State*. New York: Oxford University Press, 2008.

Ehrenreich, John. *The Altruistic Imagination: A History of Social Work and Social Policy in the United States*. Ithaca, NY: Cornell University Press, 1985.

Elam, Michele. "Passing in the Post-race Era: Danny Senza, Philip Roth, and Colson Whitehead." *African American Review* 41, no. 4 (2007): 749–768.

Ellison, Ralph. *Invisible Man*. 1952. Reprint, New York: Vintage, 1995.

———. "Romare Bearden: Paintings and Projections." *Crisis* 77 (March 1970): 80–86.

Epstein, Andrew. *Beautiful Enemies: Friendship and Postwar American Poetry*. Oxford: Oxford University Press, 2006.

Esteve, Mary. "Postwar Pastoral: The Art of Happiness in Philip Roth." In *American Literature's Aesthetic Dimensions*, ed. Cindy Weinstein and Christopher Looby, 328–348. New York: Columbia University Press, 2012.

Fabre, Geneviève. *Drumbeats, Masks, and Metaphor: Contemporary Afro-American Theatre*. Trans. Melvin Dixon. Cambridge, MA: Harvard University Press, 1983.

Faisst, Julia. "'Delusionary Thinking, Whether White or Black or in Between': Fictions of Race in Philip Roth's *The Human Stain*." *Philip Roth Studies* 2, no. 2 (2006): 121–137.

Fergus, Devin. *Liberalism, Black Power, and the Making of American Politics, 1965–1980*. Athens: University of Georgia Press, 2009.

Ferguson, Karen. *Top Down: The Ford Foundation, Black Power, and the Reinvention of Racial Liberalism*. Philadelphia: University of Pennsylvania Press, 2013.

Ferguson, Roderick. *Aberrations in Black: Toward a Queer of Color Critique*. Minneapolis: University of Minnesota Press, 2004.

———. *The Reorder of Things: The University and Its Pedagogies of Minority Difference*. Minneapolis: University of Minnesota Press, 2012.

Fiedler, Leslie. "Cross the Border—Close That Gap: Post-modernism." In *Postmodernism and the Contemporary Novel: A Reader*, ed. Brian Nicol, 162–168. Edinburgh: Edinburgh University Press, 2002.

Fine, Sidney. *Violence in the Model City: The Cavanagh Administration, Race Relations, and the Detroit Riot of 1967*. East Lansing: Michigan State University Press, 2007.

Flood, Alison. "Philip Roth Predicts Novel Will Be Minority Cult within 25 Years." *The Guardian*, October 26, 2009. Available at https://www.theguardian.com/books/2009/oct/26/philip-roth-novel-minority-cult.

Ford, Karen. "The Last Quatrain: Gwendolyn Brooks and the Ends of Ballads." *Twentieth-Century Literature* 56, no. 3 (2010): 371–395.

———. "The Sonnets of Satin-Legs Brooks." *Contemporary Literature* 48, no. 3 (2007): 345–373.

Frazier, E. Franklin. *Black Bourgeoisie: The Rise of a New Middle Class*. 1957. Reprint, New York: Free Press, 1965.

Fried, Michael. *Art and Objecthood: Essays and Reviews*. Chicago: University of Chicago Press, 1998.

Friedman, Ellen. *Joyce Carol Oates*. New York: Frederick Ungar, 1980.

From, Al, William Galston, Will Marshall, and Doug Ross. *The New Progressive Declaration: A Political Philosophy for the Information Age*. Washington, DC: Progressive Policy Foundation, 1996.

Frow, John. *Cultural Studies and Cultural Capital*. Oxford: Oxford University Press, 1995.

Galbraith, John Kenneth. *The Affluent Society*. 1958. Reprint, New York: Houghton Mifflin, 1998.

Gandal, Keith. *The Virtues of the Vicious: Jacob Riis, Stephen Crane, and the Spectacle of the Slum*. New York: Oxford University Press, 1997.

García, Alma M., ed. *Chicana Feminist Thought: The Basic Historical Writings*. New York: Routledge, 1997.

Glaser, Jennifer. "The Jew in the Canon: Reading Race and Literary History in Philip Roth's *The Human Stain*." *PMLA* 123, no. 5 (2008): 1465–1478.

Glasgow, Doug. *The Black Underclass*. San Francisco: Jossey Bass, 1980.

Goodman, Paul. *Growing Up Absurd: Problems of Youth in the Organized Society*. New York: Vintage Books, 1969.

Gordon, Brandon. "Professions of Sentiment: Culture, Poverty, and the Social Work of American Literature." PhD diss., University of California, Irvine, 2012.

Gordon, Linda. *Pitied but Not Entitled: Single Mothers and the History of Welfare, 1890–1935*. New York: Free Press, 1994.

Gouldner, Alvin. *The Future of Intellectuals and the Rise of the New Class: A Frame of Reference, Theses, Conjectures, Arguments, and an Historical Perspective on the Role of Intellectuals and Intelligentsia in the International Class Contest of the Modern Era*. New York: Seabury Press, 1979.

Grace, Nancy McCampbell. "A White Man in Love: A Study of Race, Gender, Class, and Ethnicity in Jack Kerouac's *Maggie Cassidy, The Subterraneans*, and *Tristessa*." In *The Beat Generation: Critical Essays*, ed. Kostas Myrsiades, 93–120. New York: Peter Lang, 2002.

Grant, J. Kerry. *A Companion to the "Crying of Lot 49."* Athens: University of Georgia Press, 1994.

Gross, Laurence F. "The Game Is Played Out: The Closing Decades of the Boott Mill." In *The Continuing Revolution: A History of Lowell, Massachusetts*, ed. Robert Weible, 281–300. Lowell, MA: Lowell Historical Society, 1991.

Guillory, John. *Cultural Capital: The Politics of Literary Canon Formation*. Chicago: University of Chicago Press, 1993.

Guo, Jeff. "A New Theory for Why Trump Voters Are So Angry—That Actually Makes Sense." *Washington Post*, November 8, 2016. Available at https://www.washingtonpost.com/news/wonk/wp/2016/11/08/a-new-theory-for-why-trump-voters-are-so-angry-that-actually-makes-sense/?postshare=121478883323950&tid=ss_fb.

Gutiérrez-Jones, Carl. *Rethinking the Borderlands: Between Chicano Culture and Legal Discourse.* Berkeley: University of California Press, 1995.

Hames-García, Michael. *Fugitive Thought: Prison Movements, Race, and the Meaning of Justice.* Minneapolis: University of Minnesota Press, 2004.

Haney-López, Ian. *Racism on Trial: The Chicano Fight for Justice.* Cambridge, MA: Harvard University Press, 2003.

Hannon, Philip. "The Leadership Problem in the Legal Services Program." *Law and Society Review* 4 (1969–1970): 234–253.

Harlem Youth Opportunities Unlimited. *Youth in the Ghetto: A Study of the Consequences of Powerlessness and a Blueprint for Change.* New York: Harlem Youth Opportunities Unlimited, 1964.

Harrington, Michael. *The Other America: Poverty in the United States, with a New Introduction.* 1962. Reprint, New York: Macmillan, 1969.

Hartshorne, Thomas L. "Tom Wolfe on the 1960's." In *Tom Wolfe*, ed. Harold Bloom, 85–97. Broomall, PA: Chelsea House, 2001.

Harvey, David. *A Brief History of Neoliberalism.* Oxford: Oxford University Press, 2007.

Heise, Thomas. *Urban Underworlds: A Geography of Twentieth-Century American Literature and Culture.* New Brunswick, NJ: Rutgers University Press, 2011.

Hendrickson, Roberta. "Remembering the Dream: Alice Walker, Meridian, and the Civil Rights Movement." *MELUS* 24, no. 3 (1999): 111–128.

Hogan, Wesley. *Many Minds, One Heart: SNCC's Dream for a New America.* Chapel Hill: University of North Carolina Press, 2007.

Holmes, Linda Janet. *A Joyous Revolt: Toni Cade Bambara, Writer and Activist.* Santa Barbara, CA: Praeger, 2014.

Holton, Robert. "Kerouac among the Fellahin: *On the Road* to the Postmodern." *Modern Fiction Studies* 41, no. 2 (1995): 265–283.

Howard, June. *Form and History in American Literary Naturalism.* Chapel Hill: University of North Carolina Press, 1985.

Hughes, Sheila. "A Prophet Overheard: A Juxtapositional Reading of Gwendolyn Brooks's 'In the Mecca.'" *African American Review* 38, no. 2 (2004): 257–280.

Hungerford, Amy. *The Holocaust of Texts: Genocide, Literature, and Personification.* Chicago: University of Chicago Press, 2003.

Johnson, Earl, Jr. *Justice and Reform: The Formative Years of the OEO Legal Services Program.* New York: Russell Sage, 1974.

Johnson, Greg. *Invisible Writer: A Biography of Joyce Carol Oates.* New York: Penguin, 1998.

Johnson, Lyndon. "Remarks upon Signing the Economic Opportunity Act," August 20, 1964. In *The American Presidency Project*, ed. Gerhard Peters and John T. Woolley. Available at http://www.presidency.ucsb.edu/ws/?pid=26452.

Jones, Gavin. *American Hungers: The Problem of Poverty in U.S. Literature, 1840–1945.* Princeton, NJ: Princeton University Press, 2008.

Jones, James. *Jack Kerouac's Duluoz Legend: The Mythic Form of an Autobiographical Fiction.* Carbondale: Southern Illinois University Press, 1999.

Kaplan, Brett Ashley. "Anatole Broyard's *Human Stain*: Performing Postracial Consciousness." *Philip Roth Studies* 1, no. 2 (2005): 125–144.

Katz, Michael. *The Undeserving Poor: From the War on Poverty to the War on Welfare.* New York: Pantheon Books, 1989.

Kent, George. *A Life of Gwendolyn Brooks.* Lexington: University Press of Kentucky, 1990.

Kernan, Alvin. *The Death of Literature.* New Haven, CT: Yale University Press, 1990.

Kerouac, Jack. *Conversations with Jack Kerouac.* Ed. Kevin Hayes. Jackson: University Press of Mississippi, 2005.

———. *Desolation Angels.* 1965. Reprint, New York: Riverhead, 1995.

———. *Dr. Sax: Faust Part III.* 1959. Reprint, New York: Grove, 1987.

———. "Essentials of Spontaneous Prose." In *The Portable Beat Reader*, ed. Ann Charters, 484–485. New York: Viking, 1992.

———. *Maggie Cassidy.* 1959. Reprint, New York: Penguin, 1993.

———. *On the Road.* 1957. Reprint, New York: Penguin Books, 1999.

———. *On the Road: The Original Scroll.* Ed. Howard Cunnell. New York: Penguin, 2007.

———. *The Portable Jack Kerouac.* Ed. Ann Charters. New York: Viking, 1995.

———. *Vanity of Duluoz: An Adventurous Education, 1935–1946.* New York: Coward-McCann, 1968.

Kimball, Roger. *Tenured Radicals: How Politics Has Corrupted Our Higher Education.* New York: Harper & Row, 1990.

Klein, Christina. *Cold War Orientalism: Asia in the Middlebrow Imagination, 1945–1961.* Berkeley: University of California Press, 2003.

Kornbluh, Felicia. *The Battle for Welfare Rights: Politics and Poverty in Modern America.* Philadelphia: University of Pennsylvania Press, 2007.

Krosney, Herbert. *Beyond Welfare: Poverty in the Supercity.* New York: Holt, Rinehart & Winston, 1966.

Kukrechtova, Daniela. "The Death and Life of a Chicago Edifice: Gwendolyn Brooks's 'In the Mecca.'" *African American Review* 43, no. 2–3 (2009): 457–472.

Ladner, Joyce, ed. *The Death of White Sociology: Essays on Race and Culture.* 1973. Reprint, Baltimore: Black Classics Press, 1998.

Leacock, Eleanor Burke, ed. *The Culture of Poverty: A Critique.* New York: Simon & Schuster, 1971.

Leeds, Anthony. "The Concept of the 'Culture of Poverty': Conceptual, Logical, and Empirical Problems, with Perspectives from Brazil and Peru." In *The Culture of Poverty: A Critique*, ed. Eleanor Burke Leacock, 226–284. New York: Simon & Schuster, 1971.

Lehman, Daniel. "'Split Flee Hide Vanish Disintegrate': Tom Wolfe and the Arrest of New Journalism." *Prospects* 21 (October 1996): 397–434.

Levine, Robert. *The Poor Ye Need Not Have with You: Lessons from the War on Poverty.* Cambridge, MA: MIT Press, 1970.

Lewis, Andrew. *The Shadows of Youth: The Remarkable Journey of the Civil Rights Generation.* New York: Hill & Wang, 2009.

Lewis, Oscar. *Five Families: Mexican Case Studies in the Culture of Poverty.* New York: Basic Books, 1959.

———. *La Vida: A Puerto Rican Family in the Culture of Poverty—San Juan and New York.* New York: Random House, 1966.

Liebow, Elliot. *Tally's Corner: A Study of Negro Streetcorner Men.* 1967. Reprint, Washington, DC: Rowman & Littlefield, 2003.

Lowney, John. "'A Material Collapse That Is Construction': History and Counter-memory in Gwendolyn Brooks's 'In the Mecca,'" *MELUS* 23, no. 3 (1998): 3–20.

Madhubuti, Haki. "The Wall." *The Wall of Respect.* Mary & Leigh Block Museum of Art. Accessed October 9, 2017. Available at http://www.blockmuseum.northwestern.edu/wallofrespect/main.htm.

Mailer, Norman. *Advertisements for Myself.* 1959. Reprint, Cambridge, MA: Harvard University Press, 1992.

Malewitz, Raymond. "'My Newish Voice': Rethinking Black Power in Gwendolyn Brooks's Whirlwind." *Callaloo* 29, no. 2 (2006): 531–544.

Marris, Peter, and Martin Rein. *Dilemmas of Social Reform: Poverty and Community Action in the United States.* New York: Atherton Press, 1969.

Martinez, Manuel Luis. *Countering the Counterculture: Rereading Postwar American Dissent from Jack Kerouac to Tomás Rivera.* Madison: University of Wisconsin Press, 2003.

Maslan, Mark. "The Faking of Americans: Passing, Trauma, and National Identity in Philip Roth's *The Human Stain.*" *Modern Language Quarterly* 66, no. 3 (2005): 365–389.

Masters, Joshua. "Race and the Infernal City in Tom Wolfe's *Bonfire of the Vanities.*" In *Tom Wolfe*, ed. Harold Bloom, 179–192. Broomall, PA: Chelsea House, 2001.

May, Elaine Tyler. *Homeward Bound: American Families in the Cold War Era.* New York: Basic Books, 1999.

McCann, Sean. *A Pinnacle of Feeling: American Literature and Presidential Government.* Princeton, NJ: Princeton University Press, 2008.

McCann, Sean, and Michael Szalay. "Do You Believe in Magic? Literary Thinking after the New Left." *Yale Journal of Criticism* 18, no. 2 (2005): 435–468.

McGurl, Mark. *The Program Era: Postwar Fiction and the Rise of Creative Writing.* Cambridge, MA: Harvard University Press, 2009.

Mead, Lawrence. *Beyond Entitlement: The Social Obligations of Citizenship.* New York: Free Press, 1986.

Melhem, D. H. *Gwendolyn Brooks: Poetry and the Heroic Voice.* Lexington: University Press of Kentucky, 1987.

Menand, Louis. "The Irony and the Ecstasy: Philip Roth and the Jewish Atlantis." *New Yorker*, May 19, 1997, 88, 90–94.

Mendoza, Louis Gerard. *Historia: The Literary Making of Chicana and Chicano History.* College Station: Texas A&M University Press, 2001.

Michaels, Walter Benn. *The Shape of the Signifier: 1967 to the End of History.* Princeton, NJ: Princeton University Press, 2004.

Mills, C. Wright. *White Collar: The American Middle Classes.* London: Oxford University Press, 1956.

Mink, Gwendolyn. *The Wages of Motherhood: Inequality in the Welfare State, 1917–1942.* Ithaca, NY: Cornell University Press, 1996.

———. *Welfare's End.* Ithaca, NY: Cornell University Press, 1998.

Moore, Burton. *Love and Riot: Oscar Zeta Acosta and the Great Mexican American Revolt.* Northridge, CA: Floricanto Press, 2003.

Moore, Natalie, and Lance Williams. *The Almighty Black P Stone Nation: The Rise, Fall, and Resurgence of an American Gang.* Chicago: Lawrence Hill Books, 2011.

Morrison, Toni. *What Moves at the Margin: Selected Nonfiction.* Ed. Carolyn Denard. Jackson: University Press of Mississippi, 2008.

Moynihan, Daniel. *Maximum Feasible Misunderstanding: Community Action in the War on Poverty.* New York: Free Press, 1969.

———. *The Negro Family: The Case for National Action.* Washington, DC: United States Department of Labor, 1965.

Muñoz, Carlos, Jr. *Youth, Identity, Power: The Chicano Movement.* London: Verso, 1989.

Myrdal, Gunnar. *An American Dilemma: The Negro Problem and Modern Democracy.* 1944. Reprint, New York: Pantheon Books, 1972.

Nadasen, Premilla. *Welfare Warriors: The Welfare Rights Movement in the United States.* New York: Routledge, 2005.

Neal, Larry. "The Black Arts Movement." *TDR: The Drama Review* 12, no. 4 (1968): 28–39.

Nicholls, Brendon. "The Melting Pot That Boiled Over: Racial Fetishism and the *Lingua Franca* of Jack Kerouac's Fiction." *Modern Fiction Studies* 49, no. 3 (2003): 524–549.

Nicosia, Gerald. *Memory Babe: A Critical Biography of Jack Kerouac.* Berkeley: University of California Press, 1994.

Nielson, Erik. "White Surveillance of the Black Arts." *African American Review* 47, no. 1 (2014): 161–177.

Nishikawa, Kinohi. "Between the World and *Nommo*: Hoyt W. Fuller and Chicago's Black Arts Magazines." *Chicago Review* 59/60, no. 4/1 (2016): 143–163.

Oates, Joyce Carol. *Because It Is Bitter, and Because It Is My Heart.* New York: Plume, 1990.

———. *Black Girl / White Girl.* New York: Harper Perennial, 2006.

———. *Conversations with Joyce Carol Oates.* Ed. Lee Milazzo. Jackson: University Press of Mississippi, 1989.

———. *Expensive People.* New York: Vanguard, 1968.

———. *them.* New York: Fawcett Crest, 1969.

O'Connor, Alice. *Poverty Knowledge: Social Science, Social Policy, and the Poor in Twentieth-Century U.S. History.* Princeton, NJ: Princeton University Press, 2001.

Olson, Charles. *Collected Prose.* Ed. Donald Allen and Benjamin Friedlander. Berkeley: University of California Press, 1997.

Orleck, Annelise. *Storming Caesars Palace: How Black Mothers Fought Their Own War on Poverty.* Boston: Beacon, 2005.

Park, Robert, Ernest Burgess, R. D. McKenzie, and Louis Wirth. *The City.* 1925. Reprint, Chicago: University of Chicago Press, 1967.

Parsons, Talcott. *Essays in Sociological Theory.* Glencoe, IL: Free Press, 1954.

"Personal Responsibility and Work Opportunity Reconciliation Act of 1996." Public Law 104-193, August 22, 1996. Available at https://www.congress.gov/104/plaws/publ193/PLAW-104publ193.pdf.

Pizer, Donald. *Realism and Naturalism in Nineteenth-Century American Literature.* Carbondale: Southern Illinois University Press, 1984.

Podhoretz, Norman. "The Adventures of Philip Roth." *Commentary,* October 1998, 25–36.

———. "The Know-Nothing Bohemians." In *Beat Down to Your Soul: What Was the Beat Generation?,* ed. Ann Charters, 479–492. New York: Penguin, 2001.

Posnock, Ross. *Philip Roth's Rude Truth: The Art of Immaturity.* Princeton, NJ: Princeton University Press, 2006.

Pynchon, Thomas. *The Crying of Lot 49.* 1966. Reprint, New York: Harper & Row, 1986.

Quadagno, Jill. *The Color of Welfare: How Racism Undermined the War on Poverty.* Oxford: Oxford University Press, 1996.

Rainwater, Lee. *Behind Ghetto Walls: Black Families in a Federal Slum.* Chicago: Aldine Transaction, 1970.

Rankine, Patrice. "Passing as Tragedy: Philip Roth's *The Human Stain,* the Oedipus Myth, and the Self-Made Man." *Critique* 47, no. 1 (2005): 101–112.

Raz, Mical. *What's Wrong with the Poor? Psychiatry, Race, and the War on Poverty.* Chapel Hill: University of North Carolina Press, 2013.

Reed, Adolph, Jr. *Stirrings in the Jug: Black Politics in the Post-segregation Era.* Minneapolis: University of Minnesota Press, 1999.

Reich, Charles. "The New Property." *Yale Law Journal* 73, no. 5 (1964): 733–787.

Richardson, Mark. "Peasant Dreams: Reading *On the Road.*" *Texas Studies in Literature and Language* 13, no. 2 (2001): 218–242.

Rigdon, Susan. *The Culture Facade: Art, Science, and Politics in the Work of Oscar Lewis.* Urbana: University of Illinois Press, 1988.

Riis, Jacob. *How the Other Half Lives.* 1890. Reprint, Boston: Bedford / St. Martin's, 1996.

Rotella, Carlo. *October Cities: The Redevelopment of Urban Literature.* Berkeley: University of California Press, 1998.

Roth, Philip. *American Pastoral.* New York: Vintage, 1997.

———. *Conversations with Philip Roth.* Ed. George Searles. Jackson: University Press of Mississippi, 1992.

———. *Goodbye, Columbus.* New York: Bantam, 1959.

———. *The Human Stain.* New York: Vintage, 2000.

———. *I Married a Communist.* New York: Vintage, 1998.

———. *The Plot against America.* New York: Vintage, 2004.

———. *Portnoy's Complaint.* 1969. Reprint, New York: Vintage, 1994.

———. *Reading Myself and Others.* New York: Farrar, Straus & Giroux, 1975.

Ruiz, Vicki L. *From out of the Shadows: Mexican Women in Twentieth-Century America.* New York: Oxford University Press, 1998.

Sachs, Peter. *Tearing Down the Gates: Confronting the Class Divide in American Education.* Berkeley : University of California Press, 2007.

Saldívar, Ramón. *Chicano Narrative: The Dialectics of Difference.* Madison: University of Wisconsin Press, 1990.

Sánchez, Marta. *"Shakin' Up" Race and Gender: Intercultural Connections in Puerto Rican, African American, and Chicano Narratives and Culture (1965–1995).* Austin: University of Texas Press, 2005.

Sapphire. *Push.* New York: Vintage, 1996.

Sasson, Eric. "Blame Trump's Victory on College-Educated Whites, Not the Working Class." *New Republic,* November 15, 2016. Available at https://newrepublic.com/arti cle/138754/blame-trumps-victory-college-educated-whites-not-working-class?utm _source=social&utm_medium=facebook&utm_campaign=sharebtn.

Saunders, Judith. "The Love Song of Satin-Legs Smith: Gwendolyn Brooks Revisits Prufrock's Hell." *Papers on Language & Literature* 36, no. 1 (2000): 3–18.

Saussure, Ferdinand de. *Course in General Linguistics.* Trans. Roy Harris. La Salle, IL: Open Court, 1983.

Schoen, John. "Why Does a College Degree Cost So Much?" CNBC, June 16, 2015. Available at http://www.cnbc.com/2015/06/16/why-college-costs-are-so-high-and-rising.html.

Schryer, Stephen. *Fantasies of the New Class: Ideologies of Professionalism in Post–World War II American Fiction.* New York: Columbia University Press, 2011.

Schwartz, Larry. "Roth, Race, and Newark." *Cultural Logic,* 2005. Available at http:// clogic.eserver.org/2005/schwartz.html.

Segrest, Mab. "Rebirths of a U.S. Nation: Race and Gendering of the Nation State." *Mississippi Quarterly* 57, no. 1 (2003–2004): 27–40.

Shaw, Clifford. *The Natural History of a Delinquent Career.* Chicago: University of Chicago Press, 1931.

Shaw, Clifford, and Henry McKay. *Juvenile Delinquency and Urban Areas: A Study of Rates of Delinquency in Relation to the Differential Characteristics of Local Communities in American Cities.* Chicago: University of Chicago Press, 1969.

Shaw, Clifford, Frederick Zorbaugh, Henry McKay, and Leonard Cottrell. *Delinquency Areas: A Study of the Geographical Distribution of School Truants, Juvenile Delinquents, and Adult Offenders in Chicago.* Chicago: University of Chicago Press, 1929.

Siraganian, Lisa. *Modernism's Other Work: The Art Object's Political Life.* Oxford: Oxford University Press, 2012.

Sollors, Werner. *Amiri Baraka / LeRoi Jones: The Quest for a "Populist Modernism."* New York: Columbia University Press, 1978.

Sparer, Edward. "The Right to Welfare." In *The Rights of Americans: What They Are—What They Should Be*, ed. Norman Dorsen, 65–93. New York: Pantheon Press, 1971.

Sparks, Holloway. "Queens, Teens, and Model Mothers: Race, Gender, and the Discourse of Welfare Reform." In *Race and the Politics of Welfare Reform*, ed. Sanford F. Schram, Joe Soss, and Richard C. Fording, 171–195. Ann Arbor: University of Michigan Press, 2010.

Spengler, Oswald. *The Decline of the West*. Trans. Charles Francis Atkinson. New York: Alfred A. Knopf, 1926.

Spillers, Hortense. "Mama's Baby, Papa's Maybe: An American Grammar Book." *Diacritics* 17, no. 2 (1987): 64–81.

Stack, Carol. *All Our Kin: Strategies for Survival in a Black Community*. 1974. Reprint, New York: Basic Books, 2013.

Stallybrass, Peter, and Allon White. *The Politics and Poetics of Transgression*. Ithaca, NY: Cornell University Press, 1989.

Stein, Karen. "*Meridian*: Alice Walker's Critique of Revolution." *Black American Literature Forum* 20, no. 1/2 (1986): 129–141.

Steritt, David. *Mad to Be Saved: The Beats, the '50s, and Film*. Carbondale: Southern Illinois University Press, 1998.

Stull, James N. "The Cultural Gamesmanship of Tom Wolfe." *Journal of American Culture* 14, no. 3 (1991): 25–30.

Sumner, William Graham. *Folkways: A Study of the Sociological Importance of Manners, Customs, Mores, and Morals*. 1907. Reprint, New York: Dover, 1959.

Sundquist, James. "Origins of the War on Poverty." In *On Fighting Poverty: Perspectives from Experience*, ed. James Sundquist, 6–33. New York: Basic Books, 1969.

Sutherland, Edwin. *The Professional Thief*. Chicago: University of Chicago Press, 1937.

Szalay, Michael. *Hip Figures: A Literary History of the Democratic Party*. Stanford, CA: Stanford University Press, 2012.

———. *New Deal Modernism: American Literature and the Invention of the Welfare State*. Durham, NC: Duke University Press, 2000.

Tewkesbury, Paul. "Keeping the Dream Alive: *Meridian* as Alice Walker's Homage to Martin Luther King and the Beloved Community." *Religion and the Arts* 15, no. 5 (2011): 603–627.

Thompson, Hunter S. *Fear and Loathing in America: The Brutal Odyssey of an Outlaw Journalist*. New York: Simon & Schuster, 2000.

Thompson, J. Phillip, III. *Double Trouble: Black Mayors, Black Communities, and the Call for a Deep Democracy*. Oxford: Oxford University Press, 2006.

Thompson, Julius E. *Dudley Randall, Broadside Press, and the Black Arts Movement in Detroit, 1960–1995*. Jefferson, NC: McFarland, 1999.

Thorsson, Courtney. *Women's Work: Nationalism and Contemporary African American Women's Novels*. Charlottesville: University of Virginia Press, 2013.

Thrasher, Frederic. *The Gang: A Study of 1313 Gangs in Chicago*. Chicago: University of Chicago Press, 1936.

Trilling, Diana. "The Uncomplaining Homosexuals." *Harper's Magazine*, August 1969. Available at http://harpers.org/archive/1969/08/the-uncomplaining-homosexuals/.

Valentine, Charles. "The 'Culture of Poverty': Its Scientific Significance and Its Implications for Action." In *The Culture of Poverty: A Critique*, ed. Eleanor Burke Leacock, 193–225. New York: Simon & Schuster, 1971.

Wacquant, Loïc. *Punishing the Poor: The Neoliberal Government of Social Insecurity*. Durham, NC: Duke University Press, 2009.

Walker, Alice. *In Search of Our Mothers' Gardens: Womanist Prose*. New York: Harcourt Brace Jovanovich, 1983.

———. *Meridian*. 1976. Reprint, New York: Simon & Schuster, 1986.

———. *The World Has Changed: Conversations with Alice Walker*. Ed. Rudolph P. Byrd. New York: New Press, 2010.

Walker, Melissa. *Down from the Mountaintop: Black Women's Novels in the Wake of the Civil Rights Movement, 1966–1989*. New Haven, CT: Yale University Press, 1991.

Ward, Cynthia. "From the Suwanee to Egypt, There's No Place like Home." *PMLA* 115, no. 1 (2000): 75–88.

Warren, Kenneth. *So Black and Blue: Ralph Ellison and the Occasion of Criticism*. Chicago: University of Chicago Press, 2003.

Watkin, William. *In the Process of Poetry: The New York School and the Avant-Garde*. Lewisburg, PA: Bucknell University Press, 2001.

Watts, Jerry. *Amiri Baraka: The Politics and Art of a Black Intellectual*. New York: New York University Press, 2001.

"'Welfare Queen' Becomes Issue in Reagan Campaign." *New York Times*, February 15, 1976, 51.

Werner, Craig Hansen. *Playing the Changes: From Afro-Modernism to the Jazz Impulse*. Urbana: University of Illinois Press, 1994.

West, Cornel. 1994. *Race Matters*. New York: Vintage, 2001.

White, Evelyn. *Alice Walker: A Life*. New York: W. W. Norton, 2004.

Whyte, William F. *Street Corner Society: The Social Structure of an Italian Slum*. Chicago: University of Chicago Press, 1943.

Willis, Susan. *Specifying: Black Women Writing the American Experience*. Madison: University of Wisconsin Press, 1987.

Wilson, William Julius. *The Declining Significance of Race*. 2nd ed. Chicago: University of Chicago Press, 1980.

———. *The Truly Disadvantaged: The Inner City, the Underclass, and Public Policy*. Chicago: University of Chicago Press, 1987.

Wolfe, Tom. *The Bonfire of the Vanities*. New York: Picador, 1987.

———. *Conversations with Tom Wolfe*. Ed. Dorothy M. Scura. Jackson: University Press of Mississippi, 1990.

———. *The Electric Kool-Aid Acid Test*. 1968. Reprint, New York: Bantam Books, 1999.

————. *The Kandy-Kolored Tangerine-Flake Streamline Baby.* New York: Farrar, Straus and Giroux, 1965.

————. *Mauve Gloves & Madmen, Clutter & Vine.* New York: Bantam, 1977.

————. *The New Journalism, with an Anthology Edited by Tom Wolfe and E. W. Johnson.* New York: Harper & Row, 1973.

————. *The Pump House Gang.* New York: Farrar, Straus & Giroux, 1968.

————. *Radical Chic & Mau-Mauing the Flak Catchers.* 1970. Reprint, New York: Bantam Books, 1999.

Zola, Émile. *The Experimental Novel and Other Essays.* Trans. Belle M. Sherman. New York: Cassell, 1893.

Index

Acosta, Oscar Zeta, 6, 24, 79–98. *See also specific works*

AFDC. *See* Aid to Families with Dependent Children (AFDC)

affirmative action, 153, 157–59, 162, 173

Affluent Society, The (Galbraith), 114

Aid to Dependent Children (ADC). *See* Aid to Families with Dependent Children (AFDC)

Aid to Families with Dependent Children (AFDC), 20–25, 82–85, 108, 143, 152, 164, 193n84, 193n90

alcoholism. *See* substance abuse

Allison, Dorothy, 178

American Dilemma, An (Myrdal), 135

American Pastoral (Roth), 152, 160–65, 170–71

Anderson, Sherwood, 36

Annie Allen (Brooks), 62

anomie, 29–30, 41

antiformalism, 32, 118

Arsenio Hall Show, 164, 169

artists, 63, 68, 128–29, 138–39. *See also* audiences (relationship to artist of); process aesthetics; subject matter (relationship between artist and); *specific artists*

Ashbery, John, 4, 37

Atlas, Charles, 88–89

audiences (relationship to artist of), 11, 53, 61–77, 80, 96–102, 118, 126–28, 137–40, 150–56, 179

Auletta, Ken, 123

Autobiography of a Brown Buffalo, The (Acosta), 79–82, 85–91, 95–98

Axel's Castle (Wilson), 64

Ayler, Albert, 1

Baker, Houston, 14, 126

Bakhtin, Mikhail, 85

Bambara, Toni Cade, 6, 125–27, 139–50

Banfield, Edward, 18–20, 123, 176–77, 182

Baraka, Amiri (LeRoi Jones), 5–6, 12–15, 22–24, 80, 82, 161; Beat movement and, 4, 55–56, 72; Black Artists Repertory Theatre and, 1–4, 142; Black Arts and, 51–70, 73, 95–96, 128, 137; class and, 200n9; Gwendolyn Brooks and, 63–64, 68, 77, 203n48; nationalism and, 3, 52, 61, 83; process aesthetics and, 3–4, 1034, 119. *See also* Black Arts Repertory Theatre and School (BARTS); *specific works*

BARTS. *See* Black Arts Repertory Theatre and School (BARTS)

Bastard out of Carolina (Allison), 178

Beans of Egypt, Maine, The (Chute), 177–78

Bearden, Romare, 137

Beardsley, Monroe, 4, 154, 158

Beat movement, 3–4, 11, 20, 27–28, 33, 55, 79, 101, 195n4. *See also* Ginsberg, Allen; Kerouac, Jack

Behind Ghetto Walls (Rainwater), 100

Benedict, Ruth, 14, 18

Bennett, Lerone, Jr., 110

Benston, Kimberly, 61
Bernstein, Leonard, 113–14, 116–18
Bhave, Vinoba, 112
Black Arts movement, 51–52, 62–67, 73,
    77, 80, 95–96, 125–28, 137–45, 203n48
Black Arts Repertory Theatre and School
    (BARTS), 1–2, 6, 51, 142. *See also*
    Baraka, Amiri (LeRoi Jones)
black bourgeois, 11, 19, 53–55, 57–60,
    63–64, 132, 157, 164, 170. *See also* class;
    middle class; race
Black Bourgeoisie (Frazier), 60, 63
Black Fire (Baraka & Neal), 65
Black Mountain poets, 3, 32, 55
Black Panther Party, 2, 113–18
Black Power, 2, 5, 67, 137, 153, 160
Blackstone Rangers, 6, 23–24, 51,
    64–65, 68, 75, 144, 193n82. *See also*
    delinquency; gangs
Black Woman, The (Bambara), 126, 141
Bloom, Allan, 158–59, 167
Blues People (Baraka), 55
Bogart, Humphrey, 88
Bonfire of the Vanities, The (Wolfe), 122
Bourdieu, Pierre, 37
Bowles, Paul, 48
Bradford, Walter, 67
Brando, Marlon, 27
Brint, Steven, 8
Broadside Press, 52, 64
Brooks, Cleanth, 4
Brooks, Gwendolyn, 6, 25, 51–53, 62–78,
    96, 199n42
Browder, Laura, 178–79
Brown Berets, 97–98
Brown Power movement, 79–80, 90–91,
    95, 97
bureaucrats, depictions of, 113, 120–22,
    145
Burroughs, William S., 4, 11, 32, 37, 47
Byerman, Keith, 134

Cahn, Edgar, 82–87, 92–93, 96, 155. *See
    also* Legal Services

Cahn, Jean, 82–87, 92–93, 96, 155. *See also*
    Legal Services
Calderón, Héctor, 88
Capote, Truman, 48
Cardon, Lauren, 132
Cassady, Neal, 27, 38
Chavez, César, 81, 91
Chomsky, Noam, 179
Chute, Carolyn, 6, 177–85, 216n11. *See also*
    specific works
Cisneros, Sandra, 6
civil disobedience, 84, 130
civil rights movement, 7, 112–16, 127,
    129–36, 139, 143, 148, 211n19
Clark, Kenneth, 1, 12–13, 100, 187n6
class: alienation and, 82; ambitions,
    35, 37–41, 54, 56–60, 97, 110, 133,
    161, 178, 196n10; art and, 104, 136,
    156; assimilation and, 31, 34, 184;
    awareness of, 74, 177; Baraka, Amiri
    (LeRoi Jones) and, 22n9; circular
    causality and, 76–77; community
    action and, 147; culture and, 58–59,
    62, 114, 176–77, 179; delinquency and,
    42, 116, 123; divisions of, 126, 128, 143,
    147, 183; double consciousness and,
    54–55; education and, 59, 83, 97, 104,
    131, 156–58, 165–67, 178–80, 213n16,
    216n11; families and, 43; gender and,
    81; hybrids of, 22; liberals and, 113–16;
    literature and, 119, 153, 156, 178;
    masculinity and, 81–82, 86–88, 176;
    mobility and, 45, 60, 104–5, 110, 131–
    33, 136, 153, 170–71; New Journalism
    and, 119–20; race and, 108–10, 153,
    164; style and, 114; substance abuse
    and, 89; theories of, 131, 182; violence
    and, 61, 107, 162; women and, 85;
    work ethic and, 165, 170–71, 175–76
Cleaver, Eldridge, 120
Clinton, Bill, 20, 26, 151–52, 154, 162–64,
    169, 172–73
Closing of the American Mind, The
    (Bloom), 158

Cloward, Richard, 10, 21, 23, 28, 30, 39

Cohen, Albert, 30, 42

Coleman, Ornette, 56

collective healing, 139–40, 142–43

collectivist art, 95–96

Color Purple, The (Walker), 125, 138–39

community action, 10, 83, 127–28, 141–44, 147, 179, 183, 189n29

Community Action Agencies, 1–7, 12, 79–83, 100, 126, 130, 141, 143–45. *See also* community organizations

Community Action Program, 1, 4, 6, 21, 68, 99, 123–24

community organizations, 1–2, 142–48. *See also* Community Action Agencies; *specific organizations*

Community Progress, Inc. (CPI), 82

Confessions of Nat Turner, The (Styron), 110

consumerism, 115–16. *See also* style

corner boy/college boy dichotomy, 31, 34–35

Cowley, Malcolm, 48

Cramer, Kathy, 175–77

Crane, Stephen, 23–24

Creeley, Robert, 4

Crying of Lot 49, The (Pynchon), 16–18

culture: appropriation of, 153; differences of, 142, 156; impulses and, 38; race and, 58, 94. *See also* class; gender; race

Culture and Personality School, 14, 18

culture of poverty thesis, 14–15, 19, 100, 142, 184–85, 190n41, 192n61–192n62. *See also* class; Lewis, Oscar; race

Curzon, Daniel, 109

Dante, 54, 56–57, 59

Dark Ghetto (Clark), 100

Darnell, Linda, 58–59

Davies, Jude, 102

Davis, Angela, 161–62

Dean Moriarty (character), 27, 38–41, 43–44, 86

Death of White Sociology, The (Ladner), 14

Decline of the West (Spengler), 16

delinquency, 10, 20–22, 26–49, 68–69, 75, 107; alienation and, 29; anomic, 29, 37, 39, 43, 196n10; class and, 42–43, 53, 116, 123; culture and, 116; families and, 29, 41, 76; fear and, 143; film and, 27; gangs and, 30, 60; independence and, 45; masculinity and, 24; mothers and, 86, 105; Oedipal attachment and, 29, 42, 45; psychopathological, 29, 43; race and, 27–29, 43, 53, 68, 143, 193n80; romanticism of, 60, 75; social science and, 29; style and, 116; theories of, 28–30, 34, 41, 60, 195n8; underclass and, 123; *vatos locos* and, 89; violence and, 29; writing and, 36. *See also* education; families; gangs; violence

Delinquency and Opportunity (Cloward and Ohlin), 10, 21, 23

Democratic Leadership Council (DLC), 26, 152–53, 163–64, 169, 172

Democratic Party, 8, 25–26, 66, 79–81, 142, 144, 151–53, 163–69, 175–76. *See also* Republican Party

deviant behavior. *See* delinquency

Didion, Joan, 119

Disciples, 23. *See also* gangs

DLC. *See* Democratic Leadership Council (DLC)

Dostoevsky, Fyodor, 36

Drew, Elizabeth, 64

Dr. Sax: Faust Part III (Kerouac), 44–46

Dubey, Madhu, 6, 12, 126, 137, 146

Du Bois, W. E. B., 54, 157

Duluoz Legend (Kerouac), 34, 36, 41, 43–44. *See also specific works*

Dunbar, Paul Laurence, 65

Durkheim, Émile, 29–30, 41

Economic Opportunities Act, 1, 3, 21, 51, 83

education, 97, 105, 119; black bourgeois and, 157; civil rights movement and, 134; class and, 59, 83, 97, 104, 131, 156–58, 165–67, 178–80, 213n16, 216n11; feminism and, 169; gangs and, 23, 65; humanist education and, 153–54, 157–59, 163, 167–68, 171, 173; liberalism and, 128; libraries and, 166–67; merit and, 153; multiculturalism in, 158–59, 162; postsecondary, 6, 18, 34–36, 39, 64, 153, 165–68, 170, 178, 213n16; poverty and, 9, 91, 103, 213n16; race and, 91, 97, 126, 128–29, 132, 135, 153, 157–59; War on Poverty and, 117; women and, 125, 129. *See also* class; delinquency; race

Electric Kool-Aid Acid Test, The (Wolfe), 118

Eliot, T. S., 59, 64

Ellison, Ralph, 35, 56, 62, 135

employment. *See* labor

Engle, Paul, 63

Esquire, 118

Essentials of Spontaneous Prose (Kerouac), 32

Esteve, Mary, 166, 214n26

Expensive People (Oates), 107

Fabre, Geneviève, 2

families: abuse and, 85; black bourgeois and, 157; civil rights movement and, 139; class and, 43; delinquency and, 29, 41, 76; Democratic Party and, 169; dysfunction and, 43–44, 103, 105–7, 112, 198n33; gender and, 24–25, 131, 138; masculinity and, 42, 48; Oedipal attachment and, 42, 45; poverty and, 24–25, 53, 76, 104; race and, 24–25, 42, 60, 81, 192n62; structure of, 24–25, 29, 41–44, 46, 60, 74, 76, 86, 181; theories of, 60; violence and, 103, 131. *See also* fathers; female centered households; mothers

fathers, 29; abuse and, 108; education and, 157; families and, 25–26, 60, 172;

identification with, 42–43, 45–46; masculinity and, 29; neglect and, 44; substitute figures, 43, 47; violence and, 106, 108, 157; weakness of, 29, 44, 48. *See also* families; masculinity; mothers; violence

Faust (Goethe), 45, 47–48

Faustianism, 32–38, 43–48

Fellahin, 16, 32–41, 46–47, 62

female-centered households, 10, 12, 25–26, 46, 53, 60, 75–76, 82, 86, 105, 172, 192n61. *See also* families; mothers

feminism, 101, 134, 141–42, 178, 181; education and, 169; race and, 134, 149; Southern folk aesthetic and, 134. *See also* gender; women

Ferguson, Karen, 2

Fisk Black Writers Conference, 51

Ford, Gerald, 18

Ford Foundation, 2, 4, 6, 81, 130, 141, 188n25

Forman, James, 131

Fort, Jeff, 23

Frazier, E. Franklin, 25, 60–61, 63, 200n18

Freud, Sigmund, 42, 104

Frost, Robert, 63

Fry, John, 23

Galbraith, John Kenneth, 31, 105, 114, 190n34, 214n26

Gandal, Keith, 23

Gandhi, Mahatma, 112

gangs, 21, 23, 51, 60, 75–76, 89, 92–94, 122, 144. *See also* Blackstone Rangers; delinquency; Disciples

Gans, Herbert, 100–101

Gates, Henry Louis, Jr., 14, 126

gender: civil rights movement and, 148–49; community organizations and, 148; essentialism, 179; families and, 24–25, 131, 138; gangs and, 75–76; gender roles, 132, 178, 181, 191n47, 195n8; inequality and, 25, 148; welfare and, 82. *See also* families; fathers;

feminism; labor; masculinity; misogyny; mothers; women
Generation of Vipers (Wylie), 42
genetic essentialism, 19
ghetto culture, 11, 13, 31, 43, 57, 69–77, 85–86, 94–101, 108–24, 130, 142–47, 161, 170. *See also* class; families; poverty; race; violence
Ginsberg, Allen, 4, 11, 28, 39, 47, 52, 54
Goethe, Johann Wolfgang von, 45, 47–48
Goodbye, Columbus (Roth), 154, 156–57
Goodman, Paul, 30
Gorilla, My Love (Bambara), 142
Gouldner, Alvin, 132
Grace, Nancy, 34
Grant, J. Kerry, 17
Great Migration, 6, 8, 126, 161, 166
Growing Up Absurd (Goodman), 30
Guillory, John, 162, 167
Guo, Jeff, 175–76
Gutiérrez-Jones, Carl, 90, 205n19, 205n21

Hames-García, Michael, 85, 91–92
Harlem Youth Opportunities Unlimited (HARYOU), 1–3, 5, 10, 12, 127
Harper & Row, 52, 64
Harrington, Michael, 9–10, 17–18, 57, 116, 190n34
Harvey, David, 171
HARYOU. *See* Harlem Youth Opportunities Unlimited (HARYOU)
Hayden, Robert, 63
Head Start, 126, 128–30
Hemingway, Ernest, 88
high cultural pluralism, 6
hipsterism, 27–29, 35, 43, 46
Holton, Robert, 32
homosocial behavior. *See* gender
"Howl" (Ginsberg), 28
How the Other Half Lives (Riis), 24, 123, 164
Hughes, Langston, 65
Hughes, Sheila, 72

Human Stain, The (Roth), 151–54, 157–63, 165–73
Hurston, Zora Neale, 125

I Married a Communist (Roth), 152, 160–61, 163
Inferno (Dante), 54, 56
In the Mecca (Brooks), 52–53, 66–75
Invisible Man (Ellison), 35

Jackie Duluoz (character), 34–35, 37–39, 44–46
Jackson, Jesse, 163
Jackson, Maynard, 141
James Bond (character), 89
Jim Crow, 11, 125, 146
Job Corps, 21
Johnson, Greg, 109
Johnson, Lyndon, 1, 3, 22, 28, 79–80, 99
Jones, Gavin, 13–14
Jones, James, 43, 47
juvenile delinquency. *See* delinquency

Karenga, Ron, 2, 12
Kawaida Philosophy, 12, 62
Kennedy, John F., 10, 21, 79, 81, 155
Kennedy, Robert, 81
Kenner, Hugh, 5
Kerouac, Jack, 4, 11, 15–16, 22–49, 52–55, 88, 101, 103, 110, 118–19. *See also* *specific works*
Kerouac, Leo, 44
Kesey, Ken, 118
King, B. B., 134
Kingston, Maxine Hong, 6
Klein, Christina, 37
Kundera, Milan, 157

labor: employment and, 21–22, 109, 150, 164, 169; unemployment and, 25, 60, 105, 115. *See also* class; families
Ladner, Joyce, 14
La Gente de Aztlán (The People of Aztlán), 96

Larsen, Nella, 132
latency stage, 42, 44
La Vida (Lewis), 105
Ledbetter, Huddie William, 58
Lee, Chang-Rae, 6
Legal Services, 79–80, 83–84, 86, 88, 96,
    155, 188n16, 204n13. *See also* Cahn,
    Edgar; Cahn, Jean; legal system
legal system, 82–85, 95, 205n23; poverty
    and, 82, 86; race and, 91, 94; racism
    and, 92; welfare and, 86, 205n24;
    women and, 85, 90
Letting Go (Roth), 154
Lewinsky, Monica, 151, 154, 172
Lewis, Oscar, 9–11, 14, 86–88, 94, 105,
    184, 190n41, 192n61–192n62. *See also*
    culture of poverty thesis
liberalism, 2, 20, 113–16, 121, 160, 162–63,
    166. *See also* racial liberalism
Liebow, Elliot, 100
Life of Grand Copeland, The (Walker), 126
Literary Situation, The (Cowley), 48
Lukács, Gyorgi, 108, 208n22

Madheart (Baraka), 24
Madhubuti, Haki (Don Lee), 51–52, 70,
    73, 202n42, 203n48
Maggie, a Girl of the Streets (Crane),
    23–24
Maggie Cassidy (Kerouac), 34–37, 197n24
Mailer, Norman, 22–23, 28, 100, 110
MALDEF (Mexican American Legal
    Defense and Education Fund), 98
Malewitz, Raymond, 51
Mama Day (Naylor), 146
Marshall, Kenneth, 12
Marxism, 14–15, 52
masculinity, 56–57, 89, 92; Black Arts
    movement and, 77; Blackstone
    Rangers and, 64–65, 68, 75; Chicano
    culture and, 90; class and, 81–82,
    86–88, 176; delinquency and, 24;
    families and, 42, 48; fatherhood and,
    29; loners and, 49; mothers and, 143;

process art and, 67; Pulitzer prize, 62;
    race and, 88–89, 120; violence and,
    60, 105–7. *See also* fathers; gender;
    misogyny; violence
Masters, Joshua, 122
Maureen Wendall (character), 102–12
Maximum Feasible Misunderstanding
    (Moynihan), 13, 99, 113
McCann, Sean, 17, 160
McCarthy, Eugene, 81
McCullers, Carson, 48
McGovern, George, 162
McGurl, Mark, 5–6, 48, 104, 179
Melham, D. H., 67–68
Melville, Herman, 28
Mendoza, Louis Gerard, 97
Meridian (Walker), 127–39
Meridian Hill (character), 127, 129–38
Merry Men (Chute), 179
Merry Pranksters, 118
Michaels, Walter Benn, 14
middle class, 99, 104; achievement of,
    34–36, 41, 46–47, 90, 105; art and,
    10–11, 103, 136–37; aspirations of, 109;
    culture of, 58, 114; exclusion from, 39,
    111; literature and, 103, 150; norms of,
    107; organizations, 114; participatory
    professionalism and, 6–8, 29, 113;
    privilege of, 138; race and, 17, 31, 55,
    63, 104, 112, 114, 123; rejection of, 20,
    28, 34, 39, 92, 113–14; responsibility
    and, 112; Southern folk aesthetic and,
    150; theories of, 10; values of, 19, 28,
    57–59, 109, 168; work ethic, 31, 33, 38,
    43. *See also* black bourgeois; class;
    culture; labor; race
militancy, 182; black community and,
    113, 117, 161; Chicano/Chicana
    community and, 79, 90–98, 206n27;
    ghetto culture and, 121. *See also*
    nationalism; race
Mills, C. Wright, 40
minority organizations. *See* community
    organizations

misogyny, 85–86, 88, 205n19. *See also* masculinity
Mobilization for Youth, 127, 130
"momism," 42. *See also* mothers
Morrison, Toni, 6, 110, 172
mothers, 75, 178, 208n18; delinquency and, 86, 105; estrangement from, 139; families and, 29, 60, 76; masculinity and, 143; Oedipal attachment to, 29, 42, 45; poverty and, 86, 88; race and, 42, 76, 86, 108, 132; welfare mothers, 20–26, 82–88, 108, 143, 154, 172, 193n90. *See also* families; female centered households; "momism"; women
Moynihan, Daniel, 10–11, 14, 18, 53, 192n62; black nationalism and, 190n47; circular causality and, 76–77, 107; class and, 13, 19, 99, 164; criticism of, 100–101, 110, 113, 195n95; families and, 25–26, 42–44, 60, 86–90, 105
music: blues, 55, 58; civil rights movement and, 134–35; jazz, 27, 32, 37, 40; race and, 55
Myrdal, Gunnar, 135

NAACP (National Association for the Advancement of Colored People), 114
National Book Award, 99
nationalism: Baraka, Amiri and, 3, 52, 61, 82; black community and, 2, 72–73, 147; Chicano/Chicanas and, 2, 79, 90, 94–96, 98. *See also* militancy; race
National Welfare Rights Organization (NWRO), 84
Nation of Islam, 12, 62
naturalist art, 102–6, 118, 207n16
Naylor, Gloria, 146
Neal, Larry, 1, 63, 65
Negro Family, The (Moynihan), 10, 13, 19, 25, 42, 44, 53, 60, 76, 100, 164
Negro Family in the United States, The (Frazier), 25

Neighborhood Arts Center (NAC), 141. *See also* collective healing
New Criticism, 48, 118, 155
New Journalism, 20, 117–20, 122
New Journalism, The, 120
New Left activism, 91, 99, 161–62
New Poetry, 48, 63
New Progressive Declaration, The, 169
Newton, Huey, 2
New York School, 53, 55
New York Times, 166
Nixon, Richard, 13, 18, 20, 81, 98, 100–101, 125

Oates, Joyce Carol, 6, 99–115, 124
Obama, Barack, 26
object art, 4
Office of Economic Opportunity (OEO), 2, 7, 23, 80, 96, 117–18
O'Hara, Frank, 4
Ohlin, Lloyd, 10, 21, 23, 28, 30, 39
Olson, Charles, 3–4, 11, 15–16, 32, 37, 52–55, 140
On The Road (Kerouac), 11, 24, 27, 32–33, 38–41, 43–45, 79, 86, 118
Organization of Black American Culture, 64
Oscar Acosta/Buffalo Zeta Brown (character), 80–98
Other America, The (Harrington), 9–10, 57, 116

Parker, Charlie, 66
Parsons, Talcott, 41–42, 44
participatory professionalism: civil rights movement and, 130–31; class and, 12–13, 16, 20, 22, 26, 152, 185; crisis in, 100–101, 113, 149; writers and, 3, 6–9, 51, 68, 155
patronage, 2, 6, 128, 148, 183
Patterns of Culture (Benedict), 14
Personal Responsibility and Work Opportunity Reconciliation Act, 20, 26, 152, 164, 169, 172

A Pocket Book of Modern Verse
(Williams), 64
Podhoretz, Norman, 27, 198n29
*Poetry: A Modern Guide to Its
Understanding and Enjoyment*
(Drew), 64
Poetry of the Negro, 64
Poitier, Sidney, 65
Portnoy's Complaint (Roth), 153–55, 165
Posnock, Ross, 156, 166, 213n9
postmodernism, 7, 189n27
Pound Era, The (Kenner), 5
poverty: anxiety and, 92; art and, 103;
Black Arts and, 141; Chicano/Chicana
culture and, 87; childhood influence
of, 92; civil rights movement and,
132–33; class divisions and, 87;
consumerism and, 115; crime and,
68; culture and, 13–16, 41, 53, 58–59,
62, 114–15, 142, 177, 184; cycles of,
105–6; degrees of, 114; delinquency
and, 43, 53; education and, 9, 91, 103,
213n16; employment and, 13; family
structure and, 24–26, 53, 76, 104;
gender and, 81; ghetto culture and,
100; housing and, 31, 69, 72; housing
discrimination and, 31; inertia and,
100; intergenerational, 15, 18–19, 53,
56–57, 76–77, 105, 131; legal system
and, 82, 86; liberals and, 113–16;
militants and, 116; music and, 55;
race and, 25, 32, 43, 55, 104, 112, 114;
theories of, 7, 9, 53, 56, 76, 86, 94, 100,
104, 107, 115, 123, 131; women and, 25,
82, 85–88, 105, 131; work ethic and,
175. *See also* class; culture; families;
gender; labor; middle class; race
Precious, 24
Preface to a Twenty-Volume Suicide Note
(Baraka), 52
President's Committee on Juvenile
Delinquency and Youth Crime, 10, 21
process aesthetics, 3–4, 7, 40, 48–55, 67,
103–4, 119, 127, 136–41, 146, 150–55

process art, 4, 27, 40, 49, 61, 64, 67–69, 96,
110, 119, 141, 180–81
process professionalism, 4, 12, 26
product art, 11, 22, 48
professional-managerial class, 6–7, 13
Program Era, 48, 179
Program Era, The (McGurl), 5
prostitution, 57–59, 103, 105–6, 108, 111
protests, 1, 91, 95, 99, 130. *See also* riots
Push (Sapphire), 24, 193n90
Pynchon, Thomas, 16–17

Quie Amendment, 7
Quinn, Anthony, 95

Ra, Sun, 1
race, 107; artists and, 63, 68; aspirations
and, 89; assimilation and, 31, 33;
black community structure, 52; class
ambitions and, 54, 56; class and,
108–10, 153, 164; class divisions and,
87; community action and, 143–44;
cultural origins and, 88; culture
and, 58, 94; delinquency and, 27–29,
43, 53, 68, 143, 193n80; differences
of, 122; education and, 91, 97, 126,
128–29, 132, 153, 157–59; employment
and, 109, 164; families and, 24–25,
42, 60, 81, 192n62; fear and, 120, 123,
159, 182; feminism and, 134, 149;
fetishization of, 108, 116, 122, 199n39;
housing and, 109; identification
and, 90, 113, 153, 163; incarceration
and, 152; isolation and, 146; legal
system and, 91, 94; liberals and,
113–16; literature and, 101–2, 110, 126,
130, 146, 153, 178; masculinity and,
88–90, 120; middle class and, 17, 31,
55, 63, 104, 112, 114; mothers and,
42, 76, 86, 108, 132; music and, 55;
oppression and, 129; poverty and,
25, 32, 43, 55, 104, 112, 114; privilege
and, 109; process art and, 61, 141;
relationship between artist and

audience and, 70, 80; religion and, 134; sexuality and, 132, 172; Southern folk aesthetic and, 126; stereotypes and, 120, 122–23, 163; style and, 114; substance abuse and, 89; violence and, 90; War on Poverty and, 100; white appropriation of, 110; women and, 134; work ethic and, 164–65, 170–71, 176. *See also* class; gender; poverty; racism

racial discrimination. *See* racism

racial liberalism, 2, 113, 115, 125. *See also* liberalism

racism, 8, 18, 31, 76, 92, 133, 135, 151, 155, 157–59, 162, 175. *See also* Jim Crow; race; segregation

racist romanticism, 11, 32

Radical Chic and Mau-Mauing the Flak Catchers (Wolfe), 20, 99–101, 113–18, 120–24

Rainwater, Lee, 100

Randall, Dudley, 52

Ransom, John Crowe, 4

Reagan, Ronald, 18, 194n92

Rebel Without a Cause, 27

Reed, Adolph, 19, 107

Reed, Ishmael, 6, 138

Reich, Wilhelm, 37

religion, 37, 134, 151, 153, 159–61, 211n19

Report from Part One (Brooks), 77

Republican Party, 26, 81, 151–52, 161, 164, 172, 176, 216n1. *See also* Democratic Party

Revolt of the Cockroach People, The (Acosta), 79–82, 88–98

Riis, Jacob, 24–25, 123

riots, 1, 21, 99, 108–9, 111, 161–64, 169. *See also* civil disobedience; protests

Rise and Fall of General Zeta, The (Acosta), 98

Roi (character), 53–54, 56–61, 70

Rolling Stone, 98

Roosevelt, Franklin Delano, 151, 161

Rosen, Ken, 179

Rotella, Carlo, 28–29

Roth, Philip, 6, 151–85

Saldívar, Ramón, 80

Sal Paradise (character), 32–33, 38–41, 43, 86

Salt Eaters, The (Bambara), 127, 139–50

Salvage the Bones (Ward), 177

Sanders, Bernie, 182

Sapphire, 24

Saussure, Ferdinand de, 71

scale of class cultures, 18

School on Heart's Content Road, The (Chute), 177, 179–84

Schwartz, Larry, 163

Sea Birds are Still Alive, The (Bambara), 141–42

Seale, Bobby, 2

Search for Education, Elevation and Knowledge (SEEK), 126, 141

Second Maine Militia, 177, 179. *See also* Chute, Carolyn

SEEK. *See* Search for Education, Elevation and Knowledge (SEEK)

segregation, 130, 132–33, 135, 146, 170, 194n93. *See also* race; racism

Sellers, Cleveland, 131

Senghor, Léopold Sédar, 70, 72

sexism, 88, 90. *See also* gender; misogyny

sexuality: homosocial behavior, 45, 56, 90, 183, 205n21; race and, 132, 172; women and, 132. *See also* gender; masculinity; misogyny

sexual violence, 59–60, 73, 90, 106, 109. *See also* masculinity; misogyny; prostitution; violence; women

Shepp, Archie, 1

Sherrod, Charles, 131

Shriver, Sargent, 1

Signifying Monkey, The (Gates), 126

Siraganian, Lisa, 4

Slave Ship, 3–4

SNCC. *See* Student Nonviolent Coordinating Committee (SNCC)

Social Security, 25, 194n93
Sollors, Werner, 11
Song of Solomon (Morrison), 125, 146
Souljah, Sister, 163
Soul on Ice (Cleaver), 120
Souls of Black Folk, The (Du Bois), 54
Southern folk aesthetic, 126–30, 133–34,
    136, 145–46, 149–50
Sparer, Edward, 84
Spengler, Oswald, 16, 32–33, 35, 45
Spirit House, 6, 142
spirituality, 27, 125, 127, 140, 147
spontaneous prose, 32, 38, 40, 118
Stafford, Jean, 48
Stallybrass, Peter, 85
"statusspheres," 114–15
Stembridge, James, 131
Street in Bronzeville, A (Brooks), 63
Student Nonviolent Coordinating
    Committee (SNCC), 13, 127, 130–31,
    136, 210n9
Students for a Democratic Society, 130
Stull, James, 118
style, 114–16, 121. *See also* consumerism
Styron, William, 110
subject matter (relationship between
    artist and), 101–4, 106, 118, 122–24,
    126, 137–39, 179
substance abuse, 36, 43, 89, 97
Subterraneans, The (Kerouac), 34
suburbs, 9, 31, 107, 215n31
Suicide (Durkheim), 29
Sula (Morrison), 125
Sumner, Charles Graham, 135
System of Dante's Hell, The (Baraka), 11,
    23, 52, 54–55, 61, 64, 199n8
Szalay, Michael, 10, 17, 189n27

Tally's Corner (Liebow), 100
TANF. *See* Temporary Assistance for
    Needy Families (TANF)
Taylor, Peter, 48
Temporary Assistance for Needy Families
    (TANF), 164

tenements, 69–71, 76, 194n93. *See also*
    ghetto culture; poverty
them (Oates), 99–115, 208n17
Third Life of Grange Copeland, The
    (Walker), 129
Third World Press, 52
Thompson, Hunter S., 79, 86, 88, 95, 98,
    119
Thrasher, Frederic, 31
Tillmon, Johnnie, 84
Tolson, Melvin, 63
*Treat Us like Dogs and We Will Become
    Wolves* (Chute), 177, 179–84
Tristessa (Kerouac), 34
Trump, Donald, 26, 175, 177, 182

Ulysses (Joyce), 54
underclass, 19, 28, 99, 107, 121, 123, 142,
    176. *See also* class; poverty
Underclass, The (Auletta), 123
unemployment. *See* labor
Unheavenly City, The (Banfield), 18, 176
United Mexican American Students
    (UMAS), 97
urban deindustrialization, 8, 153, 171
Urban League, 114

Vanity of Duluoz (Kerouac), 33, 36, 38
Varela, Maria, 131
vatos locos, 89–90, 92–95, 98. *See also*
    delinquency; gangs; militancy
Veblen, Thorstein, 36
Vietnam War, 161
violence, 19, 22–23, 61, 69, 89–92, 99,
    103–12, 131, 133, 143–45, 162, 172, 183.
    See also sexual violence
Violent Crime Control and Law
    Enforcement Act, 152

Wacquant, Loïc, 21
Wald, Jerry, 27
Walker, Alice, 6, 125–39, 149–50
Walker, Bill, 66
Wall of Respect, 66

Ward, Jesmyn, 177
Ward, Val, 67
War on Poverty, 1, 3, 12–13, 18, 21, 51, 81, 83–87, 98–100, 104, 117, 125, 142, 176
War on Welfare, 18, 152
Warren, Kenneth, 14, 126–27
Washington Post, 175, 179
Waste Land, The (Eliot), 54
Watts, Jerry, 12
welfare: dependency, 26, 83; legal system and, 205n24; policies, 87; politics, 53. *See also* Aid to Families with Dependent Children (AFDC); class; families; labor; mothers; Personal Responsibility and Work Opportunity Reconciliation Act; poverty; race
welfare mothers. *See* mothers
welfare professionalism, 5, 82
Werner, Craig Hansen, 74
West, Cornel, 125, 127
White, Allon, 85
white community, 89, 109–10, 156, 175–76. *See also* class; culture; poverty; race
White Negro, The (Mailer), 28
Whyte, William F., 31, 34
Wild One, The, 27

Williams, Oscar, 64–65
Wilson, Edmund, 64
Wimsatt, William K., 4, 154, 158
Winter's Bone (Woodrell), 177
Wolfe, Tom, 6, 20, 99–102, 113–24. *See also specific works*
women: Black Arts and, 137–38; education and, 125, 129; employment and, 150; race and, 129, 134; sexuality and, 132. *See also* families; female centered households; feminism; misogyny; momism; mothers; sexism; violence
Woodlawn Organization, 23, 51, 68, 75, 193n82
Woodrell, Daniel, 177
Works Progress Administration, 6, 188n25
WPA. *See* Works Progress Administration
Wylie, Philip, 42

X, Malcolm, 2, 66

Yale Law Review, 82
Yeats, W. B., 37, 156
Ylvisaker, Paul, 4–5

Zola, Émile, 102

Margaret Ronda, *Remainders: American Poetry at Nature's End*

Jasper Bernes, *The Work of Art in the Age of Deindustrialization*

Annie McClanahan, *Dead Pledges: Debt, Crisis, and Twenty-First-Century Culture*

Amy Hungerford, *Making Literature Now*

J. D. Connor, *The Studios after the Studios: Neoclassical Hollywood, 1970–2010*

Michael Trask, *Camp Sites: Sex, Politics, and Academic Style in Postwar America*

Loren Glass, *Counter-Culture Colophon: Grove Press, the "Evergreen Review," and the Incorporation of the Avant-Garde*

Michael Szalay, *Hip Figures: A Literary History of the Democratic Party*

Jared Gardner, *Projections: Comics and the History of Twenty-First-Century Storytelling*

Jerome Christensen, *America's Corporate Art: The Studio Authorship of Hollywood Motion Pictures*